Positive Parenting for Children with Autism

10 Strategies + 20 Games You Need to Know to Encourage Language in Children with Autism. Establish Here and Now an Effective Connection with Your Children

Kate Gildon

Table of contents

Introduction

In the Introduction of this book, I want to explain to the readers the reason why I decided to write a book about positive parenting for children with autism. Since I was young, I loved to interact with people and listen to their stories, especially older people. I loved when they told me all the things they had to fight in life, their feelings when they thought everything was lost, what they learned from good and bad situations. Later in life, I had the possibility to keep going on with this passion I had because of my studies and my career. After all my studies, at the beginning of my career I was excited because for the first time I had not only the possibility to listen to other people, I was able to understand and help them.

During my career, I have helped several parents. Working with parents is hard but also the most beautiful thing to do in my field. Being a parent is very hard; it is the hardest thing you will do in your life. I am a mother; I know how hard it can be. Every parent knows that life is hard and has to accept that their beloved son or daughter will have to fight against the bad things in life. The question every parent has asked himself at some point in his or her life is: "am I preparing my child in the right way for the future?"

When you are a parent of a child with disabilities, you ask yourself this question a lot more because you are afraid your child won't be able to make it in life without your presence by their side.

I decided to write this book in order to help those of you who struggle with this fear, who want to do their best to raise your kid in the best way, to help them become the best version of themselves.

I'm not saying that after this book you will never ask yourself that question ever again, but I want you to answer that you are really trying.

Being a parent of a child with autism can make you feel lonely and lost, without a good plan to follow. Those feelings often affect parents of autistic children because everyday life for them is full of challenges and they would like someone at their side, teaching them how to win those challenges in a constructive way for their children, without hurting, making them feel uncomfortable or unable to do anything.

This is why I decided to write this book, to always be by your side during the difficulties that life can present everyday.

This book is full of tools & tips to follow for every situation, from the young age to the world of work.

I used all of my experience in this field and also did plenty of research in order to give some practical and useful advice.

The first thing I want to say is that every kid is different. Being affected by autism doesn't make them all the same, what might work for someone might not work for your kid. Autism is complex, but some characteristics are really common among kids with autism.

For example, let's talk about the reason why our kids are often angry, upset, annoyed and we can not understand why. What for us can be considered "normal" or "without anything relevant" for them might be a reason for discomfort and rage. Our brain filters thousands of multisensory inputs, your kid's brain can not do that.

What are those inputs? For example things that we see even if we are not directly looking at them, like cars, people walking around us, birds flying on the trees, advertising hoardings etc.

The same thing can be said about what we feel, hear, smells, etc. all at the same time. This traffic might be too much for your kid and he or she might feel the same way as you when you're stuck in the traffic of the city and you can not do anything to change the situation even if you want.

Another thing that is very common is that your kid will not automatically tell you what is wrong. If you want to help your kid you have to think about what might be going on in his or her brain at every moment and what might be causing him a problem, you can't expect your kid to tell you what's going on. Communication and interaction are two things that are difficult to do for your kid. You have to catch the signals and understand your kid without words needed and I am going to help you with that.

Children with autism need to be loved in a different way, they need you to think outside the box, they have specific needs you should know and act as a consequence if you want to help them and love them the way they deserve.

With a good doctor and this book by your side you will be able to do so. I'm happy and grateful to help you and your kid.

Now, let's begin our journey...

Chapter 1: The Truth About Autism

I decided to name this chapter "the truth about autism" not because I am going to say something new, something never heard before, but because nowadays with the internet and social media it is easy to be fooled by fake news or information.

It can be difficult to understand the difference between what is real and what is not on the internet. Fake news is made to look real and you should not blame yourself if at first you believed one of them was real. On the internet everyone seems to have an opinion about everything, even if they have never done research about the matter and don't know anything about it. Moreover, lately we have the so-called "conspiracy theories". They are theories told by people who want to make you believe they have discovered something that the authorities or the doctors for some reason won't tell you.

Fighting against those people is really hard. Even if you answer with information taken by science or even good sense they will tell you that the society is manipulating you. Often those theories are totally absurd, but many people fall for them. I have to admit that they can make you doubt everything you believe in. Moreover, they are an easy way out from reality. Think about it, sometimes it is more convenient to believe a lie than to accept a hard truth. It is easier to complain, be angry, indignated than to be strong enough to face a difficult situation you didn't want and no one caused it intentionally.

Falling for one of those conspiracies sometimes is the best way to escape from reality and don't deal with real problems.

Before everything you should think about your kid's situation and how to help them, how to raise them, how to love them in the way they need.

It is normal to have some questions, to feel lost in a sea of different information. I am here to help.

So, what is the truth about autism?

The only way you can learn something real about your kid's sindrom is listening to science. All of the information you will read in this chapter does not come from me and my mind or opinion, they are facts told by science.

Scientists have studied and worked with autism for a very long time, we should trust them because they studied all of their lives to have the capacities to say what they are saying and do what they are doing in order to help us know more about how we are made.

This chapter will provide answers (taken from science) to the most frequently asked questions that may arise about autism. I am sure that many of you will already know the answers to certain questions but science always makes progress and sometimes a different explanation of a topic can lead to a better understanding of itself.

What is autism?

Autism spectrum disorders are neurodevelopmental disorders.

This is the scientific definition; you can find it everywhere, starting from books to social media. I am sure that a lot of doctors have already provided you with all of that information but sometimes it is useful to have them where it is easy for us to find.

In a person with autism the way the brain is connected (the peculiarities of neuronal connections) affects development.

In fact, there is a wide range of studies showing anatomical evidence in the brains of autistic people. Such abnormalities would alter the structure of the brain. Several scholars, including Rémy Lestienne, are convinced that autism is due to "insufficiency or an abnormality in the elimination of synapses during embryonic development, as well as in the reorganization of neuronal connections in late adolescence."

Neuroscience studies therefore show that the autistic brain has too many connections between the nearest areas and too few between the more distant areas, which would cause synchronization problems between these areas. The brain, therefore, would have a problem of general "balance". And if there is an imbalance, some stages of normal brain development cannot take place.

When we talk about balance, we are referring to the condition of stability that the organism as a whole tries to preserve to ensure its survival. This is homeostasis, a fundamental principle that characterizes the human body and any other biological system. A disturbed system will try to maintain internal balance by returning to its initial state. For example, when we feel cold, our body reacts by increasing body heat production. Meanwhile, the brain can consciously decide that it is appropriate to raise the heating! When we feel very hot, however, our body sweats to try to lower its temperature. External information changes all the time, and our perception too.

Autistic people have a different way of managing the relationship between the changing environment and their body. In neurotypicals, the effort to regain internal balance in front of the changing external environment takes place quickly and without apparent effort. The neurotypical brain, for example, is able to react to cold based on its past experience, because it easily creates reaction patterns through learning.

Autistic people also feel the cold, but they are not always able to handle this information, because at the same time they are besieged by other information. They must associate "manually" or "consciously" data from the senses. Their body tries to react to external information without the help of reaction patterns, because their brain is unable to recover them. All neuronal resources are absorbed by perception.

Neuroscience has shown that the particular connections of the autistic brain cause it to be connected in a 'perceptual' way.

The perceptual brain primarily processes concrete data, information not related to sociability and details. This peculiarity of the brain is independent of the will. An autistic spontaneously perceives the panels on the ceiling of the room in which he is located, but not the people who are present inside it. His brain tells him almost instantly how many panels are on the ceiling, but it tells him nothing about the mood of the people in front of him.

Research shows more and more convincingly that this is a hyper connection problem: the perceptual brain collects an excessive amount of information and fails to get rid of it. He must learn to regulate the influx of information to avoid sensory overload.

Also in terms of operation, autistics show peculiarities. Comparing the brain to a car, we could say that neuro typical have an automatic transmission that performs a series of background operations fluidly, while autistics have a manual transmission. An autistic person must process every single piece of information consciously, one at a time, through enormous cognitive effort; this explains, among other things, why autistics need more time to process information.   It is evident that managing a "manual" brain requires constant effort: this is why many autistics get tired quickly and that some suffer from terrible headaches that last for days on end. We must not forget that, although an autistic cannot say "I'm sick", his body suffers.

For example, the sense of hearing provides us with an immense amount of information. We instantly acquire and interpret the qualities that make up sound — volume, height, frequency, vibration — as well as its directionality. We turn our heads in search of rumors, footsteps and traffic noises. When hearing is calibrated in the typical configuration, we sharpen our ears to understand something that is whispered to us, and only really loud sounds make us back down, cover our ears or protect us in other ways. For many individuals with autism, the auditory sense is the one that most commonly exhibits malfunctions. Hyperacute hearing can cause excruciating pain.

The sounds of a typical day are too loud, too sharp, too sudden, too penetrating, too intrusive. The child with autism may hear things that are indistinguishable to you, and that only exacerbate an already chaotic world with deafening dissonances.

The child probably lacks the ability to exclude and/or filter sounds, to distinguish your voice in the middle of the sounds of the washing machine or television, or the teacher's voice amid the murmurings and movements of other pupils. Environments that appear ordered to a random observer can be a minefield of noise and confusion for the child with hearing hypersensitivity. Sounds that are loud for us too, such as gang music, the noises of a basketball game in the gym, a crowded bar, the voice of children at the park and the sirens of rescue vehicles are examples of a daily hustle and bustle that can cause physical pain.

Loud, sudden sounds, such as a fire bell or car horns, can trigger a level of panic from which the child recovers with difficulty, sometimes after hours. In extreme cases, there are children who can hear other people's heartbeats in the room. And when on the beach you enjoy the rhythmic lapping of the sea foam beating on the shore, forget about the foam. Think that it is incessant and that it gives headaches.

Less obvious but equally invasive or intolerable are ordinary, seemingly non-threatening noises. The child does not go into hiding in his room because he doesn't love his family: he is fleeing the dissonances of the dishwasher, coffee machine, washing machine, television and teenage brother on his cell phone that all make noise at the same time. It's almost like it's inside him, in the washing machine basket. When he gets back to school, his classmates listen to the speaking teacher.

But the child with autism can't identify the teacher's voice as the primary sound they need to pay attention to. For him it is indistinguishable from the creak of pencil sharpener, from the buzz of the fly on the windowsill, from the cliff of the lawn mower in the garden, from the persistent cough of the child behind him. But even hyperacute hearing brings with it numerous problems. It affects language development and use, social learning, and school life. Children may miss pieces of what is said, fail to distinguish certain types of sound, or perceive what they hear as a succession of sounds instead of words or phrases of complete meaning. Seemingly lazy or disobedient behavior could result from a sensory defect that prevents the child from filtering and/or processing the normal sounds of everyday life. The child with under stimulated hearing also struggles to make sense of information from sounds. He could talk too flat or too loud, look for noisy environments or equipment (lawnmower, hair dryer, blender) to have more sensory input, slam toys or other objects to create noise, be attracted to noisy water flows (waterfalls, open taps, toilet drain) or toys that emit vibrations or buzz.

An auditory processing problem, whether due to excessive or poor stimulation, is to be suspected if your child or student is able to perform the instructions well if they are visual but not if they are oral.

Even our skin records an incredible amount of information: from slight touches to deep pressures, a wide range of temperatures, different types of pain or irritation, vibrations and other movements, as well as textures from liquid to rough.

Hypersensitivity to touch is called tactile defensiveness. The child with autism, trapped in his own skin, is unable to regulate the annoying sensations that rain on him in the form of uncomfortable clothing, unwanted contact with other people (affectionate hugs can be torture for him) and unpleasant textures of things he is forced to touch or eat. For the child with tactile defensiveness, clothing labels, buttons, zippers, rubber bands around the neck and ankles and other textile trimmings cause constant distraction. Walking barefoot is not available, either at home or outdoors (does the child walk on tiptoe?). It may escape your hugs, wriggle desperately for not having to cut your hair, shampoo, brush your teeth or cut your nails. Practical activities such as finger painting and sand games can produce more stress than fun. Hyposensitivity, on the other hand, induces the child to seek tactile sensations. He passes his hands on the walls from one class to another, Wants to touch everything and everyone, he may not suffer temperature changes. It could exhibit extravagant, sometimes puzzling, and potentially dangerous behavior. He may have self-harming stimming behaviors (deads, pinches, pressure applied with various objects, too intense use of the toothbrush) and not notice the intensity of his actions given the high pain threshold and insensitivity to temperatures. She may prefer tight, heavy or rough clothing or apply herself in strange activities such as bathing dressed. He could touch certain objects or bump into something or someone on purpose to stimulate the senses, only to avoid trying new motor activities because he doesn't want to be perceived by others as clumsy. Since children with hypocritical processing constantly seek contact, parents could characterize them as "sticky" and others may find their contact intrusive and inappropriate.

For an autistic, everything passes through the eyes, even tactile sensations and sounds...

Incoming information is processed one at a time by the brain, which processes only those it recognizes as already seen and to which it has attributed a reaction pattern. For many children with autism, the visual sense is the strongest. The good news is that although they rely primarily on visual inputs to learn and navigate the world, this sense may be the first to become hyper stimulated. Bright lights or objects, reflective surfaces, too many objects in the field of view, or objects moving quickly or at irregular speeds can cause distortion and sensory chaos. Although the visual sense may be the most solid in many children with autism, for some it is hypoactive or disorganized: this can manifest itself when a child swings sideways or back and forth (attempts to change the angle of the view), is disturbed by elevation changes (steps, stairs) or is fascinated by moving objects (trains, mills). At the base there could also be limits of a physical nature. Some children may not have depth perception or have a limited field of vision.

What causes autism?

Unfortunately, this is a question to which, even today, we do not know how to give an answer: in most people with Autism the cause remains unknown. The number of clinical symptoms and other alterations that can be highlighted with the support of instrumental investigations, however, suggest a multiplicity of causes. Thanks to studies conducted in recent years, many researchers today believe that among these causes are genetic and environmental ones.

About **genetic causes**, some research done on twins have shown interesting facts. High concordance (70–90%) for Autism was observed in identical (monozygotic) twins. This means that if, e.g., we consider 100 pairs of twins in which at least one of the twins is autistic, there will only be about 80 pairs with both autistic twins. In non-identical (dizygotic) twins, concordance is much lower (0–10%). These data are in favor of the existence of a genetic basis for autism as monozygotic twins have the same genetic makeup, while dizygotic twins share only 50% of their genes. The existence of a genetic basis for Autism is also supported by the observation that in families with an autistic child the risk of having a second autistic child is 25 times higher than that of any couple in the general population. Then there are numerous studies that confirm the genetic hypothesis as they report genetic or chromosomal alterations (mutations) that can be highlighted by the analysis of the cells of subjects with Autism. For example, mutations in particular genes have been observed to greatly increase the risk of contracting the disease. Cases of this type are well illustrated by the association of autism with hereditary diseases such as Fragile X chromosome syndrome, Tuberous

Sclerosis, Angelman syndrome. In all these cases the pathology is caused by mutations in a single gene.

In addition to genetic causes, many researchers believe that ***environmental factors*** are also among the causes of autism. This hypothesis finds support for example in the observation, reported above, that in about 20% of monozygotic twins (same genetic heritage) Autism is present in only one of the twins. This is indirect evidence of the existence of other etiological (non-genetic) factors. We still know very little about the nature of these environmental risk factors and it would be desirable to know more. In fact, at least in theory, it is much easier to imagine therapies for autism based on the removal of environmental risk factors than therapies that aim at a "correction" of genetic risk factors. Among the environmental causes that are believed to be of some importance in Autism is the exposure of mothers during pregnancy to viral infections such as rubella virus and cytomegalovirus or to chemicals such as thalidomide or valproic acid.

Genetic and environmental risk factors in Autism should not necessarily be considered separately. For example, it is possible that a particular combination of genes gives an individual only a susceptibility, that is, a latent risk, for Autism and that it is instead the presence of one or more environmental factors that converts that potential in the full-blown appearance of the typical symptoms of the disease.

It is very likely that Autism is the result of an alteration of the normal course of the development of the central nervous system. Genetic and environmental factors that can act either alone or by cooperating with each other play a role in causing these alterations. Different factors can take action at different times, before, during or after birth. Although the specific nature of brain damage during development may be different depending on the type, mode and time of action of the causative factors (genetic and/or environmental), the final event will always be the same: the appearance of deficits that we collectively define with the term Autism.

Today it is widely believed that the measles vaccine may be among the causes of autism. This is another false belief related to an unpleasant incident that occurred in 1998 when a doctor from Wales, Andrew Wakefield, hypothesized that vaccination against measles, mumps and rubella could cause autism.

This doctor, after confessing that he had invented the data for personal interests, was then removed from the UK medical order and all subsequent publications showed that neither the measles vaccine, mumps and rubella nor other vaccinations can be associated with autism.

Indeed, on the contrary, the measles vaccine is very important as severe respiratory complications or acute encephalitis can arise with measles. Precisely because of these two factors, death can occur in certain cases.

What is certain is that measles mortality represents a very low percentage in industrialized countries, about 1 in 10,000 cases, but this must not let your guard down.

Vaccines not only do not cause autism and protect against major diseases, but do not carry any kind of risk. It is true that following a vaccine you can witness phenomena such as some fever line, lack of appetite, irritability or slight swelling at the point where the injection was given, but these are side effects of transient duration that resolve spontaneously or with the administration of symptomatic drugs.

It should also be remembered that vaccines do not contain carcinogens. In the past there has been some controversy over the presence of metals in vaccines. On this point it is necessary to clarify why vaccines currently have neither mercury nor its derivatives inside them and consist only minimally of aluminum salts (0.25-2.5 mg) that strengthen their effect and play a fundamental role in the stimulated immune response. Suffice it to say that with our diet we take a much higher amount of aluminum (5-20 mg) daily, especially through vegetables, an amount that is then eliminated normally by the kidneys without causing toxicity.

So the commitment of us doctors and scientists must be to transmit correct information and make families understand that vaccines are useful, necessary and absolutely safe. Administration of vaccines is strongly recommended in children, but also in adults and pregnant women. Research shows that pregnancy vaccinations help protect the newborn from infectious diseases in the first few months of life.

How and when was autism discovered?

The word autism, derived from the Greek autos, meaning itself, was first used in psychiatry by Eugen Bleuler to describe one of the symptoms of schizophrenia, consisting of self-folding characteristic of certain stages of the condition. In 1943, Leo Kanner, a German pediatrician who emigrated to America used the term "early childhood autism" to describe a complex of symptoms (a syndrome) found in a group of 11 children. In his article Kanner described eleven children, between the ages of two and ten, whose behavior was quite peculiar and very far from normal, but with characteristics that were repeated within the group. In the context of a generalized inability to communicate, there were serious and completely peculiar disorders of language. Three children were mute and in the rest the stages of language development were abnormal.

The first words spoken consisted, in some cases, of mechanical repetition, without understanding, of nursery rhymes, biblical verses, lists of animals and so on. Immediate or delayed echolalia were often present, that is, repetition, direct or at a distance of time, of sentences heard by others, pronounced outside of a context that gave them meaning and without communicative intent. They had pronominal reversal: "you" instead of "I" and vice versa; difficulty acquiring the concept of the words "yes" and "no". If and when the child acquired the ability to speak, he tended not to use it communicatively, not to answer questions, not to porn to others and not to tell things that happened to him. Some also had unwarranted fears of moving objects or mechanical noises and oddities in food preferences.

The physical appearance was completely normal and the gaze seemed absorbed and gave the impression of regular intelligence.

Actually the answer to this question might be a little more complex. The psychiatrist Fitzgeral believes that Leo Kanner may have plagiarized the Austrian neurologist Asperger, the first to provide a comprehensive description of the syndrome of the same name.

Officially Leo Kanner published the article on autism in 1943 and Asperger the following year, in 1944. But Kanner would not have referred to an earlier 1938 Asperger article, named "Das psychisch abnorme kind", which provides a first complete description of autistic disorder. The researchers suspect that Kanner had the opportunity to read the article and used it to identify and define the descriptive characteristics of the syndrome that takes its name from him. Fitzgerald considers the hypothesis that Kanner had contact with a doctor who, to save himself from the dangers of war, had taken refuge in the States and brought with him a copy of Asperger's article. It is estimated that over 200 doctors landed in America. Except that we must not forget that Kanner, having been born and lived in Austria, knew how to speak German, the language of his Austrian colleague.

Asperger's daughter, Dr. Maria Asperger Felder, interviewed by Feinstein, said her father used the term "autistic" in 1934 in letters to colleagues on trips to Leipzig and Potsdam in Germany (presumably in the modern sense and not schizophrenic). In fact, she quotes a letter dated April 14, 1934 in which her father writes about difficulties on diagnostic definitions suggesting the possibility of using the term "autistic". Feinstein also recalls that Kanner, having been born in the Austro-Hungarian state, knew German well, the only language with which Asperger wrote his articles...

The question remains open. Apparently it seems that, based on some elements, Kanner was not entirely original. But is there a completely original discovery in the history of science? I have my doubts. Both doctors made a fundamental contribution to their discipline. Subsequently, research differentiated the syndromes they described, whereby Asperger's syndrome has different neuropsychological characteristics from that outlined by Kanner, dissolving the historical nodes of the issue.

Why is autism increasing?

The issue of autism prevalence among younger people for some time in the USA was returned to the center of attention in the United States after the ex President Donald Trump said that there is "a huge increase in the incidence of autism in children." Limiting itself to diagnoses, the claim is correct and confirmed by statistical assessments from many universities (including Penn State in Pennsylvania), who noted an inexorable increase in certified cases from 2000 onwards. In less than twenty years, it has gone from 0.3% to 1.5% of certified cases, taking the age of 8 as a reference.

Today it is estimated that in schools about 1 in 66 children have been diagnosed with autism, with a much higher prevalence in males.

However, the number of diagnoses is the combined effect of a number of factors, ranging from clinical to bureaucratic, administrative and social aspects. A more in-depth analysis of the dynamics of this phenomenon has led to the conclusion that a good - if not most - of the increase in cases is not attributable to a real increase in the incidence of autism.

When we talk about autism or autism spectrum disorders, we include a wide range of possibilities, ranging from difficulties in social interaction to communication deficits, from concentration defects to problems in performing repetitive tasks. In addition, the severity of these symptoms is very variable, which can range from a mild disorder to more severe cases. Sometimes symptoms of autism are also considered nervousness due to a change in daily routine, slowness in sentence building and poverty of language skills. The case count alone, therefore, provides a very partial photograph of the current situation.

To date, researchers have failed to find a neurological, genetic, or symptom aspect that is uniquely associated with autism. Blood tests, brain screening or other clinical investigations do not allow the presence or absence of the disorder to be established. More or less promising attempts at clinical diagnosis are underway, but prudence is still a must. As a result, the diagnosis is based on common sense, experience, and subjectivity of the assessment physician, with the sole help of World Health Organization Guiding Criteria, which generally defines what is meant by autism.

Not only can different doctors come to opposite conclusions, but the same doctor could make different assessments from year to year due to the continuous updating of the aforementioned international guidelines.

Today there is more awareness about autism. Doctors and families have gradually become aware of the existence and characteristics of this disorder. This is undoubtedly a positive cultural aspect, which could however be the main cause of the increase in recorded cases. If autism was little considered in the past, it is natural that the recognized cases were fewer. In support of this thesis, some scientific studies have shown a correlation between the number of cases of autism and other social factors such as the degree of education of the population, the number of pediatricians and the synergy between schools and hospitals.

Statistics in hand, the increase in autism cases went hand in hand with decreased diagnoses of other disorders, such as intellectual disability and mental retardation. The decline in these diagnoses would be enough to justify at least two-thirds of the increase in autism cases. The disorders mentioned share most of the symptoms, so patient cataloguing is often at the discretion of the doctor in charge of the diagnosis.

Despite numerous explanations that would justify increasing diagnoses as an effect of social and bureaucratic factors, scientists say it is still plausible that autistic patients are really growing. Some studies have shown a link between the incidence of autism and the age of parents. The data on fathers do not allow us to say with certainty that there is an aging, while with regard to mothers the increase in the average age at the time of childbirth has undoubtedly increased in the last twenty years, at least between Europe and the United States.

Can autism be cured?

At the moment there is no cure to treat autism.

The treatments that can be used are supportive and aim to reduce, as far as possible, the symptoms induced by the disorder.

Cognitive-behavioral therapies, family therapy and educational interventions are very important. These therapeutic strategies, in fact, seek to improve patients' communication skills and social and behavioral skills.

Pharmacological treatment, on the other hand, when necessary, is generally aimed at treating any associated disorders (such as epilepsy or attention deficit hyperactivity syndrome) and improving symptoms such as irritability and aggression (for which, usually, the doctor resorts to the use of antipsychotic drugs).

For the treatment of sleep disorders associated with autism, however, melatonin intake may be useful.

Autism spectrum disorders have always been immersed in an aura of uncertainty: doctors do not know what determines them, nor how to treat their symptoms. But perhaps we know something more, thanks to a study appeared in Nature Communications that sees the participation of the Italian Institute of Technology: the step forward derives from the study of an important mechanism underlying the appearance of autistic behaviors in children suffering from Fragile X Syndrome, which shows the "corrective" action of molecules that will be the starting point for the development of new targeted drugs.

Among the known genetic causes of autism the most common is Fragile X Syndrome (FRAX), determined by a gene mutation that leads to the loss of the Fragile X Mental Retardation Protein (FMRP) protein. However, the negative consequences that this mutation has on signal transmission between nerve cells, neurons, are still little known. The IIT group then tried to study the role of the FRMP protein in neuronal communication, using genetically modified mice carrying the same gene mutation found in people with FRAX.

The study showed that the FMRP protein intervenes in controlling the transmission of 2-arachidonoylglycerol (2-AG), a particular 'endocannabinoid' – that is, a marijuana-like substance (cannabis in Latin) produced by the brain – found in neurons. When FMRP protein is absent, as in FRAX patients, neurons in certain regions of the brain lose the ability to produce 2-AG appropriately, resulting in the onset of nerve transmission deficits and autistic behaviors.

The team then sought to identify pharmacological instruments that can correct the compromised neuronal mechanism in FRAX. Through the use of new molecules that increase the effects of 2-AG, stopping its normal process of destruction by neurons, the researchers were able to restore the proper production of the endocannabinoid in neurons. As a result, the treatment resulted in the disappearance of both neuronal dysfunction and autistic behaviors.

These results are important because they demonstrate the existence of molecules that can normalize the effects of the disease on behavior.

Unfortunately, this does not mean that we already have a cure for autism, but that we have discovered a promising way on which to direct pharmacological research to identify, in the coming years, innovative therapies that can treat the symptoms of this often underestimated pathology in humans.

It is highly recommended to children with ASD follow intensive and early behavioral intervention programs.

This approach refers to the use of psychoeducational strategies for teaching and acquiring skills aimed at compensating for difficulties in multiple evolutionary areas. Within this approach, different models place emphasis on different goals and use various strategies. Some factors are common to all treatment models of documented efficacy: precocity (intervention must begin as soon as there is a strong suspicion of autism diagnosis); intensity (at least 20 hours per week of specifically planned psychoeducational activity); adaptation of educational strategies and learning objectives to the chronological age and age of development of the child; the use of evaluation tools to determine the profile of Of communication, socialization, and adaptive behavior; the reference to educational strategies inspired by the cognitive-behavioral model, but within a vision that takes into account the characteristics and preferences of the child and his family; the use of strategies for generalization and maintenance of acquired skills; and the preparation of periodic evaluations and adjustments of the plan.

Interventions must be customized to the needs of each child, shared with the family and structured according to differentiated intensities for each age group and functional profile. The methods and strategies used must be proven effective, indicated in national or international guidelines. The formation of the environment in which the child will be found (school, places of aggregation, etc.) must be guaranteed, so that he knows how to relate to him and offer him positive opportunities for development. We need support for the family, which needs clear, precise, continuous information to be able to consciously face each event and choose the most appropriate path for their child, in continuous dialogue with the operators.

Since autism spectrum disorders are relatively more prevalent than they used to be – also probably due to greater diagnostic sensitivity of clinicians – it is possible that "innovative" therapies are proposed that, unfortunately, often do not rest on solid scientific evidence. As far as possible, parents must the transparency and commercial disinterest of the proposers carefully evaluate the plausibility of the proposed treatments, and, with the help of the pediatrician or neuropsychiatrist of reference, verify the reliability of the studies carried out in support of the therapies proposed also starting from the level of the journals that hosted them.

Since there is certainly no known effective cure for autism, we will talk about "treatments", indicating some of the best known (and sometimes discussed).

Chapter 2: Therapies and Methods

Etodynamic Method, A.E.R.C.

The Ethodynamic Method starts from the ethological observation of the behavior of both the subject with Autistic Disorder and of the people with whom he interacts and articulates himself according to the sequences with whom normal relational development takes place, in particular the primary and secondary inter subjectivity of which we talked about earlier (Trevarthen, 1979, Zappella The ethological principles taken into consideration may concern those activities that take place in a context of approach to the other: for example, the affectionate, friendly, exploratory ways of the other that can be particularly reduced in some autistic subjects. In these cases there are ways of relationship, especially based on the face-to-face reciprocity relationship that, especially in younger children, can be useful both in improving this type of direct and collaborative relationship.

Relationship modalities go hand in hand: for example, a three-year-old boy who has previously had an autistic regression has often lost many of the modes of relationship that are typical of primary inter subjectivity: for this reason the relationship with him must reappear with ways of bodily and verbal reciprocity that in a younger child favor the understanding and expression of One of the main objectives is to create a positive motivation in the child both to interact and to collaborate.

it is for this reason that it is often useful to make use of various forms of activation, verbal and motor, such as taking the child by the hand and running or jumping, putting him in a state of availability and contentment so, immediately after, he becomes ready to collaborate for various cognitive goals.

On these premises is based the intervention called Emotional Activation Therapy and Body Reciprocity (AERC) proposed by Zappella (1996). This methodology always integrates with other educational methods such as the Portage Method, a behavioral educational method, whose function is to give parents guidance on the most appropriate activities to propose to the child.

The Portage Method also allows you to periodically assess your child's changes during therapy. For children who do not speak Augmentative and Alternative Communication (see J.Cafiero) it can be a very important tool and can often integrate with an ethodynamic approach: both, in fact, refer to sensorimotor intelligence that often represents the real cognitive level of many young autistic children and also the prevailing cognitive form of other older autistic subjects, given their Zappella also often proposes an organization of the day that, however, rarely takes on the strictest characteristics of other methods. For autistic people with higher language and intellectual skills it integrates with other educational modalities.

The results of this method change depending on the syndromes and disabilities present and are better, in particular, in dismativa syndrome with early-onset family complex tics and mood disorders for the simple reason that these are probable neurotransmissive disorders in which the reversibility of autistic disorder is greater. The results are better in young children both because at these ages the plasticity of the nervous system is greater and because in them the sensorimotor intelligence has greater expression. In other cases and age groups there may be improvements of varying degrees depending on the condition and degree of disability. The setting in which the intervention takes place consists of a large one, equipped with a one-way mirror and equipped for video recording in which there is enough space for the child to feel free to move and must be equipped with equipment such as table, chairs, armchairs or sofas, as well as a number of games.

The parent is offered to try to establish a relationship with their child and collaborate with him on activities such as drawing, building a tower of cubes, looking at and naming figures, and others like that. The attempt to establish a relationship with the child is carried out by one parent along with one of the therapists, while the other parent with the other therapist assist behind the mirror.

The therapist is tasked with representing a relative model for the parent (and not so much, and not only, giving rational explanations) who is generally frustrated by the repeated failures experienced in the past in an attempt to capture the availability of the child. During sessions the parent experiences an emotional bodily relationship with the child, in the direction of secondary inter subjectivity. The goal of some of these interventions can be strategic and that is, to aim to change and improve the type of parent-child relationship in a short time. A few weeks usually pass between sessions, during which parents devote about an hour a day to play and direct relationship activities with the child similar to those done in session.

The historical precedents of this intervention are partly due to Tinbergen's introduction of ethology into child psychiatry and holding, a therapeutic practice also supported in particular by Tinbergen (1983). In holding the child was kept in a close bodily relationship by one of the parents, face to face, seeking emotional attunement and repeating his vocal expressions which were then modified and enriched by the adult (Zappella, 1987, a). This was followed by a free, festive and collaborative interaction. In the eighties, holding allowed some children to lose autistic behavior and become normal adults: for some of these they were subjects suffering from dismativa syndrome with early-onset family complex tics (Zappella, 1999). It allowed others with obvious organic damage to develop verbal language. The type of sensor-motor interaction that characterized this approach facilitated these advances.

Holding, however, schematized in an unnatural, rigid and separate way, forms of interaction of the type of primary and secondary inter subjectivity as well as interventions that facilitated the articulation of language. In other words: in common life it never happens that a child is kept for a long time in the arms of the parent in a face-to-face relationship: vice versa, the confrontation of bodily reciprocity is constantly articulated with moments of play and movement. For this excessive schematism, holding became inappropriately constrictive. Having clarified these aspects and in the light of the new knowledge on the different autistic syndromes, which in the eighties were much smaller, holding today must be considered an outdated method.

TEACCH program

The TEACCH Program has been developed, during the thirty-year experience, initiated by E. Schopler and his collaborators, in autistic schools in the U.S. state of North Carolina. This program has also achieved great success outside the United States, and has also spread in recent years in Europe and Italy, thanks to the translation of some books (Schopler et al., 1980, 1983) and the activation of training courses.

The TEACCH Program includes numerous educational activities to be carried out with children with Generalized Developmental Disorders or communication disorders. However, the use of these activities must be contextualized and individualized from time to time; the implementation of these activities must be based, in particular on four criteria, which the authors call: model of interaction, development prospects, behavioral relativism and training hierarchy (Schopler et al., 1980).

The concept of interaction model refers to the need to contextualize a certain intervention technique within the relationship system in which the child finds himself. The child's special needs and learning potential can best be grasped in the context of the child's interaction with his daily life, family and school environment.

The second concept that of developmental perspective emphasizes the need to be taken into account, in defining rehabilitation intervention, the level of global development of the child in the different areas. Both its weak areas and those where it shows the greatest capacity will have to be taken into account.

Relativism of behavior is intended to describe and take into account a particular phenomenon that is observed in children with Generalized Developmental Disorders; that of the difficulty, sometimes impossibility, to generalize, to areas other than the one in which it was learned, a behavioral response. It is therefore important to define specific educational goals for each context.

Finally, the concept of the training hierarchy indicates the need for priorities to be defined among the problems to be faced with the autistic child. Educational intervention should be aimed at modifying, firstly, behaviors that put the child's life at risk; secondly, those problems that affect the child's ability to adapt to the family environment. So, as a third priority, there is adaptation to the school context and, as a fourth, adaptation to the extracurricular community.

A logical consequence of what has been said so far is that educational intervention must be tailored to the child, his family and his school (Schopler et al., 1991, p.16).

The rehabilitation intervention will therefore make use of an individualized evaluation that lays the foundations for the formulation of a psychoeducational project.

The TEACCH Program was built to develop imitative skills, perceptual functions, motor skills, oculo-manual integration skills, linguistic comprehension and production, behavior management (autonomy, social and behavioral skills). The enabling project must include objectives that cover different areas: those of communication, leisure, autonomy and domestic skills, social skills and learning in the strict sense.

The conduct of the program is entrusted to parents and teachers, who share the same strategies and work closely together. Doctors and psychologists guide the intervention of parents and teachers, taking into account the level of development achieved by the child, his context of daily life and the propensities of the child.

An important part of the program is evaluation, which takes place through three different ways. The first that involves the use of intellectual tests and standardized scales, concerns the evaluation of development. The second mode is to observe the child's patterns of behavior. The third is the collection of information made in interviews with parents, which also identifies their expectations of the child and the main problems they face. Developmental assessment uses a specific tool called Psychoeducational Profile (P.E.P.): P.E.P. allows you to determine the child's development in the areas of imitation, perception, motor skills, ocular-manual integration, and cognitive abilities. Next to the P.E.P. another tool called A.A.P.E.P. has been prepared, which is used for the evaluation of adolescents and autistic adults.

The expectations and goals expected to be achieved, for each child, are divided into:
1) long-term expectations,
2) intermediate expectations between 3 months and a year
3) immediate educational goals.

Appropriate intervention will need to involve coordination between the three levels. The intervention should also first develop those skills that are implicit in others; if, for example, the child has not developed the ability to imitate, this must be developed first, before proceeding with language stimulation.

The procedure described so far is aimed at defining educational goals; the next step is to formulate, starting from educational goals, specific educational objectives. Each specific educational goal is then translated into educational activities, built taking into account all the variables mentioned above, both individual and contextual. Alongside specific teaching activities, behavior modification techniques are used, especially with regard to problem behavior management.

One of the fundamental principles of the intervention is that the acquisition of skills by the autistic child requires an adaptation and modification of the child's living environment, both family and school. It is important, in particular, that the learning environment is structured and predictable and that the activities proposed to it are precise and, especially for children who do not speak, understandable beyond verbal indications. Structuring must cover both spaces and working times; for example, images describing the various times of the day can be used, and the child is taught to associate each with a specific time/activity of his day.

Schopler and collaborators, provide many concrete examples of specific teaching activities, adapted to the different level of development at which the individual child is located, and related to different skills.

The Therapie d'Echange et Développement (TED)

The starting point of TED is some neurophysiological research that has investigated phenomena such as cross-sensory association and free acquisition and imitation. Cross-sectional sensory association means that phenomenon that is observed when electroencephalographic responses resulting from a sound and a light stimulus that follows the sound by one second are recorded. What is observed is that after some presentations of this pair of stimuli, the first (sound) evokes a response in the occipital visual zone, the one that is usually activated by the light stimulus. No form of reinforcement (such as food) is required for this association to occur. It is, in fact, a cognitive process that occurs spontaneously, and that is present, albeit irregularly, in the autistic child.

In autistic children, moreover, the phenomenon of free acquisition is also observed under certain conditions, unconstrained by any reinforcement and not constrained by the presence, during learning, of a predefined timeline.

Alongside the presence of free acquisition, the free imitation acquisition is also observed: this has been demonstrated through an electroencephalographic recording made with children watching a movie in which gymnastic movements are projected. It is observed that during the perception of gymnastic movements electroencephalographic modifications occur in the motor areas of the subject, synchronized with the movements projected on the screen. The autistic child is in possession, according to these authors, of a capacity for free imitation, albeit poorly structured.

The results of this research highlight a natural physiological curiosity, the biological tendency to associate, understand and seek meanings. The therapist must organize the setting and activities to be proposed to the child taking into account these abilities that the autistic child also possesses, albeit to a reduced and unstructured extent. From these premises Barthelemy, Hameury and Lelord (1995) draw the inspiring principles of TED, which cross all the activities proposed to the child, which as we have seen aim to develop the different psychophysiological functions. These principles were defined by the authors: "tranquility", "availability" and "reciprocity".

Now let's define in particular the setting in which the intervention takes place. This typically consists of a small, bare room, where there is a table and two chairs. Often there is a unidirectional mirror that allows direct observation of the session. In this room calm dominates and no disturbing external noises are felt. The main source of interest for the child is the therapist who, through an exclusive and careful mode of interaction, offers him one activity or one game at a time.

This organization of the setting aims to maximize the child's attention and decoding of messages, minimizing the presence of distracting or confusing stimulation.

The therapist's availability (second principle) is aimed at facilitating the child's openness to the outside world and fostering his natural curiosity. Attempts by the child to break his isolation are encouraged and attempts are made to develop his spontaneous initiative; even the smallest manifestation of attention by the child is encouraged.

Reciprocity is expressed through games and activities that involve an exchange of objects, gestures, vocalizations, emotions, etc., between therapist and child. The purpose of reciprocity is to stimulate communication.

The activities that are proposed to the child are those contained in the Individual Educational Project, based on functional analysis, and concern attention, perception, association, intention, traction, ability to contact and communication. The overall therapeutic project, which may also include medical care and interventions by different practitioners, is defined by all team members who participated in the evaluation, and agreed with the family. Active family involvement is another key feature of TED. Periodic checks are planned between the members of the team, who make use of video recordings of the sessions and the evaluation made through the use of purpose-built stairs.

The intervention is conducted in the context of a "Hopital de Jour", and involves inclusion in groups and activities (such as kindergarten) inside the hospital.

TED is preferably conducted in the classic setting described above; however, it can also take place in other areas, without prejudice to the general principles of tranquility, availability and reciprocity. The speech therapy room, that of psychomotor skills, or in special cases the water of a large bathtub, can be as many places where TED is conducted.

The intervention can also be conducted with two children at the same time, if the main purpose is to promote socialization. These situations are typically triggered after a classic TED has been done, with children still having socializing problems, often with an aggressive component. The child is joined by another child with similar abilities, in need of developing communication, but calmer.

TED is flanked by interventions with larger groups of children, but even in this case the inspiring principles of the intervention are those seen above. The context in which this intervention takes place must be reassuring, predictable, with precise time sequences, stable.

Psychoanalysis and therapy of childhood psychoses

The problem posed by childhood psycho psychotherapy has sparked the interest of psychoanalytic authors, well before Kanner's description of childhood autism. Already in 1930, in fact M. Klein wrote that one of the main tasks of child analysis should also be to study and treat childhood psychoses (Klein, 1968).

Mahler (1972), starting from her distinction between primary autistic psychoses and symbiotic psychoses, identifies some principles in the analytical care of psychotic children.

The first therapeutic objective will be according to Mahler to involve the child in a "corrective symbiotic experience" (Mahler) that allows the child, over a rather long period of time, to reach a higher level of relationship with the object, also reliving the previous stages of development.

This can be achieved if the child retraces the various stages of development (presymbiotic, symbiotic and separation - detection) with the support of a therapist acting as an auxiliary self. The therapist will also have to provide the child with those functions of the Ego that serve to protect him from excessive stimulation from the outside and, at the same time, from threatening inner stimuli.

The psychotic child is on a state of panic and anguish in which the fear of the loss of ego boundaries and the inability to contain aggression emerges. The therapist will have to put limits on the child, especially his aggressive and self-destructive impulses, e.g. by intervening and helping him better organize a game that tends to be fragmentary and incomprehensible. It can also perform a pedagogical function with the child: According to Mahler, individual therapy is more suitable for the autistic child, necessary to get him out of his isolation. Certain pedagogical interventions cannot be beneficial until the child has begun to develop some kind of symbiotic relationship.

This does not apply to the primarily symbiotic child who will be able to profit from educational interventions as soon as his typical panic reactions have disappeared and will be ready to establish diversified relationships that replace the state of fusion with the mother.

Starting from the deep panic reactions that autistic children often have in the face of trying to break their isolation, Mahler suggests trying to pull the child out of isolation with the help of music, using pleasant stimulation of his sensory organs, using inanimate objects; not using, therefore, the direct approach especially the corporeal one.

Mahler proposed, particularly for symbiotic psychoses, a therapeutic method that sees the presence of the mother next to the child and therapist. These are engaged in sessions lasting 2 or 3 hours during which the mother and therapist work jointly for the rehabilitation of the child. The involvement of the mother is one of the substantial differences between Mahler's therapeutic model and that of another important psychoanalytic author, B. Beththeleim. The latter considers it appropriate to separate the child from the mother and to care in a specially prepared institution.

The goal of therapy is to prevent the child from retiring to an autistic defensive position. It must be encouraged to relive with a mother's substitute an exclusive, more rewarding, albeit regressive, symbiotic-parasitic relationship. This relationship must be freely made available to the child and become a defense for him at the time when he must get out of the vicious circle of his deformed relationship with his mother.

Mahler therefore proposes a therapy model that, for symbiotic psychosis in particular, holds the mother-child dyad together and differs from the classic one of child analysis. Manzano and Palacio Espasa (1983) believe that Mahler's intervention, as well as most North American authors, tends to focus on a corrective emotional experience and not so much, or otherwise to a lesser extent, on the analysis of transference. The latter approach is for example developed by F.Tustin and other Kleinian authors who, in fact, focus their therapeutic procedure on the analysis of transference.

In recent years, some authors of psychoanalytic school have emphasized the need for the taking charge of the child to be early and include alongside individual psychoanalytic psychotherapy, other interventions, pharmacological and educational, that take into account the heterogeneity of the paintings shown by autistic children.

Systemic family therapy

The family therapy proposed in the case of the psychotic child partly follows that for the adolescent, in particular in the sequence with which members of the nuclear family and those of origin are involved.

The first session involves members of the nuclear family and a significant extended family member, summoned on the basis of the information collected during the first phone call. Typically, the extended family member who was summoned was the maternal grandmother. This choice may appear to be a logical consequence of what has been described as a typical dynamic of these families, in which the relationship between mother and maternal grandmother is often disturbed and sees continuous interference of the latter in the maternal functions of the former.

In the first session, the presence of an extended family member makes it possible to focus on the frequent interference of their families of origin in the interaction of the nuclear family and also represents the ideal context to bring out any "negative prediction" about the outcome of the couple's marriage (see previous section).

At the end of the first session, the member of the extended family who participated is thanked for the collaboration and discharged, with the explicit invitation to stop interference and psychological pressures that, as emerged from the session, can disturb the normal parental function of the couple.

Only members of the nuclear family are present in the second session, including the "designated patient" child. This session is dedicated to deepening the couple's relationship and the relationship of each member with the little patient.

The child is able to provide important information with his behavior, even if he does not speak and appears closed in his world. It is in fact common for the child to privilege the relationship with one of the parents and intervene by disturbing, at particularly significant moments of the sessions.

This allows the therapist to redefine the child as an actor in family play, endowed with intentionality. This definition replaces that of a sick and passive child even if, in general, it is not accepted without objection or resistance by parents.

The central phase of therapy sees only the presence of parents; in these sessions the therapist tries to more clearly relate the child's disorder with the relationship "stall" situation of the couple (cf. Selvini Palazzoli et al., 1988). This also implies personal work on each parent, aimed at better understanding how their way of relating to the partner is largely determined by the relationships established in the past with their families of origin.

The presence of parents alone at this stage of therapy emphasizes, pragmatically, that therapeutic work is directed primarily at them. Some deliveries are also proposed to parents, which concern activities to be done with the child.

A proposed activity that has proved particularly useful is a daily period of holding, that is, of forced relationship with the child in which the parent (usually the mother), strongly embraces the child forcing him to an intense bodily and visual relationship. The child, especially at the beginning, generally opposes this activity, showing an intentionality and usually unexpressed energy.

It is at this point in therapy with the couple that, according to Sorrentino, it becomes appropriate to offer the child individualized rehabilitation interventions, both on the learning and social skills side.

The harmonization of these rehabilitation interventions aimed at the child, with the therapy of the parental couple, is an indispensable prerequisite for achieving an improvement in symptoms and, in some cases, healing.

Pharmacological therapies

Therapeutic intervention in pervasive developmental disorders must be typically intensive, prolonged and integrated, with the association of functional, psychological, social, family and pharmacological rehabilitation educational interventions. Poor knowledge on the neurophysiological basis of autism means that the pharmacological approach to this pathology is still primarily symptomatic, aimed at fostering more adequate and socially acceptable behaviors, or is aimed at containing associated manifestations in comorbidity. Current data indicate that drug intervention has a very marginal impact on the natural history of autistic disorder.

The phenomenal multiplicity of "autistic pictures" and the lack of knowledge about the pathogenesis of this disorder justify the multiple therapeutic attempts with pharmacologically even very different substances of which attempts have been tried from time to time to exploit the specific activity on a symptom. The prevailing objective of the pharmacological intervention therefore becomes that of the control of symptomatic manifestations that can negatively affect the quality of life and other therapeutic interventions.

Treatment should be preceded by careful functional analysis highlighting target symptoms, which can be very different in various subjects (stereotypies and aggressive conduct, attention disorders, mood swings, sleep disturbances). The use of these substances in developmental age requires special attention for the onset of possible side effects.

Pharmacological intervention in Autistic Syndromes must be a tool that makes psychoeducational, rehabilitation and psychotherapeutic approaches aimed at the child more effective.

Since autism disorder cannot be cured, but only its most disabling symptoms, there is a risk of incurring polytherapy that would represent a "pharmacological bombing"; to overcome this it is advisable to use those with a broader spectrum as first choice drugs.

These are neuroleptics or SSRIs. When drugs are not effective individually, they may be combined, bearing in mind that the combination changes the plasma level of both, and in case of further ineffectiveness to replace them with the drugs indicated for target symptoms.

The indication for the use of the drug is to limit it to acute phases, not yet having sufficient data on prolonged treatments, evaluating that the administration of psychopharmacological therapy has meant only if associated with an overall care of the autistic child and his family.

Delacato Method

C. Delacato was initially part, with G. Doman and R. Doman, from a working group with a clear medical physiatric approach, dedicated to the rehabilitation of cerebroharm children.

1 of the conclusions of the working group was that the child's development proceeds in stages, which, if they are skipped, prevent the child from reaching their potential. The task of the rehabilitation program is to have the child repeat the stage that has been skipped, and have him retraced in order to stimulate his brain to develop (Delacato, 1974). In addition, it was found that there are different degrees of brain injury, from severe to mild, and that the most common factor of mild brain injury was perception problems (tactile, visual or acoustic).

Later Delacato began working with normal children from a motor point of view, but who had serious behavioral disorders. From here he went on to study autism.

From the observation that many of the symptoms of brain-injured children are similar to those of autism, he begins to consider autistic attitudes as a consequence of a sensory or perceptual problem.

Autistic children are considered as cerebrolesis with serious sensory problems: not being able to exploit the stimuli that come from outside, because the channels of communication with the brain are defective, they try to normalize the route through repetitive behavior that stimulates the channel itself.

Autistic children are therefore not psychotic, that is, they do not behave like this for psychological causes but for neurological reasons.

3 types of sensory deficit are identified:

1) **Hypersensitivity:** Pass too much information to the brain and creates an overload.

2) **Hyposensitivity:** too small a part of information passes which therefore cannot be adequately processed and processed.

3) **White noise:** Perception is disturbed by internal sensory interference, meaning the very activity of the inefficient sensory system creates interference in the system.

To treat this disorder, it is therefore necessary to first help the child survive stimuli and then proceed to normalize his sensory system.

In summary
- Autistic children are not psychotic but brain-injured
- Brain injury causes perceptual dysfunction
- Sensory pathways are abnormal, of three types: hyper, hypo and white noise
- Autism (stereotypies) are symptoms of brain injury
- They are here called sensory attitudes, and are attempts to normalize the injured sensory pathways
- The child tries to cure himself
- Trying to do it he distracts himself from reality
- From the observation of behavior, the injured ways can be identified
- You can tell if the deficit is hyper, hypo or white noise
- Pathways can be normalized by offering the child the right experience and stimulation through that specific compromised pathway
- When the channel is normalized, repetitive behavior ceases
- When this behavior ceases, the child can focus on the real world
- At this point you will treat him as you treat mild brain injuries, giving him the opportunity to retrace the stage that was somehow skipped.

Facilitated Communication

The Facilitated Communication technique was developed in the late 1980s by Chosley and Biklen and later spread mainly in the United States and Australia.
Facilitated Communication means a method of facilitating communication in which a licensed therapist - the facilitator - offers support to the hand or arm of an individual

with a communication deficit to help them indicate images or letters or use a keyboard to type text.

The assumption of this is that this method would help people who are autistic or with severe mental retardation communicate.

According to the supporters of this technique, in fact, the autistic individual would find it difficult to communicate not because he does not want or does not know how to do it, but because he cannot order in sequence what he has to say, and he cannot make the right movement to indicate or write what he would have to say but does not succeed. In this difficulty autism is united with apraxia, that is, the communication difficulty would be caused by the apraxia that autistic individuals suffer from.

In support of this hypothesis it is noted that a period of training is enough to associate words-images, indicate or beat on a keyboard made by offering support to the arm of the person subjected to such training, after which the help is progressively decreased until it touches only the hand of the person who in the meantime has learned to communicate using more and more words and an increasingly structured language.

The aid is subsequently further reduced by switching to a facilitation made by placing the hand on the shoulder or knees (Bicklen, 1999).

The method has garnered numerous criticisms and objections, including that of the American Psychological Association, who object that the method is devoid of scientific validity, that it has been proven that the product of facilitated communication is often directed or systematically determined by the facilitator, and that no scientific studies have been done aimed at determining whether therapists or facilitators are aware of their degree of influence.

For these reasons, the APA opposes the use of facilitated communication as it would pose a threat to override the rights of patients who are treated in this way.

The answer to such criticisms provided by supporters of this method is that it must be taken into account the fact that the laboratory situation envisaged for a type of research that can give scientific validity would certainly negatively affect the performance of subjects, and that this is one of the reasons why so far the results of the tests made have come at the expense of this communication technique.

In favor of CF, it is instead considered the fact that it has been useful for many people because it has allowed them to communicate, and that if the theoretical and research foundations are not entirely firm, this is not a sufficient reason to eliminate it completely without offering other alternatives anyway. In the future, therefore, it is proposed to make greater efforts in research aimed at improving and consolidating this powerful means of communication.

Auditory Training

Two methods are presented here that rely on auditory stimulation in order to improve listening and auditory processing skills in the individual: Guy Bérard's auditory integration training and Alfred Tomatis' audio-psycho-phonological approach.

Additive Integration Trainings

The AIT was developed by Guy Berard in Annecy, France, to help people with hearing stimuli processing problems. According to Berard, there can be processing problems if one hears certain frequencies of sounds much better than others, and if one is hypersensitive to certain frequencies. The frequencies on which a person is hypersensitive are called "auditory peaks," and these spikes in the audiogram are visible as mountains.

Before the initial session, an auditory test is done to determine if the person has hearing spikes. Then, after five hours of treatment, a second test is done, to see if there are still hearing spikes and if there are new ones. At the end of the training a third test is done. According to Dr. Berard, at the end of training all frequencies should be perceived equally, and the person should no longer have spikes in hearing.

Symptoms of autism begin to be apparent between 18 and 36 months. Often doctors and parents understand that some form of disorder is present in the child already in the early hours of birth. As has already been said, intervening immediately guarantees excellent results for the development of the small patient. In this way, in fact, parents are more likely to identify the early signs and symptoms of autism through detailed and precise monitoring of their children's development, trying to identify any deficits or arrests.

In the course of growth, moreover, children go through a process in which fundamental skills are learned and mastered, defined in pediatrics as the basics of development. These are physical skills, such as gesticulating, sitting, standing, walking; social skills, such as smiling or imitating others; and communication skills, such as talking. Since the pace of growth varies from child to child, there are times by which certain basic skills should be achieved. If the child has not achieved these skills on schedule, this would already be a first wake-up call.

The AIT is done by a device that randomly selects high and low frequencies from a piece of music, and transmits them in headphones to the person. If the person has particular auditory spikes, as highlighted by the audiogram, these frequencies are filtered from the song completely (are removed) or partially (are slightly changed).The program includes two AIT sessions per day of thirty minutes, for ten consecutive days. During the first five hours of AIT, the sound level is equal for both ears. For people who have language problems, after five hours of training the sound level in the left ear is reduced.

Because the right ear is connected more directly to the left hemisphere than the right one, and because the left hemisphere is responsible for language processing, Dr. Berard believes that a higher sound level in the right ear can stimulate the left hemisphere more.

Unexpected behavior problems during the ten days of training, such as agitation, hyperactivity, and rapid mood changes, were observed in some individuals. Although the cause of these behaviors is not certain, that is, it is not known whether they are directly caused by AIT, or by changes in diet and activity level during training (it has been noted that children are often offered many sweets and snacks during training for them to be good), Dr. Bérard and his collaborators stress the importance of advising parents both before and after treatment, so as to prepare and inform them of such possible changes.

For example, a possible change is an increase in attention span. If a child has short attention spans, it may be quite simple to distract them from a game or activity. But if attention span increases, the child may become more stubborn is harder to distract because his attention has improved. Other changes could be an increase in the affective sphere (such as anger, crying, reactions to other crying people), independence (leaving a place without permission), and social maturation (an increase in interaction)

At the moment, it is not known exactly how AIT can affect the behavior of a person with autism. One possible explanation is that the AIT actually conditions the person to shift attention more easily. Dr. Eric Courchesne, of Children's Hospital in San Diego, recently found that autistic children have a hard time shifting attention from one stimulus to another. Because high and low stimuli are randomly transmitted, AIT could teach a person to quickly and with less effort shift attention; as a result, the person could learn to pay more attention and better understand contingencies related to sounds and movements (such as gestures). Another possible explanation refers to the fact that autistics often don't seem to know how to "tune" with others in the environment.

When random ups and downs sounds are sent, the person cannot anticipate the sounds, and therefore cannot stay out of tuning. As a result, you see that the person is taught to "tune" with others. Finally, it is possible for a person to begin to perceive sounds in a better way, especially language; as a result, it could improve their ability to relate a sound to a behavior, object, action or event. Then there are two other hypotheses that could explain the effect of Berard's AIT, the opioid hypothesis and the melanin hypothesis.

According to the opioid hypothesis, by Jaak Panksepp, some individuals with autism would have a high level of opioid activity at the brain level, and there is evidence of the presence of an uncharacterized variant of beta endorphins.

Beta endorphins are substances similar to endogenous opium in the brain; high levels of these substances are associated with both pleasure and anesthetic effects.

According to this hypothesis, modulated music stimulates the production of endogenous opioids, but verification of such a hypothesis has not yet been done. The results of a study done on chicks who underwent music soon after birth were published in the journal "Autism research Review International" (1995, Vol.9). Another hypothesis, by Lisa Boswell, concerns melanin.

According to some studies, the circadian rhythms of melatonin in the pineal gland in autistic subjects are not normal. Melatonin helps, among other things, regulate sleep and wake rhythms and autoimmunity functions. According to this hypothesis, AIT would help normalize the pineal functions and rhythms of melatonin, with effects also on autoimmune symptoms. This hypothesis would explain among other things an effect noted by Dr. Berard, which is the attenuation of allergic disorders such as asthma, hay fever and skin eczema following treatment with AIT.

Audio-psycho-phonological approach of Tomatis

Tomatis' method is based on a psychological-emotional hypothesis, and aims to improve listening and communication skills. The method was introduced around the 1950s by Dr. Alfred Tomatis, a French ENT doctor, with the aim of re-educating and improving listening and learning skills, communication, creativity and social behavior. The method is aimed at children with learning disabilities, attention deficits, autism, and motor problems and sensory integration.

The theory developed by Dr. Tomatis over the years is centered on the different functions of the ear and the connections between hearing and voice. The functions of the ear that have been examined in more detail, in addition to hearing, are vestibular and cochlear function. The first is responsible for balance, coordination, verticality, muscle tone and eye muscles. The vestibule also plays an important role in transmitting and coordinating the sensory information our body sends to the brain. Problems at this level cause sensory integration problems.

The second function studied, the cochlear one, is responsible for sound analysis, and therefore is closely related to language comprehension.

The vestibular and cochlear system then filters and processes sensory information, both auditory and visual and tactile.

According to the theory further elaborated by dr. Tomatis, high-frequency sounds can give energy to the brain, while low-frequency sounds take away energy. This is because high-frequency sounds activate the vestibular system and make the body move reflexively, as can easily be seen in people who listen to pop music and dance spontaneously.

Another important function of the ear, detailed in Tomatis theory, is to listen (not hearing). This function allows us to filter out what we hear, excluding what we don't need to hear, and to organize auditory information into meaningful hierarchies, rather than being submerged in sounds. The development of this function depends on several factors, including pregnancy, childbirth, disease, or trauma and events that can affect hearing and the ability to communicate. When this function is disturbed, negative consequences in school, social and communication skills are noted. Communication skills, especially those related to voice, such as intensity, timbre, rhythm, fluency in expression, also depend on ear dominance. In fact, if it is the right ear that is dominant over the left, information processing is more effective and faster, and the individual is able to better control the components of verbal communication indicated above. In addition, individuals with right auditory dominance would have greater ability to manage their emotional experiences. The training then aims to regain the ability to listen in a balanced way and improve the efficiency of the right ear. When the listening function is recovered and balanced, there will also be positive repercussions on the voice, which is closely connected with the auditory system, and with it also on self-expression and behavior.

In analyzing the development of ear and hearing functions, Dr. Tomatis attaches particular importance to all stages of the child's development, beginning with fetal development and uterine life. Since it has been proven that hearing is the first sense to be developed, being already completely effective when the fetus is 4.5 months old, the Tomatis method attaches great importance to uterine life, and tries to retrace all its development through symbolic experience.

The program proposes, in fact, in a first phase, sounds or the voice of the mother, suitably filtered, as would be perceived by the fetus. Retracing these early stages, and the "therapeutic use" of the mother's voice, has been mistakenly regarded as making the mother guilty of the child's problems, in the specific case of autism. What the doctor tries to do instead. Tomatis with this type of intervention is to create or restore a healthy attachment bond between mother and child, a bond that for various reasons could not develop in a normal way. At this stage, high frequencies are used, which infuse energy and charge the brain. In the second phase the sounds that would be perceived after birth are recreated; these sounds include songs, repetition of words, stories, and the frequency of sounds is high, as in the first phase. In the third phase, aimed at integrating written language, the patient reads aloud.

This addresses the problem of auditory processing both from a functional point of view (auditory stimulation and balancing) and from a psychological point of view.

In the particular case of children with autism, with particular difficulties of integration and auditory sensitivity, highlighted by the tendency, on the occasion of certain noises, to cover their ears, or to have crises of anger, or to indulge in self-stimulatory activities, the audio-psycho-phonological approach aims to reduce hypersensitivity and integration deficit, going to desensitize the child's hearing. These behaviors are in fact interpreted as a natural defense for listening to particular auditory stimulations, which are perceived as painful, not only at the level of hearing, but also through the skin and skeleton, or are mistakenly associated with other types of sensations (for example, sounds are seen as lights, or vice versa), creating confusion in the child's mind and excessive overload.

Training is done with the use of sound stimulation done with a special device, called the electronic ear, which in addition to headphones also has a piece resting on the skull, which transmits vibrations and sounds directly on the bone. At first stimulation is intense, typically 2 hours a day, for 15 days; subsequent stages are shorter and occur at intervals of 1 or 2 months.

Early Behavioral Intervention by Lovaas (Method A.B.A)

Lovaas and his collaborators (1987) say that early and intensive behavioral intervention performed at home, using **Applied Behavior Analysis (A.B.A.)** methods allows many autistic children to get to have a normal life. O. I. Lovaas believes that the treatment of autistic subjects is better if it is carried out in their living environment without hospitalization. The most important purpose is to help children live and function in a real world and not in an artificial one as it is an institution; for this reason the place of treatment is the natural one of the child (home, school), and the way to intervene is the teaching entrusted to parents and relatives.

Applied Behavior Analysis uses methods based on scientifically established behavioral principles (operating learning) in order to build socially useful behavioral repertoires and reduce problematic ones.

According to the behavioral analytical point of view, autism is a syndrome of deficits and behavioral excesses that have neurological basis, but still subject to change as a result of specific, carefully programmed and constructive interactions with the environment, since children with autism do not learn easily from typical environments, but can learn if they receive appropriate instructions. Emphasis is placed on teaching the child how to learn from the normal environment. Behavioral analytical treatment for autism focuses on the systematic teaching of small, measurable units of behavior; each skill is divided into small steps, each of which is taught separately by presenting a specific set of instructions (explicit and clear). The rule for starting to teach a behavior is to choose a simple (fixed) one; meals are a perfect opportunity to start teaching.

The student thus comes to master at the beginning the first units that are then coordinated and put together until they form a single whole later. Sometimes help (such as physical help) is added to get started, which is then progressively decreased to prevent the child from becoming addicted to it. Appropriate answers are followed by consequences that function as reinforcement: when a child does something good, they are rewarded immediately: as soon as the correct behavior occurs, the child must be rewarded instantly, behavior and reward should be almost contemporary. At first the rewards (which must last only 3 to 5 seconds and be varied) can be remarkable and concrete (frozens, kisses, words of praise), and you have to be emphatic in the tone of voice to make learning fun, then as the child develops such rewards become thinner (a look, even minimal recognition).

You have to move the reward from food to other more normal and natural types as soon as possible, such as social ones ("good", "good"); then you move from a continuous reward to a partial one, rewarding only once in a while. Problem responses (whims, stereotypes, self-aggressive behavior, withdrawal) are not reinforced. A priority purpose is to teach the child to discriminate between different stimuli (colors, shapes, letters, numbers, appropriate and non-appropriate behaviors). Teaching tests are repeated many times, initially in quick succession, until the child gives an answer easily and without the help of the adult.

The time and speed of teaching sessions, practical opportunities, and consequences are determined precisely for each child and each skill, the instructions are highly personalized and adapted to each child's learning style and speed.

The results of research conducted by Lovaas and collaborators (1987) on early behavioral intervention for autism would show:

Effectiveness: early intervention based on the principles of Applied Behavior Analysis would produce large, lasting, and significant improvements in many important domains and the reduction of problematic behaviors; for some these improvements can achieve normal and complete intellectual, social, academic, communicative and adaptive functioning. Only a small portion (about 10%) made no improvement. The most documented positive result is the increased intellectual functioning measured by standardized IQ tests or with development scales. Successful integration into the regular course of schools would be another positive effect.

Age for optimal efficacy: the optimal age to initiate early behavioral intervention is before 5 years of age; the best results have been reported for children who have started treatment at 2 or 3 years. There may be an optimal period during which the young evolving brain is very modifiable: in some children with autism the repeated and active interaction with the physical and social environment that is ensured by early behavioral intervention can modify their neural circuit, correcting it before the neurobiological correlates of autistic behavior become permanent.

Nature of the intervention: Behavioral intervention is a "package" of treatments that are applied intensively and sustainably (with carefully planned learning opportunities). An important feature of A.B.A. is that it is highly individualized. Intensity: The best results would be obtained, according to supporters of this methodology, for those children who have followed behavioral intervention for at least 30 hours a week, every day. Duration: the best outcomes would be with children who have practiced this intensive surgery for at least 2 consecutive years, if not longer.

Environment: in general, quiet and distraction-free environments are preferred for the first time, bearing in mind that then the treatment must be extended to other environments to produce lasting and generalized effects. In addition, parental involvement in treatment can be a crucial component for intervention on young children, especially if it takes place at home.

Greenspan floortime

Stanley Greenspan is a child psychiatrist and psychoanalyst, as well as a professor of psychiatry and pediatrics at a medical school in the United States. His approach is the result of a long experience of working with young children and their families.

The short presentation that follows on his method is taken from the book "The Child with Special Needs" by S. Greenspan and S. Wieder, a manual that by integrating clinical experience with research work on the mental and emotional development of the child, provides parents of children with special needs with very practical guidance to help them grow and educate them directly and serenely, through direct interaction and play.

And indeed, it is really about play in this book, that is, how to find a way to play with your child and make play a tool to involve him emotionally and cognitively. "Floor - time", literally "time spent on the ground, on the floor", means exactly that, spending 20-30 minutes on the ground with your child playing and interacting with him.

This is the central node of Greenspan's approach, play, but the underlying basis from which play benefits to guide and foster the child's development is represented by human relationships, which nourishes the human brain and mind and without which one cannot generate, in Greenspan's words, sense of self-esteem, initiative and creativity, and higher functions such as logic, judgment, abstract What therefore distinguishes this type of approach from other traditional points of view on cognition and learning is that the emotional "lesson" precedes the cognitive one, and is indeed its basis, the starting point for mobilizing the intellectual and emotional growth of the disabled and able-bodied child.

This growth will be mainly affected by three factors. The first is represented by the neurological potential with which the child is endowed and the biological limits that prevent its functioning.

The second is the way the child interacts with parents, teachers, operators or other reference figures, and the third is represented by the type of family, the underlying culture and the environment in which he lives, with the expectations and ability to process and accept that follow.

Fundamental in this approach is therefore the work of parents with the child, parallel to that of therapists and teachers, and the work of parents on themselves, their responses and styles of interaction, play and emotional response to the demands and needs of the child as he grows up. The parent thus becomes a playmate and a guide who takes the child on the evolutionary path. The "Floor - time" is therefore a so-called "evolutionary approach", as it is a systematic method to help the child who has problems acquire and master the different stages of development and related skills. Greenspan identifies 6 stages and skills in the mental growth of the child, fundamental for every type of learning and intellectual development, and for the possibility of interacting with the world.

The first skill that the child must learn to master is the ability to stay calm and be open and interested in stimuli from outside; later he will have to learn to interact and feel good with others, especially with parents and other reference figures, sharing intimacy and security with them.

The third stage is the ability to create reciprocal communication exchanges, that is, open and close the so-called "communication circles", starting from responding to the mother's smile to get to give a gestural or verbal response to a proposal that comes from the other and trying to understand her intention and communication. This may seem like the point of arrival for many children with Autism and the starting point for emotional and intellectual development, but neither the previous stages nor the subsequent goals should be forgotten.

From here, in fact, the child proceeds towards the acquisition of the ability to create complex gestures, to sequence a series of actions in an elaborate sequence of logical reasoning, the ability to create new ideas and finally the ability to create a bridge between ideas and make them real and logical, which essentially means being able to express ideas and feelings through play or language and to be able to put them together according to a logical and original thought.

The method on which this type of approach is based is, as we said, based on direct and interactive play with the child, done by therapists but above all by parents. A game therefore as spontaneous and fun as any other moment of play and free time, but always keeping in mind that, unlike spontaneous play, the parent has a leading and master role here, and must therefore always try to be a very active playmate.

The type of game is inspired by a few very clear principles, not always simple to follow, among which the most important is to always try to follow the child's guidance and initiative and play with anything that attracts his attention, even if it is just looking out the window, but in such a way as to encourage interaction. However, following the child's interests does not mean being passively transported by his game or refusal to play with the other, but it means building on what the child does and forcing him, literally, to open and close more and more circles of communication.

The work is carried out intensively by therapists and parents, but it is above all the latter who have to commit to carving, in the approximately 12 hours that a child typically has of wakefulness, 6 or 10 "Floor-time" sessions of 20-30 minutes each day. It should also be noted that this approach, which at first seems to enter the daily routine and upset it, then often becomes a philosophy of life and a general approach to solving problematic behaviors or problems in acquiring new notions and skills.

In his research and practice work on cases of Autism and Global Developmental Disorders, Greenspan introduced the term "Multisystem Neurological Disorder," to refer to children with communication problems and repetitive behaviors, but who may or have the potential to relate to others with warmth and joy. In his experience of working with children with these types of problems he noted that, contrary to many pessimistic prognoses that generally accompany a diagnosis of Global Developmental Disorder, when spontaneous affective interactions based on very consistent, or gestural or verbal, exchanges, are introduced and intensified, idiosyncratic or perseveration behaviors decrease and increases the ability to relate.

Cafiero's Natural Aided Language

Joanne M. Cafiero has developed an approach methodology to autism that is based on Augmentative and Alternative Communication. Cafiero starts from the observation that many of the early indicators of autism represent indispensable prerequisites for developing communication; their absence or severe impairment in autism requires interventions that favor the development of communication precursors such as eye contact, gesture communication, declarative indication, joint attention, etc.

In addition, problems on the communication side are one of the main stressors also at the family level. Cafiero points out that about 50% of autistics do not speak and the possibility of improving communication skills is a fundamental variable for improving the quality of life.

Augmentative and Alternative Communication concerns that set of strategies, which can also be supported by technological tools, aimed at "increasing" the verbal communication skills already present or introducing "alternative" modalities to language where it has not developed.

The methodology proposed by Prof. Cafiero represents a type of CAA that is defined by the author as "Natural Aided Language". The N.A.L. represents an augmentative communication strategy in which iconic and verbal symbols (typically Mayer-Johnson's Picture Communication Symbols) are used in natural game and learning situations, in order to facilitate interaction between participants. These iconic and verbal symbols are used both to foster understanding of the activities carried out, and to facilitate spontaneous communication and decision-making by children.

The symbols can be used individually (e.g. the symbol - image + word - of soap bubbles can be given by the autistic child to the teacher as a way to request the desired game); or they can be placed on a table (Interactive Language Board) divided according to the function, into pronouns, names, verbs etc. The intervention of Natural Aided Language requires the collaboration of all the people who are part of the life environment of parents and aims to stimulate communication methods that through the visual channel create the conditions for the organization of a linguistic thought.

Cafiero's strategy takes into account the specificity of the communicative disability of autistics, which in most cases are lacking precisely on the side of communicative intentionality; this requires that CAA strategies are also calibrated on the specific type of disability, creating relational situations that can favor communication exchanges through the sharing of a symbolic system.

Speech therapy

Studies on cerebral electrical responses show, as already mentioned, that there are natural modes of acquisition (cross-sensory association, free sensory acquisition, cross motor association, free motor acquisition, free imitation), in situations of tranquility, which are considered as a physiological basis for the mechanism of operation of exchange and development therapies and which differ from other characteristics assumed at the foundation of approaches such as analytical psychotherapy and behavioral therapies.

Practically the autistic subject is physiologically predisposed, albeit with peculiar expressions, to a curiosity and a need to acquire spontaneously, as well as to a natural tendency to imitate both in terms of movement and emotions.

These characteristics inspire the general principles of TED, which consist in making communication exchange situations characterized by tranquility, availability and reciprocity available to the subject, in the process of implementing the individual project.

The therapeutic project envisaged by TED, as already mentioned, is multidisciplinary and also involves the family, and within this individual project developed for the child and placed in a more global approach logopedic work is integrated.

The role that the language therapist plays in a multidisciplinary team has two main modalities: on the one hand a direct intervention on the child with regard to individual or group speech therapy interventions, and on the other a more indirect action through participation in psycho-educational treatments, collaboration with the family, information and daily dialogue with the attending team.

It is about helping the child express his needs, rejections, joys and fears and helping the environment adapt to this child who has strange behavior.

The approach rests on some essential clinical elements, which lead to defining language disorders in autism as complex, heterogeneous, and variable.

They are complex disorders because they are inserted into a more global pathology than development and social interactions and relationships with the environment. Then because they concern linguistic disorders related to real autism at the same time, but also possibly disorders related to other associated syndromes, again because they concern language but more widely communication in all its forms: verbal communication, non-verbal communication". Finally because they concern various levels of linguistic organization: phonology, lexicon, syntax, semantics and finally the social use of language, the pragmatic component.

These are heterogeneous disorders because they cover very different clinical realities in etiology, diagnosis and prognosis (some children do not acquire language, others access rudimentary language that maintains characteristics such as echolalia; others possess language but have difficulty using it conventionally), and because children can also have very different levels in different sectors of language.

Finally, they are variable disorders because they vary expression in the same subject. Faced with this "polymorphic semiology" three modes of speechopedic approach to the autistic subject are identified: the first makes use of usual techniques, the second uses means from experience in the various sectors of disability, where the aim is to promote the adaptation and integration of the individual into his environment. The third level is more specific to autism and is based on "a central idea: this central idea is that intervention must prioritize communication at any time. Language is usually built through communication and with it, while also having other functions, such as cognitive function. The autistic child has difficulties when it comes to understanding, when it comes to handling the codes that oversee this social use of language. It is therefore not a question of teaching the child how to speak correctly, it is rather a question of pushing the child to communicate effectively

From this derive some guiding principles:

- The intervention is based on a so-called ecological conception of the logopedic approach", that is, it takes place not only in the rehabilitation room but "makes the environment participate in the complex process of building language and communication".
- The active collaboration of the family, "first partner of communication for the child", is fundamental, and with it a "joint work of mutual information and harmonization of points of view" is conducted, which represents the first stage of the intervention.
- To prevent a whole host of consequences, the intervention must be as early as possible, and it aims to "harmonize the child's abilities in the various sectors of language" inspired by the normal stages of development.

Multimodal communication (use of visual codes, gestural, graphic symbolization of sounds ...) is privileged, with the use of all potentially suitable channels, and "the use of alternative communication systems must be taken into account whenever there is a need to do so, without waiting for the failure of traditional methods.

The theoretical model referenced is that of J.S.Bruner, who investigates "the emergency conditions of language and the implementation of communication in able-bodied children". Bruner identifies forms of shared activity between the child and the other, which he calls "formats" or "communication sets", which make it possible to establish communicative exchange and the appearance of language; these situations respond to three fundamental properties: repetitiveness, predictability and systematicity.

Precisely these characteristics help the child discover the basic mechanisms of communication.

The speech therapy intervention, which involves an in-depth evaluation and is part of the multidisciplinary individual project, can be depicted as articulated mainly on three levels: a level that concerns communication within the family context, a second level of communication in all situations of activities shared between the child and the environment (meals, bathroom, games ...), a more specific third level, aimed at the most direct work on language and communication. The work can be done individually, in communication workshops or in larger groups.

The language used is adapted to the subject's abilities: a "language bath" is carefully avoided, on the contrary, "exaggerated accentuation and pronunciation, repetitive intonation, slower speech, accentuated use of mimicry and gestures, simplified vocabulary, use of particular words, use of short and simple sentences with little varied construction. Inappropriate behaviors, such as echolalia, are ignored while resuming and encouraging moments of intentional communication, referring and completing the child's productions, commenting on the environment and objects.

The picture that tends to be created is that of "a context of activities shared by the child and the therapist (...); the "sceneries" of communication thus established are reproduced stably and then gradually enriched according to his progress". In such situations "continuity, the stability of the child's activity is encouraged both with the choice of simple material, with clearly described tasks, and with a distinctly perceptible purpose and with actions that are easy to anticipate.

Psychomotor therapies

Psychomotor therapies draw their roots from H intakes. Wallon and J. Piagetche, in the first half of the 20th century, related motor skills with affective and cognitive emotional development.

The specific scope of psychomotricity, characterized by its pathologies and related therapeutic modalities, was defined by exponents of neuropsychiatry and psychology in Francophone-speaking environments in the 1950s and 1960s. Studies and practice on psychomotor disorders lead to clarifying how psychic and motor functions are deeply rooted functions; over time psychomotor therapy has also come to apply to personality and identity disorders, defining itself as Relational Therapy to Body Mediation.

In the treatment of autistic children, psychomotor therapy tends to open up communication through the relationship with the therapist: this allows the child to be recognized in his uniqueness, to be able to manifest his desire, his fears and his suffering hidden by his inability to express himself.

Starting from the skills and modalities proper to each one, the therapist guides the child to organize and integrate functions, to differentiate, to access new modes of action and relationship and to the pleasure of doing, thinking, knowing and communicating. The specific tool that identifies psychomotor therapy is the body in its tonic and emotional dimensions, in its postures and gestures. The therapist uses muscle tone as a detector of his emotions and, based on the emotional variations that the autistic child - apparently absent, actually very present - sends him, manages to communicate with him even without words.

The operational tools of psychomotor therapy are: the structuring of a constant space-time containing, sensory and emotional tonic stimulation, the possibility of sharing the experience of sensory-motor pleasure, the proposal of experiential objects, the use of the voice and putting simple words on the emotional experience of the child.

It is essential, in this approach, a specific personal training of the therapist so that he is able to decode nonverbal messages, who knows and masters his own bodily communication modalities. The training is complemented by knowledge of the child's pathology and must avail itself of supervision.

The conduct of a psychomotor therapy must be included in a multidisciplinary therapeutic intervention operation and requires to be integrated into a networked organization of territorial resources in collaboration with the family, school and caregivers.

In this historical phase in which we witness the multiplication of rehabilitation interventions, there is often the risk of forgetting the person of the child and his identity, chasing the mirage of obtaining services in the most differentiated fields. Psychomotor therapy draws attention to the basic needs of the child's person.

Eto-behavioral approach to psychomotor therapy

This section presents one of the approaches to psychomotor therapy, the eto-behavioral one, with particular reference to the work of A.M. Wille (1994). The following material is mainly taken from the work of this author, based on a long experience of observation and intervention in the field of Autism

Wille offers us an in-depth story, made on the basis of a rich conceptualization rooted in practice, of the change that the child, and in particular the autistic child, experiences and realizes in the psycho-motority room, where he modifies his adaptive and communication modalities in the relationship he lives with the Therapist.

Wille's text is characterized by a considerable thickness of content, giving rich food for thought and causing a great difficulty in describing here, if not in the essential traits, the complexity of the argument, full of references, ideas, concepts, descriptions of the world of the child and specifically of the autistic subject.

After taking a position against a use of interpretation and labeling of behavior, present in other settings, the author declares her choice for an ethological perspective. Ethology adheres to the observation of what is seen, and in particular profoundly elaborates a theory and practice of observation and description of behavior by identifying the conducts "typical of the species"

In this perspective, aspects such as spontaneous behavior, play, conflicting behavior motivated by internal conflicts and acting as signals are considered.

In the study of autism, the ethologist N. Timbergen, referring to the concept of motivational conflict to explain behaviors "that at first glance do not seem to have a clear function, and which the inexperienced observer tends to define as 'bizarre', proposes considering them from the perspective of the value they have in the social context.

Evolutionary tendencies, ambivalent behavior, redirected behavior, substitution activities, the mechanism of disinhibition are some of the forms of reading behavior identified by human ethological studies. Likewise, the concept of releaser explains how the world of objects, the structuring of space, the body and the actions of the other can strongly trigger responses and influence the behavior of the child.

In a therapeutic perspective "the ethological approach does not aim to search for the cause of autism, whose biological origin is now universally accepted, but aims to help the child emerge from his cognitive chaos to become a person.

The psychomotor approach as implemented by Anne-Marie Wille has as its purpose the humanization of the autistic child: it is based on a great respect on the part of the therapist who with deep humility accepts to be an "object among objects and not even the most fascinating of them", to propose himself to the child without imposing himself, to help him to give meaning to his actions and to broaden his cognitive horizons through play and the body".

Observing the child's spontaneous behavior in the specific context of the psychomotor environment, stable environmental structure, the finding is that an internal thrust of the organism is "simply" welcomed, then collected by the environment.

If this happens, there is a change in the subject (at any level of his neuro-psychic organization) that coincides with a global improvement in the evolutionary situation."

It is necessary to know how to "choose carefully in the environment a specific structure that harmoniously influences the biological processes of ontogenesis (...). It is the ability to select subordinate to the consciousness of the purpose of our actions that allows us to hierarchize, in the multitude of stimuli that surround us, those that are currently most "convenient". And it is this same ability that qualifies the therapist's intervention, if he manages to produce a change in the monotony of autistic behavior.

The child, the PA (small inhabitant), is offered a path in a particular environment, the GfbV (psychomotor environment), which includes both the physical structure (a room containing "stable" objects and "unstable" objects), and the actions that the Therapist performs there.

Some characteristics of the size and shape of the room, cladding, lighting, acoustics, and furniture will be respected: stable objects have characteristics as neutral as possible so as not to be distracting, while unstable objects, whose function is to induce action, have physical characteristics that define, not uniquely, their influence on behavior, also depending on the situational and relational context.

There are fundamental unstable objects (conseverally used in the process of change) and auxiliary objects.

The "action space" includes a territory, tracks followed in travel and neutral areas, for example those occupied by containers.

One of the purposes of the GfbV is to induce the subject to the global use of the body. Another purpose is to activate curiosity, interest in objects, through the exploration and creative use of the material.

In the GfbV the unstable object commemorates the events that belong to the history of the process of change of the subject , symbolically evokes a situation, a gesture, an emotion" .

Basic strategies are applied: suppression of verbal language by the Therapist, high rate of emotionality, absence of explicit requests, respect for the duration (45') of the meeting.

There will be a temporal regularity between meetings and an organization within each of them.

Avoidance, rapprochement, exploration, play, learning and acquisition are the stages that are observed in the evolution of the child within the GfbV, with different times and modalities from individual to individual.

Behaviors can arise that are an obstacle to the process of change (PDC) and that are called "toxic conduct", as well as moments of stagnation, which make it necessary to introduce novelties into the proposals.

The eto-behavioral psychomotor mode of taking charge provides for the initial involvement, and for a more or less long period, of the mother of the autistic child, to ensure that those natural characteristics of the relationship that autistic difficulty has made difficult or absent develop between mother and child; it is also underlined the importance of maximum collaboration between all those who are subjects of reference for the child.

Music therapy

A particularly exhaustive definition of Music Therapy is that of Scardovelli (Scardovelli, 1985, 1986, 1987, 1988) which defines it as a tool or a way of observing, listening, perceiving, acting within a therapeutic (but also rehabilitation or educational) relationship in order to facilitate the process of interpersonal communication.

Poetry is a modulation of existence", as Marleau Ponty says, and we could add that just as essentially music is intonation of existence, it is a transition from dream to life, where music and the dynamics it urges evoke and represent "a vitality of dream" and "a dream as essential to life".

Neurophysiological reflections on the musical experience

Listening to music, making music, individually or in "ensamble" is a solo experience that involves our minds and emotions entirely. In this globality of listening, in this emotional and aesthetic loss, where the boundary between dream and reality blurs, it is also necessary to recognize a biological basis represented by hemispheric dominance.

This dominance is genetically determined, but the "plasticity" with which the nervous system operates allows modifications and adaptations.

There are numerous studies on the neurophysiology and neuropathology of music since the end of the nineteenth century, when Dr.Ballet correlated speech speech disorders (aphasias) with musical language disorders (amusie), demonstrating the presence of aphasia and amusia in the same patient. Subsequent works have shown the existence of amusia without aphasia (Henschen, 1920), or musical deafness without deafness for the word.

Famous is the case of maestro Shebalin, a Russian composer who had preserved, despite a right paralysis with dysphasic disorders (for left hemispheric injury), an excellent perception and musical creativity, continuing to compose symphonies.

There are numerous studies on the neurophysiology and neuropathology of music since the end of the nineteenth century, when Dr.Ballet correlated speech speech disorders (aphasias) with musical language disorders (amusie), demonstrating the presence of aphasia and amusia in the same patient. Subsequent works have shown the existence of amusia without aphasia (Henschen, 1920), or musical deafness without deafness for the word.

Famous is the case of maestro Shebalin, a Russian composer who had preserved, despite a right paralysis with dysphasic disorders (for left hemispheric injury), an excellent perception and musical creativity, continuing to compose symphonies.

An experimental study of the neurophysiology of music listening was represented by the "dichotic listening technique", which starts from the neurophysiological assumption that the temporal cortex of a hemisphere is preferentially connected with the ear on the opposite side. The dichotic listening test involves the simultaneous presentation to the two ears of different musical messages in frequency, timbre and intensity.

Based on neurophysiological knowledge, the best and fastest perception with the right ear will mean a prevalent participation of the left hemisphere and vice versa.

The following studies showed from the studies:

1. The right hemisphere is dominant, but not for all musical tasks; in fact, it is dominant in "naive" listeners (non-musicians) who perceive music in a more global, gestaltic form.

2. The left hemisphere is dominant: a) for tasks that require analytical and sequential elaborations; b) for musical perception and performance in the context of more sophisticated, differentiated and analytical listening.

We then witness a transmission of functions from the right to the left hemisphere that becomes "the hemisphere of musicians".

As for singing, from a neurophysiological point of view, words are the responsibility of the left hemisphere, the melody of the right hemisphere. Again, language has a musicality whose specific characteristics can go beyond intrinsic meaning, transmitting archaic feelings and very primitive modes of communication capable of evoking deep emotions.

Application aspects:
- Taking Scardovelli again (1989), "being Music therapy means knowing how to grasp and know how to respond adequately to temporal-rhythmic aspects, energy aspects and individual logical-cognitive ones in any communicative behavior. Through the mediation of Music Therapy it is thus possible to reflect the physiology and the emotional-cognitive map of the world of the other.

- A Winnicott holding company is created (Winnicott, 1941) where the elements at stake are represented by the operator, the patient, the sound-musical element that mediates the relationship through a tracing of the map of the other: taking on oneself "as if" were proper the rhythms (the cardiac, the respiratory one), the times, the energetic variations, up to Ideas, values, beliefs of the other, his language (verbal and non-verbal), his silences, his "physiology", therefore globally his Being.

After all, we reproduce that wonderful audio-visual-kinetic symphony that binds two human beings, the mother with her child, which prevails over random fluctuations, turmoil, disorder. This symphony creates emotions that the child is not able to understand and that therefore "rejects", emotions that are taken up by the mother empathetically, rationally elaborated, and that are empathetically and rationally returned to the child thus creating his internal world and a mind capable of growing and being able to choose.

In autism, in particular, Music Therapy can become an effective augmentative communication tool, colluding with seemingly more regressive, symbiotic-fusional aspects. Moreover, it mobilizes deep structures of reception-expression of emotions, managing to evoke those relationships between minds and bodies, between internal and external, between internal objects and external objects, between pleasure and pain that cannot be communicated through the verbal channel. In our opinion, the role of Music Therapy, in all situations as specifically in autism, plays the role of mediation between us and the world, between our individuality and individuality outside of us, helping to calibrate ourselves on the other, to accept him, to trust in a less structured context than the reassuring and consolidating one that is the potential emptiness of the word.

Animal Assisted Therapy

In this type of therapy the animals enter the scene and become co-protagonists of the therapeutic process. There are several ways this can happen. In hippo therapy, or therapy with the horse's medium, some physical characteristics of the horse are exploited, along with psychological and social values related to the horse and the riding stable environment. The particular movement of the horse offers from a physical point of view stresses to the rider's neuromuscular system, which can bring different benefits to the psychomotor development of the person, and improve coordination, balance, muscle tone, fine and global traction, breathing and so on.

It is therefore easy to imagine that this type of stimulation will also have effects at the level of sensory integration, which in autism is often deficient. But in addition to physical characteristics, the horse, and the environment in which it lives, also offers other advantages, with implications in the psychological area and interaction with others. On the one hand, in fact, the horse lends itself to being a companion, a friend, an animal to take care of, but at the same time, on the other, he takes the child on his back and carries him around. Similarly, the horse lends itself on the one hand to being a container, that is, another being that contains, carries around, offers very precise boundaries dictated not only by its size and intrinsic danger, but also by the rules that have always accompanied horse care and horse riding.

On the other hand, the horse is not container but contained, as it offers the exclusive possibility for the child to guide it, to bring it, to learn a new language, made up of gestures and movements and even vocalizations, to take it wherever he wants. In addition to these aspects, specific to the horse, we must not forget the values and benefits related to any type of recreational-sports activity, individual or team, such as motivation, self-esteem, attention span, independence, in the sense of willingness to carry out a new activity as a protagonist, in continuous interaction and harmony with another living being. Finally, there are the psycho-social benefits of a therapeutic process closely linked to a recreational-sports activity done in a public and open environment, non-medical and reserved for pathology, which offers a new opportunity for social integration.

Another type of animal-assisted therapy is dolphin therapy. This is the only example of animal-assisted therapy that uses a non-domestic but wild animal, or rather aquatic, such as dolphins. This species, which lives precisely in a marine environment, therefore very different from ours, has always been recognized as a particular ability to come into contact with human beings, and to interact and play completely spontaneously with them.

Another very favorable feature of these cute animals is that they are social, non-lone animals, which have a complex communication system for communicating with each other, made up of sounds and ultrasound that seem to have a particular beneficial effect on people. In addition, dolphins have a particular ability to understand certain types of human language, such as sign language. For these characteristics, combined with a strong intelligence, the idea of using dolphins for therapeutic purposes in autism and in cases of depression or other mental disorders was considered.

The main effects that have been studied are an improvement in the integration of some aspects of personality and corporeality, such as the perception of neglected body parts, stimulated by the movement of dolphins and the water around them; the ability to express and spontaneity, favored by the fact that in water, in the company of dolphins, there are fewer rules, or are otherwise different from ours; movement, also stimulated by the particular vivacity of dolphins and their propensity for play; the willingness to contact, also favored by the aquatic environment.

Chapter 3: What are the symptoms of Autism?

An autistic person could show the first symptoms and signs of the disease around 2-3 years of age.

However, autism is generally a condition that unequivocally manifests itself with the start of school, when the patient – who has problems with interaction and socialization – comes into contact daily with many other people.

The symptomatology of autism is highly variable, both in terms of the extent of symptoms and severity.

As a result, each autistic patient represents a case in its own right, different from others.

In an autistic child, the symptoms and signs of autism that denote problems with communication and interaction with others are:

- A delay in language development.
- The tendency to avoid spoken language.
- Frequent repetition of a set of words or phrases.
- Speak in a tone that sounds monotonous and uniform, as if it cannot adapt to current situations.
- The tendency to interpret anything heard literally and the lack of ability to recognize a sarcastic or humorous idiom or phrase.
- The tendency to communicate with individual words rather than phrases.
- Failure to respond to the pronunciation of one's name by other people. Because of their oddity, autistic individuals sometimes look like individuals with hearing impairments. In reality, however, their hearing abilities are almost always very regular.
- Total disinterest (disinterest that sometimes seems virtually annoying) towards "pampering" and gestures of tenderness, addressed by parents and other people.
- Preference to stay and play alone.
- Respond angrily or aggressively for no particular reason.
- The tendency to avoid eye contact.
- Failure to use gestures and facial expressions to communicate.
- Do not have fun in pleasant situations for peers, such as birthday parties.
- The little, if any, interest in making friends with their peers.
- The tendency to be intrusive.

Some of these issues – including delayed language development or preference to play alone – are found as early as preschool.

Some classic abnormal behaviours of an autistic child include:

- Doing some repetitive movements, such as swinging back and forth or banging your hands.
- Use toys in different ways than their actual purposes.
- Depend strongly on certain habits, so much so that a possible upheaval of the latter represents a real drama.
- Experience strong attraction or significant repulsion to foods, depending on their colour or preparation.
- For unexplained reasons, the tendency to smell toys, objects, and people.
- Have very few interests, but maniacal. It is widespread for autistic subjects to develop a particular attraction for certain activities or things and dedicate most of their daily time to it.
- Demonstrate a specific sensitivity to intense lights, certain sounds, or physical contact (even when not painful).

• Be in constant motion.

Among people with autism, some have a below-average IQ and poor learning skills, others with normal intelligence, and more — but that's an absolute minority — with specific skills in mathematics or art.
Many individuals with autism show coordination problems and clumsiness in movements. In adulthood, a person's difficulties with autism can improve – in some cases even clearly – or remain unchanged, if not even worsen.
In the opinion of doctors, parents should subject their child to specialist checks if:

• At six months, he does not smile or denote any signs of joy/cheerfulness.
• At nine months, it makes no sounds and shows no particular facial expressions.
• At the age of 12 months, he does not vocalize.
• At the age of 14 months, he does not perform any return gestures, does not indicate, does not stretch, etc.
• At the age of 16 months, he doesn't talk.
• At the age of 24 months, he does not say two-word phrases.

Which tests should I do?
Typically, assessment analyses and tests include:

• An objective examination serves to establish the exact nature of the symptomatology. For example, a child who doesn't respond to their name may suffer from an undiagnosed hearing disorder. Doctors clarify this and other aspects of the same kind with the objective examination.
• An analysis of the genetic profile to clarify whether the individual under examination suffers from some genetic disorder among those previously reported (fragile X syndrome, Rett syndrome, etc.).
• A specialist test evaluates social interaction, communication skills, and behavior. For this type of evaluation, it is essential to compare what has been observed by the test driver and what has been observed by parents and school teachers so far.
• A specialist test establishing language development.
• A neurological examination for mental health assessment.
• A questionnaire aimed at parents serves to clarify whether, in the family, there are (or have been) relatives with disorders similar to the individual under examination.

ABAS BEHAVIORAL ASSESSMENT TEST FROM 5 TO 21 YEARS OLD
I think it would be a good idea for you to try the abas test, but first, let's see what it is. ABAS-II is structured in 5 questionnaires (with a variable number of items from 193 to 241) that must be completed by the subject himself or by some reference figures (teachers, parents, family members, caregivers, or other people who participate in the daily activities of the examinee), who can verify the presence and frequency of behaviours. The adult questionnaire can also be used as a self-administration.

The tool investigates ten adaptive areas attributable to 3 domains:

- Conceptual: Communication, Preschool/School Skills, Self-Control;
- Social: Play/Leisure, Socialization;
- Practical: Self Care, Home/School Life, Use of the Environment, Health and Safety, Work.

To these is added the Mobility area, which is limited to evaluating children from 0 to 5 years.

KEY FEATURES

- Comprehensive assessment of lifecycle adaptation skills.
- Multiple sources of information compete with the evaluation.
- Evaluation in different contexts: school, home, work, social centers.

IT IS USEFUL FOR:

- Diagnose and classify disabilities and disorders, measuring their incidence in leading autonomous lives in subjects of all halves.
- Measure adaptive areas in different contexts – school, work, family, social centers – to get a complete picture of an individual's functional skills.
- Develop treatment plans, document and monitor progress over time.
- Even just reading it and evaluating your children gives us an idea of what skills are missing, those in which you can work, those that are a more significant challenge.

Chapter 4: Why is my child acting in this way? Manifestations of autism

The autistic lives in exactly the same world as non-autistics, with the difference that his static brain, with its particular internal functioning, processes incoming information differently.

First of all, it is necessary to distinguish autistic manifestations from behavioral disorders. When the information received is too complex to manage and organize internally, the autistic structure faces a destabilization comparable to an earthquake or an inner storm that manifests itself on the physical plane. The autistic person instinctively tries to regain their stability, particularly by putting pressure on a particular area of the head. For this reason it is common to see autistic children kick their heads.

In this gesture there is no self-harming or self-stimulation intent, but only a survival reaction to a very unpleasant physical phenomenon that causes severe discomfort. In these cases, the autistic needs help.

This mechanism of "survival" is what sets in motion the chain that allows access to the work of cognitive organization that leads to self-consciousness. It is essential for an autistic to learn how to manage this mechanism as soon as it manifests itself and becomes accessible.

Unlike neuro typical, autistics must manage the link between information from outside and the internal condition of their body at all times. If their brain senses a change on the outside, the internal balance undergoes an upheaval and they have to restore it according to what has changed. They move to find or return to a balance point. For an autistic, movement is a normal reaction of the body to the way the brain is stimulated by the changes it perceives around itself.

Since everything that is external to his body changes continuously, the autistic gives priority to research of internal balance and this research goes through constant movement. Its movements are not random: it is a survival mechanism.

Autistic people have a very complex relationship with physical contact. Everything enters through the eyes: if an autistic is touched but does not see contact and the brain cannot associate an image with the perceived physical sensation, contact cannot be recorded and thus causes deep discomfort. But this is not emotional distress; what the autistic person faces is an inconsistency in information processing. In order to be transmitted to the brain, physical contact must be seen.

Whenever physical contact occurs, the autistic person's brain must process the sensory information received. Until this information is processed and classified, the brain cannot devote itself to anything else. It is more or less what happens to a neuro typical person when in the garment they wear there is a label that irritates the skin of the neck or back. Until the discomfort caused by the label has been eliminated, that person will struggle to focus on the present! Once the label is removed, it can immediately switch to something else; the autistic person, on the other hand, will not be able to get rid of the feeling of discomfort from the presence of the label for hours. This phenomenon, which would be caused by hyper connection of the autistic brain, is not a sensory modulation problem and has nothing to do with affectivity. Because of this hyper connection, the sensation caused by contact, be it with a person or with an unknown consistency, is received in an "exaggerated" way by the brain, which places it in the row of information to be processed. This phenomenon related to information processing recurs similarly for all types of external, tactile, auditory, or visual stimuli. Because the autistic brain processes data one at a time, handling information from tissues of various textures and/or colors at the same time is very complicated. The choice of clothing does not follow the same criteria as neuro typical. Autistic people, in fact, do not care about the appearance of clothes, they limit themselves to choosing those that help them in autistic management, which force them to process the minor As much cognitive information as possible. It's a matter of survival.

In some cases, clothes may also be directly associated with specific activities or contexts. The autistic brain is very skilled at making associations, but struggles to organize and synthesize information. An autistic might wear a certain pair of pants to walk the road to school, but once there take them off, because it is impossible for him to wear them in what he perceives as a different occasion or function. Once the school-garment association has been done, it is very difficult, if not impossible, for the autistic person to modify it. In order to behave differently you will need help.

Autistic people try to meet some internal needs, the needs of their 'manual' brain. It's not about tantrums. You have to be patient with them; after cognitive organization work has been done, they will learn to make different choices as well.

When we touch an autistic for the first time, or when he is in a new context or tired or anxious, we absolutely must avoid moving, talking and asking questions. Let's limit ourselves to static contact: let's put our hand on him without moving. In this way, we help the autistic to process the contact more quickly; later, when he gets used to static contact, we can gradually introduce non-static contact.

 In this way the autistic person may be able to process these contacts more easily. Autistics apparently overreact to sensory stimuli from their surroundings. The noise of the coffee machine, for example, is 'twisted' for an autistic: it is irregular, unstable and full of small variations that he is unable to handle. It is not noise but its irregularity that attacks its information processing system.

Since the autistic gets tired quickly in the presence of sounds of this type, he instinctively tries to avoid them.

These noises make him "bad", that is, they cause a real physical pain in his head, a pain that however has nothing to do with what you feel, for example, when you bang your big toe against something while walking. An irregular noise is an aggression, which will continue to rumble in his mind and will not fade until it is processed. The autistic person, therefore, must face too intense a stimulus, and manage excessive sensitivity.

It is necessary to ensure that it "sees" the noise of the lawnmower; to locate and process the noise, the autistic must be able to associate it with the object that produces it the moment it produces it. The lawnmower itself must be placed in a space-time context, otherwise a feeling of discomfort will be generated: **will this object make this noise forever?**

Autistics are visual thinkers, it's true, but we need to help their minds make the necessary connections.

We should Activate their internal visualization, thus favoring cognitive organization, otherwise the connections will take place only through external visualization, the one that captures the surrounding environment, and not the one that organizes thoughts. It will be like depriving them of the (static) camera and giving them a (moving) camera!

When autism was believed to be a disease, autistic behaviors were considered symptoms to be gone. No one wondered why all the autistics in the world behaved the same, nor what they used for. Also, no studies have ever shown that countering these behaviors

When the brain struggles to process complex information, the body intervenes to help it maintain the necessary balance. It can be said that physical gestures are manifestations of the body that help the brain, and spontaneously recede or fade as soon as the brain can work on its own.

Let's not forget that the human body is intelligent and that it never does anything by chance. You should never try to hinder the spontaneous behavior of an autistic. This is a stage of development that all autistics go through. These behaviors manifest at a specific stage and their presence is crucial to understanding what kind of intervention and support it needs.

Some people are convinced that the "hand flapping" should be prevented, that is, the action of quickly shaking the hands typical of autistics. And when they think autism is "healed" because it is no longer visible!

Hand flapping is not only about autism, it is typical of human development; all children, around nine months old, make this gesture, which then disappears over time. Who would think of preventing a nine-month-old baby from moving his arms? To no one, of course! We would find it nice for the child to express himself and give him time to grow up.

In autistics, hand flapping manifests itself later and does not disappear. It occurs in two circumstances: as an indicator of a positive emotion that is trying to pass or when there is a mix of emotions in a pre-crisis condition. The presence of hand flapping in an autistic person is excellent news, because it indicates the achievement of a certain stage of development. Hand flapping is the motor expression of an emotion, and not a behavior to repress. It is a sign that the brain begins to be able to grasp positive emotions (for example, the person waving hands expresses His own contentment).

It can be said that hand flapping is a manifestation of the body that helps the brain capture a positive emotion, joy, which is the emotion that communication feeds on. As soon as the brain manages to process the information conveyed by this emotion, the hand flapping loses meaning, becomes useless to the autistic and disappears.

Autistic people often hold objects When you try to take them away from them, they react exaggeratedly.

An object that is held in the hand is mistakenly considered a transitional object. For an autistic, however, it is a stable sign or unit of measurement that helps him place his body in motion in space. If on the one hand the position of the body changes continuously, forcing the autistic brain to seek a new balance, on the other this concrete point of reference remains constant; its presence is therefore essential to anchor the individual in physical reality, and at the same time allows him to concentrate his cognitive functions elsewhere.

When an autistic person begins to locate their physical presence in the environment, they touch the walls and furniture, a bit like they are blind: this allows the brain to follow the movement of the body and orient itself in space. Afterwards, he will help by holding an object that will allow him to cross An environment. The object serves as a concrete unit of measurement for the brain: in this way, the autistic will be able to follow the measurement of his body in an environment and his ability to decipher his surroundings will improve.

There is no right age to resort to an autistic management object.

If we try to deprive him of this type of object, the autistic will have a violent reaction: he will be afraid of no longer being able to move and his brain will stop collaborating. At that point, he will have to return to the environment he knows and touch the furniture or walls with his fingers, before he can continue the movement that has been interrupted, otherwise he will not be able to orient his movement.

The autistic brain processes what it recognizes. Watching a spinning top or a fan on helps your child process information, because it is a smooth, stable, continuous and predictable movement. The regularity of the movement gives him a feeling of deep well-being.

When the autistic has reached a certain stage of development, his information processing "system" will become more sophisticated and his fondness for what is regular can be directed towards more complex activities such as mathematics, calendars, public transport schedules, physics etc. (according to Mottron, 2004). The study of these regular systems has a calming effect for the autistic.

There's nothing wrong with letting your child observe the regular movement of these objects, as long as they don't do it for hours. Let's not forget that this type of activity corresponds to one phase of its development, and that it needs help to move on to the next phase.

Conversely, any 'unstable' or irregular stimulus – noise, light or physical contact – can deeply make the autistic uncomfortable.

Many parents tell us that they have great problems cutting their autistic son's hair. The little one does not want to, he reacts strongly, cries and is scared. Parents need to devise a number of strategies that very often cause great anxiety in the child. Many cut their child's hair while he is asleep, others instead postpone as much as possible.

We now know that, until he reaches a certain stage of development, the autistist does not know that his hair grows back. You may think they will stay short forever! Also, he doesn't have the cognition of time. Cutting his hair means altering his "image", modifying an image that must remain stable. The child cannot project this image over time because for him the present is immutable. The fact that it is altered by the haircut is therefore a source of great anxiety.

For autistics, everything passes through the eyes, and tactile sensations are no exception. The eyes need to locate every single touch, including the feeling of water falling on the skin. During a certain phase of movement reconnaissance, by dint of measuring each of the drops that touch the skin, the brain turns into a machine gun. This is why the child is afraid of the shower or says that "water hurts".

If, on the other hand, it is in another phase, it may be that, not possessing the cognition of time, he cannot understand that the Shower has a beginning and an end. He cannot cognitively organize the sequence related to the action of taking a shower, its development. In addition, trying to verbally communicate to him the concept of "shower duration" (for example, repeating several times to the child that it will not take long, that there are only a few minutes left) could fix this activity over time, make it "static", which would further complicate things.

In other cases, however, the child is not able to place his body in the physical space of the shower (compared to the base, walls, ceiling), which makes the different phases of the action of showering very laborious. In the midst of these unstable landmarks, he has the impression that he is continuously in a vacuum. Every movement he makes to wash a part of the body requires a lot of concentration and a huge expenditure of energy.

Due to the hyper-connection of the brain, those who are autistic perceive the sensation of every single drop of water falling on the skin; they cannot get rid of it by processing the information, and thus bring the concentration back inside, because to achieve this it it should no longer be stressed externally by the other drops that continue to fall on their skin, one after the other. The first drop is immediately followed by the second, which must in turn be processed starting from contact with the skin, and the eyes are immediately asked to process it.

The effects of autistic structure are very noticeable in nutrition, at different levels. It may be that the autistics, at a certain stage of development, does not realize that he is hungry and that all the points of reference he needs to understand that he needs to eat are outside, in the surrounding environment. For example, he may want to eat exclusively from his blue plate, otherwise it's not a real meal. She could only eat mom's spaghetti, because Grandma's spaghetti is different, despite the fact that the recipe is identical. He may want to drink water only from his yellow cup, or eat a dish only if served at his usual temperature. An autistic is able to do a diet of only five foods without getting tired.

If the people surrounding the autistic are not aware of this problem and the landmarks are all external, in the surrounding environment, meals can become very nerve-wracking moments. Meal misunderstanding, at different levels, is a serious problem for autistics, particularly misunderstanding of food textures and shape. At a certain stage of development, the autistic may not be able to recognize the sense of food. He may not know that the thing on his plate is food, and this is because the object has changed shape. For an autistic, washer carrots are not the same as stick carrots. The image is completely different, the internal reference too.

The autistic may also need all the resources of their brain to be able to eat. Being surrounded by talking people can prevent them from concentrating. This is why many autistics refuse to eat or sit at the table with friends. The more mature will tell us to shut up because they are eating.

Because they don't feel hungry (the person never thinks about eating) and the concept of "meal-related sociality" is absent, some autistics don't understand why they have to sit back and swallow the food in front of them. For many, meals are not an opportunity for sociability, but something necessary to stay healthy. If the autistic has not yet visually received the sense of information, he will have no way of knowing that the time to get up from the table is after finishing the dessert. Since the food on the plate is never perfectly identical and the quantities vary, it is difficult for him to calculate how long he can get up.

So, to understand the meaning of what is happening, some autistics always ask for the same foods. During meals, it would be better to reduce as much as possible the surrounding sensory elements (television, music, noise, etc.), which constitute a useless source of stimuli for the autistic. Calm is the best ally. There is no point in working on multiple learning sessions at the same time. Priorities need to be set. The common point of all these examples is that the autistic child's brain works differently, first of all because he cannot process the information in a fluid way, then because all the information must pass through the eyes first. Knowing these two general principles it will be more possible to give explanations in the face of strange behaviors or behavioral manifestations of the disorder. For example, it will be easier to understand why your child shakes for a cut while instead does not seem to show a suitable reaction for more serious injuries. Ask yourself why. We said that the brain of the autistic child reasons through the eyes, all information passes through the eyes, sight is the most developed sense. As a result it is normal for the child to get scared by a cut because it modifies his person, his body, the perception that he has of himself. A broken bone hurts more, of course, but it does not agitate the child because it cannot see it, its figure is not altered.

The fact that the autistic brain works in this way, through the eyes, also explains how we have already said for example why the child does not want to cut his hair but also why the child does not want to cover himself in winter: the cold cannot be seen, consequently the child does not understand why he should do it.

Movements in the space of an autistic child are also conditioned by the sense of sight. It often happens to see autistic children or teens with hoodies, hoodies or various headgear. Autistic people often use these headgear as a landmark that follows their body all the time, remaining regular, unaffected and thus better allowing the brain to do its job... This is a gesture of defense.

Diagnosis, tests and doctors

Neurodevelopmental disorders manifest themselves in the early stages of development and are characterized by deficits in personal, social, school or work functioning.

The deficit ranges from very specific limitations of learning to the global impairment of social skills and intelligence.

Intellectual disability, communication disorders, autism spectrum disorder, attention deficit/hyperactivity disorder, specific learning disorder, and movement disorders were included in neurodevelopmental disorders. This complex of disorders involves a high health, social and economic burden.

Normally parents notice during growth characteristics of behavior that they consider worrying and the pediatrician participates in it. Observation of behaviors that deviate from expected can also take place in non-family environments, such as kindergarten or primary school. In any case, the comparison between parents and their pediatrician of reference is the first step to verify the hypothesis of a diagnosis of autism. In the event that the pediatrician, based on his observations and the doubts brought by the family, thinks he has encountered symptoms consistent with autism, a specialist visit will be required that can substantiate the diagnosis. Diagnosis must be supported in specialized facilities recognized by the National Health System on the basis of the grid of criteria defined by the two main international reference diagnostic manuals (ICD and DSM) and with appropriate standardized tools. The DSM 5, recently introduced in Italy, foresees significant changes regarding the diagnostic category of autism spectrum disorders (ASD).

Diagnosis must be complemented by a functional diagnosis involving an overall clinical evaluation performed by a multifunctional team.

Evaluation team National and international experience (Guidelines section) supports the need to carry out the functional diagnosis and definition of the rehabilitation therapeutic project, through a multi-professional team that provides for the presence of at least the following figures: neuropsychiatrist, psychologist, neuro psychomotor therapist of developmental age, speech therapist, and educator. The team must have clinical experience and up-to-date expertise in pervasive developmental disorders. The evaluation path is in fact an articulated path that must establish the behavioral profile from the cognitive point of view (ability to understand), communicative (language), social (relationship), and emotional point of view of the child that can allow the definition of the enabling therapeutic project.

Meetings dedicated to parents In such meetings it is intended to obtain mutual knowledge between parents, and more generally family members, and the team. This report will allow, in addition to collecting anamnestic data, to obtain information on the behavior of the child in environments (home, school, or other environmental situations) and his ability to adapt. In these meetings, it will also be possible to deepen the characteristics of the environment where the child lives through an evaluation of personal, family resources and more generally of the social context in which the 'family system' is inserted (availability of territorial services, socio-economic aspects, cultural aspects). Such meetings, on the other hand, will allow family members to acquire the team as a constant point of reference in the phase of diagnosis and concretization of the therapeutic project. The complex characteristics of autism may necessitate a diagnostic process involving an articulated series of investigations. The objective and neurological examination aimed at excluding the presence of pathologies that are most frequently associated with autism and identifying the specific health characteristics of the child. It will be important to verify the auxological parameters, audiometric parameters and in particular cases, which emerged from the family history, genetic and / or metabolic investigations may be necessary. The neurological examination aims to check for major and minor symptoms for assessing the integrity of central nerve structures. In some cases, an instrumental investigation through the electroencephalogram may be necessary. Behavioral examination consists of a complex assessment that can be strenuous for the child. For this reason, the behavioral exam includes meetings distributed over several days, during which through the use of different methodologies (observation, interview with the child, administration of standardized evaluation tools) the team will then verify:

- The presence of behavioral symptoms encoded by the reference international classifications
- The assessment of cognitive and language skills
- The evaluation of emotional development
- The evaluation of the functional profile (daily skills, adaptability, etc.)

Significant progress has been made since the first clinical description of autism in the ability to diagnose this disorder, but there is ample room for improvement in this specific area. In particular, there is an international consensus on the importance of developing tools that allow the diagnosis to be made as early as possible during development, as well as on the need to identify early symptoms indicative of an increased risk of manifestation. Clinical research suggests that the effectiveness of therapeutic interventions is greater the earlier these are initiated during the child's development. In this sense, the awareness on the part of parents, but also of kindergarten and primary school operators, of the 'expected' (typical) profile for social, behavioral and cognitive development (including language) that characterizes the developmental age must be increased. At the same time, the involvement of pediatricians at local level (health district) should be encouraged in order to support a specific surveillance program for preschool development that can identify and collect any reports of developmental disorders with reference also to autism. There is a set of tools that have been developed for the surveillance of risk signals for autism spectrum disorders, in order to identify early abnormalities that indicate the need to follow and evaluate the child at intervals due for a check. These instruments, although validated in the clinical field, have some limitations. They have a high specificity with respect to the disorder but have a sensitivity (85%) not totally satisfactory, which can determine the possibility of misdiagnosis, that is, the non-recognition of the disorder.

Chapter 5: Autism and other disorders

This section will talk about autism compared to other disorders or what other diseases autism can involve. Many times I have heard questions such as "what is the difference between autism and ..." or "what if my kid is not autistic, but he is ..." or " my kid is autistic but also..."
To understand something, you should know what is and what is not and compare it with all the other things you have around. Let's go deeper now into the process of really knowing what autism is.

Asperger

Autism is a complex syndrome, a set of symptoms and signs that vary significantly in both type and intensity from child to child and has onset in early childhood.
It is configured as a disability that will accompany the person throughout his life with characteristics that may vary, depending on the period of growth and interventions, throughout the life path.
Due to differences in characteristics and symptoms present in the various subgroups that can be defined along a continuum, the term Pervasive Developmental Disorder has been replaced in the DSM-V by the new category: Autism Spectrum Disorders. Let's now see the differences between the previous nosographic and current classifications.
In the old DSM-IV, autism also included Asperger's Syndrome, Rett syndrome, and childhood disintegrative disorder, among other syndromes. Symptoms were defined within three significant areas:

- Qualitative impairment of social interaction
- Qualitative impairment of communication

- Restricted, repetitive, and stereotypical modes of behaviour, interests, and activities

Currently, the new DSM-V introduces the Autism Spectrum Disorders category, which includes all subtypes of pervasive developmental disorders except for Rett syndrome, which falls under neurological disorders.

In addition, the three domains become two:

- A deficit in Communication and Social Interaction
- Restricted and repetitive interests and behaviors

DSM-V introduces "unusual sensitivity to sensory stimuli" as symptomatology between "repetitive behaviors." Another novelty is the indication of the severity of the symptoms of autism spectrum disorder on a 3-level scale that identifies the need for intensive support or not.

According to some authors, conceptualizing autism as a "spectrum" rather than a definite diagnostic entity is in line with existing research, and the proposal to eliminate Asperger's disorder as a "distinct" clinical entity has also been supported by difficulties in being able to delineate clear boundaries that separate it from other autistic disorders. With the new DSM, it would be possible to replace the definition of "Asperger's Syndrome" with "Autism spectrum," specifying that the person concerned has no intellectual disability and does not need intensive support. It will always be necessary to take into account specific individual profiles. As, moreover, also happened with DSM-IV, when trying to classify people who did not meet all the requirements for Asperger's Syndrome, but with discrete levels of autonomy and cognitive and language development, in the definition (not provided for in the Manual) of High Functioning Autism.

But what is Asperger's Syndrome?

The term "Asperger's Syndrome" was coined by English psychiatrist Lorna Wing in a 1981 medical journal; he named it in honor of Hans Asperger, an Austrian psychiatrist, and pediatrician whose work was not recognized until the 1990s.

According to the old DSM-IV, people with Asperger's Syndrome are characterized by persistent impairment of social interactions, repetitive and stereotypical behaviour patterns, very narrow activities and interests. Unlike classical autism, they have no significant delays in language development or cognitive development.

People with Asperger's Syndrome are often socially isolated but are likely to relate to others, although their approaches may be inappropriate and strange. They can, for example, engage an interlocutor, often an adult, in unilateral conversations characterized by an endless, pedantic way of speaking and aimed at a favourite topic, often unusual and limited. Also, even though they look lonely, they show a great interest in making friends and meeting people. These desires are invariably hampered by their clumsy approaches and insensitivity to other people's feelings, intentions, and nonverbal and implicit communications.

Being chronically frustrated by their repeated failures to relate to others and make friends, some of these individuals may develop symptoms of depression. In primary school, Asperger's Syndrome may not be noticed. Still, it is often the teachers who report the child's discomfort in integration: for this reason, and because these individuals are often bullied and socially isolated, it is vital that teachers are trained, that there are awareness meetings and projects to promote integration.

The intense interests demonstrated by individuals with Asperger's Syndrome can also be used to grow the child's self-esteem and inclusion in school, favouring their development and expansion.

With strategies aimed at acquiring the skills necessary for everyday life and with adequate interventions such as the cognitive-behavioural approach, people with Asperger's Syndrome can improve their social skills and the management of their emotions and find their way to live in the world while feeling good about themselves and others.

Schizophrenia

Autism Spectrum Disorders (ASDs) and Schizophrenic Spectrum Disorders (DSS) represent two highly disabling psychiatric conditions. Although they have different classification criteria according to the DSM-IV-TR, the extension of overlap areas related to clinical presentation and underlying etiological mechanisms has been a subject of scientific discussion for a long time. In the 1940s, Kanner, who first described autism, defined the term from Bleuler, who had coined it to expose the closing and isolation behaviors characteristic of adults with schizophrenia. Research from the 1960s and 1970s, on the other hand, found that the two disorders are entirely different in terms of age of onset, gender and family history of patients, clinical expression, and outcome.

Retracing the classification of autism in the DSM, it can be noted that in the first edition (1952), this diagnosis did not exist; children with autistic symptoms were diagnosed with schizophrenic reaction, childhood type label. Even in DSM-II (1968), autism was not included as a separate diagnostic category: children exhibiting autistic, atypical, and introverted behaviors were diagnosed with childhood schizophrenia. Following clinical, family, and follow-up studies, autism is classified as a shot diagnostic category in DSM-III (1980). Initially, there was only talk of childhood autism. Then, following disputes related to the adjective "childhood," in 1987, the diagnosis was changed to autistic disorder. In later editions of DSM-III, IV, and DSM-IV-TR (1994), we moved on to the category of pervasive developmental disorders and their different subtypes (autistic disorder, Asperger's disorder, Rett disorder, disintegrative childhood disorder, and pervasive developmental disorder not otherwise specified).

So, over the years, the diagnostic boundaries between autism and schizophrenia have become more pronounced. However, the conception of the two separate disorders has been expanded, and we have moved on to the conception that there are a spectrum of autistic disorders and a spectrum of schizophrenic disorders, with possible areas of overlap.

Several arguments aimed at explaining the association between schizophrenia and autism have been traced in the literature. It was noted that developmental disorders could in themselves be a risk factor for schizophrenia. In fact, indicators of early fetal damage such as prenatal viral infections have been associated with both pathologies, and it appears that this underlies the immune involvement that has recently been found in both ASDs and DSSs. The hypothesis is that such a maternal infection can activate an immunological cascade that begins during the early stages of development and determines a state of permanent immune dysregulation at the brain level, mediated by abnormal expression of pro-inflammatory cytokines such as interleukin 6. It is interesting to note that rare chromosomal abnormalities and/or Copy Number Variations (CNVs) detected in individuals with Childhood-Onset Schizophrenia (COS) are more common in patients with a premorbid DSA than in those with an adverse remote pathological history and this, again, could be related to an early developmental disorder.

In fact, several studies trace as a pathophysiological connection between the two disorders a common alteration in brain neurodevelopment that is dated, for both disorders, approximately to the age of onset of the same and which will then be the determinant of the phenotype characterized by cognitive impairment and negative symptoms, typical of the two disorders. In support of this thesis, genetic data show overlaps in risk genetic loci associated with both conditions, including a set of CNV loci and specific genes such as CNTNAP2 and NRXNI

These data document that these CNVs are not pathology-specific, but it will be their interaction with epigenetic and environmental factors that will determine the dysfunction of specific neuronal networks underlying each specific clinical condition.

In the literature, some authors suggest different hypotheses. Crespi et al. consider autism and schizophrenia as diametrically opposed psychiatric disorders, one characterized by underdevelopment, the other by an unregulated hyper development of the human social brain; at the genetic level, these two disorders are supposed to be mediated by mutual variants; the deletion of one of these variants would predispose to autism while the duplication to schizophrenia.

It has been suggested that the physiological basis of the characteristic imitation deficit of autistic subjects could be at the mirror neurons level. This system is located in the premotor area and is activated both when the subject performs a specific action and when he sees it performed by others. Such a neuronal system is essential for developing gestural communication and language.

The finding of the mirror neuron system is relevant to understanding the imitation and communication deficits typical of autism, and several studies have confirmed that autistic subjects do not show the regular activation pattern of this system, evaluated with functional imaging methods; Transcranial Magnetic Stimulation (TMS) and electroencephalography.

Recent studies have identified mirror neuron system deficits also in schizophrenia 191. Enticott et al., the first authors to demonstrate abnormalities of this type in people with schizophrenia using TMS, suggest that perhaps there is a functional deficit of mirror neurons, but also wonder if there is no more significant connectivity deficit, which may underlie discoveries about the mirror neuron system, standard in autism and schizophrenia.

Studies that trace such connections with modern neuroimaging techniques support the hypothesis that there is an anatomical connection between the two disorders. Compared to healthy controls, Toal et al. conducted a study comparing in vivo MRI in patients with ASD with psychotic symptoms and patients with ASD without psychosis. It turned out that subjects with ASD (with or without psychosis) show, compared to controls, a significant reduction in gray matter in temporal lobes and cerebellum bilaterally. Instead, they have an increase in gray matter in striatal regions.

HOWEVER, the ASD group with psychosis has a significant reduction in the gray matter contained in the frontal and occipital regions and, contrary to expectations, also a reduction in the gray matter of the right insular cortex and cerebellum bilaterally, which extends to the fusiform gyrus. Therefore, since patients with ASD already have abnormalities in the development of brain regions also implicated in schizophrenia (frontal and striated lobe), an additive abnormality in the island cortex (involved in emotional and sensitive responses), fusiform gyrus, and cerebellum (responsible for inhibitory control and the face recognition process) is sufficient in them to develop the positive symptoms of psychosis. According to the authors, the presence of these neurodevelopmental abnormalities, generally associated with ASDs, could represent an alternative entry point to a common final pathway to psychosis. It is also proven that in both DSA and DSS, there is a fundamental deficit in understanding the mental state of others and processing internal stimuli: therefore, it could be this that makes patients with ASD more susceptible to psychosis rather than an additional insult to specific structures related to delusions and hallucinations. Another study carried out in this direction is that of Cheung et al., who considered the "anatomical likelihood estimation" of a sample of patients with ASD and one with schizophrenia compared to a control group. Nor has there been a reduction in gray matter volume in the limbic-striated-thalamic circuit (right posterior track, right Parahippocampal gyrus, putamen, insula, and left thalamus) in either ailments. As more specific characteristics of the two disorders, in schizophrenia, a reduced gray volume emerged in the amygdala, caudate, and frontal and medial gyrus, and in ASDs, a reduced volume of the left putamen. Such common structural abnormalities affecting the limbic system may partly explain the overlap of socioemotional symptoms. In contrast, those of the basal gan-the system are implicated in the 'sensorimotor gating' deficiency present in both disorders.

These results show an overlap of gray matter abnormalities in some brain regions under two conditions that exhibit common behavioral traits, supporting the hypothesis that ASD and DSS are related.

In 1985, Baron-Cohen et al. hypothesized that autistic children could have a deficit in Theory of Mind (TOM), a subject's ability to attribute the mental state of others. Several authors will then confirm this hypothesis over the years, who will show that TOM deficits are more common in autistic subjects than controls or people with other developmental disorders. However, in the face of this evidence, it will be ascertained that TOM deficits are not specific to autism and are also found in a group of individuals with average intelligence, such as schizophrenic patients. Some authors have suggested a direct correlation between TOM deficits and the presence and severity of delusions and schizotypic symptoms. In addition, family members of people with schizophrenia have faced greater difficulty performing TOM tasks than the general population.

Closely connected with the concept of TOM is that of "social cognition," defined as "the mental operation that is underlying social interactions and that includes man's ability to perceive the intentions and dispositions of the other" . Deficits in this cognitive ability have been detected in both autism and Schizophrenia. Sasson et al. note that autistic subjects and schizophrenic subjects share abnormalities in using facial information to assess emotional content in social scenes but differ in tracing socially relevant "codes," starting with complex stimuli. Abdi et al. suggest that autistic and schizophrenic both exhibit persistent deficits in social connectivity, as demonstrated by reduced activation of the prefrontal and frontal cortex, i.e., brain areas implicated in tasks using TOM.

Other authors analyze neuronal activation of different brain regions implicated in social cognitiveness and the processing of socially complex faces in patients with DSS, ASD, and a control group. The result is significant activation of the cognitive-social network in all groups, but subjects with ASD and paranoid schizophrenia show a substantial reduction in neuronal activation of the right amygdala, fusiform area, and left ventrolateral prefrontal cortex compared to controls and in the left ventrolateral prefrontal cortex compared to subjects with non Such data suggest that there is a specific neuronal mechanism underlying impairment in social cognitiveness, both autism, and paranoid schizophrenia.

Another interesting study is Couture et al., which compares a group of people with schizophrenia with a group of high functioning autistic subjects (HF). As a result, both groups are deficient in different social tasks than controls but do not differ from each other. In particular, in terms of impairment in the pattern of social cognitiveness, individuals with HF autism are much more similar to people with schizophrenia with negative symptoms than those with paranoid symptoms.

It emerges, therefore, that autism and schizophrenia share a similar social cognitive profile but with different underlying neuronal mechanisms.

Recent studies have pointed to the concomitance of autistic and schizophrenic symptoms in individuals.

A good number of these studies focused on the presence of pathologies of the schizophrenic spectrum in patients with ASD, noting the possible overlap between the two disorders. Negative symptoms and disorganized symptoms were reported in both adults and adolescents with ASD, while clear positive symptoms, typical of DSS, was not found in individuals with ASD. Follow-up studies have indicated that a significant proportion of children diagnosed with ASD developed DSS over a lifetime, with a conversion rate to such diagnoses of 34.8%. This suggests that several children with ASD then arrive, during development, at schizotypy.

In these cases, subclinical schizotypal traits are more likely to have already been present in adolescence, as emerged from a recent study in which patients diagnosed with ASD showed more features belonging to the schizophrenic spectrum in adolescence than subjects in the control group; moreover, the overlap between autistic traits and schizotypal.

It is not limited to negative symptoms alone but extends to positive and disorganization symptoms.

On the other hand, other studies focused on the presence of high levels of autistic traits in patients with DSS. The most pronounced overlaps in terms of phenomenology are appreciated, especially in those disorders placed on the margins of autistic and schizophrenic spectra and appear in different functional domains. Although the two conditions have differences, such as the high prevalence of mental retardation in autistics compared to people with schizophrenia, there are also many similarities. Both are characterized by motor abnormalities, cognitive deficits, communication deficits, and deficits in social functioning.

Even very recent data indicate that autism and schizophrenia are conditions that can easily be found in the same patients and families themselves. Several studies in adult populations have suggested a connection between the two disorders, and epidemiological and population data have shown that familiarity with schizophrenic-like psychosis poses a risk factor for autism.

In many studies, it is mainly COS that reveals, as a premorbid condition, a high rate of developmental abnormalities: in a study conducted in a group of subjects with COS, 39% of a sample composed of 33 patients had autistic symptoms years before the onset of schizophrenia.

The same group of researchers then looked at an additional group of 52 subjects with COS, finding that 55% of the sample had a history that allowed them to diagnose autism or pervasive developmental disorder according to DSM-III-R criteria (23). In the more extensive study of 101 children and adolescents with schizophrenia onset before the age of 13, according to DSM-IV criteria, there was a total of 28% comorbidity with ASD pathologies, in particular with Pervasive Developmental Disorder Not Otherwise Specified (PDD-NOS), which represented a persistent and stable diagnosis in those cases, with onset before five years of age.

A particular category of PDD-NOS, called Multiple Complex Developmental Disorder (MCDD), has been considered by some authors as a possible bridge diagnosis between schizophrenia and autism. MCDD has been observed in individuals aged 12 to 18 and is characterized by a deficit sensitivity to social stimuli and thinking disorders, bizarre and disorganized thoughts, inappropriate affectivity, and mood lability. Although these subjects, compared to autistics, are less disturbed in terms of social interaction, communication, and rigid and stereotypical behaviors, they are, however, more disturbed concerning obvious thinking disorders, anxieties, and aggression.

The diagnosis of very early-onset schizophrenia has been considered and recognized by MCDD construct pioneers, who estimate it as a rare clinical occurrence compared to MCDD, from which several subjects can then develop schizophrenia in adulthood. Follow-up studies have shown that, in adolescence and adulthood, 22% and 64% of subjects, respectively, developed psychotic spectrum disorders, including schizophrenia.

At the neurobiological level, a faster and more intense reduction in gray matter is observed in the PDD-COS group than in forms of schizophrenia not associated with PDD. As Sporn et al. observe, this could be due to a summary or, in any case, interactive effect between excessive neuronal pruning typical of schizophrenia and deceleration of brain growth, which in autism occurs during adolescence and follows a previous, initial acceleration.

They could, therefore, be the same genes that cause both disorders, but the different genetic variants or different environmental factors produce a different timing or mode of neuronal interaction that determines the expression of a specific phenotype rather than another. Thus, the two disorders, which had been distinguished from the DSM-III, are still considered connected using modern research methods.

In order to resolve diagnostic doubts, several studies have tried to develop tools that differentiate the two disorders. Bölte et al. analyze the profile that emerges at the Revised Wechsler Intelligence Scale (WAIS-R) administered to 20 autistic adolescents, compared to what appears if the same test is administered to 20 schizophrenic subjects. The result is that autistics perform better at the "Similarities" scale, while people with schizophrenia report a higher score at the "Understanding" scale, suggesting that cognitive structure data reported by WAIS may differentiate subjects with autism and those with schizophrenia with greater than 80% accuracy. Naito et al. examine the validity of the Autism Spectrum Quotient (AQ), a self-administered scale that measures the level of autistic traits in adults with normal intelligence in differentiating high-functioning ASD from schizophrenia.

As a result, the ASD group showed a significantly higher score at AQ than the schizophrenic group, but neither AQ nor its subscales, nor even the S scale investigating psychotic symptoms, could completely distinguish high-functioning autism from schizophrenia. Therefore, the use of AQ alone in differentiating the two disorders is limited, so more studies are needed to analyze better schizophrenic patients who have a high score to AQ and studies aimed at patients with schizoid or schizotypic personality disorder and with onset schizophrenia in childhood or adolescence.

As we have seen, the term "autism" was coined to indicate one of the characteristic symptoms of schizophrenia, whereby initially, the two concepts were intimately connected. Over the years, however, the two disorders have been progressively differentiated, giving rise to two separate diagnostic entities, which could be distinguished quite well based on medical history and psychopathological phenotype. Over time, the diagnostic boundaries of schizophrenia and autism have expanded, reaching the concept of autism spectrum disorders and schizophrenic spectrum disorders, and it is at the extreme limits of these spectra that there may be areas of overlap at various levels (pathogenetic, neuroanatomic, neuropsychological and clinical), to which the constant flow of scientific research.

In clinical practice, all this results in difficulty distinguishing the two disorders, especially in adult subjects with forms of high-functioning autism, who can often also develop psychotic-like symptoms. At present, however, there are no diagnostic tools that allow the two disorders to be differentiated, while it would be appropriate to define test batteries that, in addition to clinical observations, help to resolve differential diagnostics and identify areas of overlap between autistic and psychotic spectra.

Anxiety

A high percentage of people with autism suffer from depression and anxiety disorders. Anxiety disorders seem pretty common among adolescents and autistic children, with between 42% and 80% of incidence. The most effective interventions are behavioral DRI gradual exposure.

Gradual exposure consists of identifying feared events, building a hierarchy of them according to an increasing level of elicited fear, and exposing the individual benefiting from treatment to them, progressing from those with lower emotional intensity to those with higher emotional intensity. In people with autism, particularly in the absence of language, great attention should be paid to the selection of the feared events and subsequent exposure to them, as these patients cannot accurately report their levels of fear concerning the events. Therefore, some prudence will be used in proceeding from the lowest to the highest levels of the hierarchy to reduce the risk of escape from the task and having conditioning of the people, materials, and places involved in the exhibition.

Differential reinforcement of incompatible behaviors (DRIs) should be adopted, mainly when the patient uses dysfunctional ways to reduce anxious states, such as self- or hetero aggressive behaviors and/or self-stimulations that significantly impair their level of functioning. DRI consists of reducing problem behaviors by reinforcing functional behaviors incompatible with problem behavior (Cooper, Heron, and Heward,

2014). It is essential that the alternative behaviors selected are reinforced so that they can be adopted more or less quickly and naturally by the patient and can capture their attention by diverting it from the anxiety stimulus. For example, suppose the functional behavior to reduce anxiety is "scratching the skin," and the patient is interested in bright objects. In that case, it is possible to teach the patient to activate a luminous object and manipulate it whenever a feared situation is presented, or an anxiety state is experienced.

In the treatment of patients with an adequate cognitive level and good communication skills, it may be helpful to integrate the behavioral strategies mentioned above with cognitive strategies that promote a greater understanding of their emotional states (Attwood, 2007; Moscone and Vagni, 2013), the ability to functionally monitor and modify one's dysfunctional thoughts, to reflect on one's experience to undertake adequate paths of action (e.g., Rotheram-Fuller and Mac Mullen, 2011).

It is vital to emphasize that the symptom-focused event acquires greater effectiveness when accompanied by psychoeducational treatment, which allows the individual to perceive himself as an effective agent in their physical and social world. Trainings aim to increase autonomy skills, reduce dependence on reference figures and improve one's sense of competence, favoring the individual's ability to face. Similarly, social skill training promotes skills helpful in acting more effectively in the social world, reducing the risk of peer group expulsion and, consequently, levels of social anxiety.

Eating disorders

Children who have autism spectrum disorders have a high incidence of problems related to the sphere of nutrition, whose manifestations are atypical eating behaviors. Atypical eating behaviors include food selectivity, eating too much or too little, rumination, and pica.

Among these, the behavior most associated with autism spectrum disorder, with an incidence of 70% (in the range between 67 and 83% of autistic children), is precisely food selectivity, to the point of becoming part of the diagnostic criterion "restricted, repetitive and stereotypical interests and behaviors" of the autistic triad, which, in addition to this, the compromise of Specifically, food selectivity manifests itself in the following ways: rejection of one or more foods, aversion to specific flavors, colors or textures of food, selection of particular food categories. Food selectivity, as is understandable, is a significant cause for discomfort for the families of people with autism, and that is why the Neaclinic team has paid specific attention to these issues, implementing behavioral interventions to increase variety and promote healthy eating among children with an autism spectrum disorder.

The kind of intervention to be carried out (systematic desensitization, operating conditioning, etc.) to deal with such a delicate aspect is established and planned after a careful evaluation aimed at understanding the function(s) of such conduct, And it is therefore personalized on a case-by-case basis, in agreement with the parents or tutors, based on the needs of the family, which is an appropriately involved in the treatment.

Sleep disorders

Sleep disorders are frequently reported by parents or caregivers of children with autism spectrum disorder, with a prevalence exceeding 50% of cases. Nighttime agitation, co-sleeping, poor sleep hygiene, and early final awakening are also often reported. Insomnia in these children is actually linked to an early alteration in circadian rhythm and physiological melatonin secretion. In addition, in a minority of cases, behavioral insomnia can be the spy for other sleep disorders such as periodic sleep movements, obstructive apnea, bruxism, and epilepsy. After excluding the presence of other sleep disorders, the treatment of choice for behavioral insomnia in children with autism spectrum disorder is twofold: behavioral therapy /Parent training in which the "sleep routines" take on fundamental importance and the creation of an adequate environment to promote sleep and sleep hygiene, possibly associated with melatonin, under the supervision of the Neuropsychiatrist.

Aggressive conduct

Most children with autism are not aggressive, but many act straight, self-aggressive conduct when facing difficult situations or when they don't get what they want. They don't react in this way to create difficulties, but because they don't know how else to react. Using some simple strategies, you can help a child with autism limit emotional crises and whims and even increase their self-control. After careful observations, interviews, and evaluations of the functions of problematic behaviors, the team develops behavioral interventions using strategies mainly aimed at teaching simple and complex functional communication, teaching tolerance responses, and increasing compliance with the requests of others, with the effect of significant reduction of problematic conduct.

Epilepsy

In People with autism, epilepsy occurs in about 30-40% of cases (epileptic comorbidity), percentages that increase in the presence of intellectual retardation and, therefore, more severe autism. In a third of cases, epilepsy occurs in the early years of life (Volkmar et al., 2004), but in most cases, seizures arise in adolescence and take on the characteristics of complex partial and generalized tonic-clonic seizures. In general, epileptic abnormalities, responsible for behavioral disorders, have an even higher incidence in people on the spectrum.
It is advisable that those who take care of people with autism, starting with their parents, know how to recognize them and intervene in case they arise and this is the goal of this article: to provide the basic knowledge sufficient to identify a crisis and above all the instructions to behave adequately when crises arise.

Tonic-clonic crisis

Clonic tonic seizures are generalized attacks affecting the entire brain. It's the kind of crisis most people refer to when they think about epilepsy. Shortly before the episode begins, some people may experience an 'aura', such as a feeling of déjàvu, a strange feeling in the stomach, or a strange smell or taste. The aura is itself a simple partial seizure.

During a clonic tonic crisis, the body of those affected stiffens, and the person falls to the ground (the tonic phase). The limbs contract with strong symmetrical, rhythmic movements (the clonic phase). The person may drool from the mouth, turn blue or red in the face, or lose control of the bladder and/or intestines. Although witnessing this type of seizure can be fearful, attacking itself can hardly cause harm to the person affected. It, however, can vomit or bite its tongue and can sometimes get injured if it bumps into surrounding objects when it falls or is in the throes of seizures. The crisis ceases typically after a few minutes, after which the person is usually confused and numbing. He may suffer from headaches and want to sleep. This drowsiness can last for a few hours.

Stay close to the person – stay calm.

√ Take note of the time/duration of the crisis (important!!).
√ Protect the person from injury – remove any heavy objects from the area they are in. Put something soft under his head. Loosen clothing that is too tight;
√ Gently move the person to one side as soon as possible to help them breathe.
√ Try to communicate with the person to make sure they have actually regained consciousness.
√ Reassure it
√ Keep the curious away
What not to do:

✗ Don't limit the movements of the person.
✗ Don't try to forcibly put anything inside your mouth (important!!).
✗ Don't give the person water, pills, or food until they are fully conscious.

After the crisis is over, the person should be put on his left side. Remember that there is a slight risk that the person may vomit once the crisis is over, before they have fully regained consciousness. Therefore, the head should be placed so that vomiting can be expelled from the mouth without being inhaled. Stay with them until they recover (5 to 20 minutes).

Call an ambulance if:

√ The crisis has an active duration of more than 5 minutes or a second attack follows soon after.
√ The person has not regained consciousness within 5 minutes of the end of the crisis.
√ The crisis takes place in the water.
√ The person got hurt.
√ The person has diabetes.
√ You know, or believe, that it was the first epileptic seizure suffered by the person.
√ If you are in doubt.

Complex partial crises

This type of attack affects only part of the brain, but the person's state of consciousness is altered. The person can often appear confused and stunned and perform strange actions such as fiddling with their clothing, swallowing movements, or making unusual or weird sounds. The crisis usually lasts for one or two minutes, but the person may remain confused and sloping for a few minutes or hours after the seizure is over. Especially in cases of severe autism, these crises are not easily recognizable.

During a partial complex attack, you may need to gently guide people to avoid obstacles and move away from dangerous places.

✓ As soon as the crisis ends, try to communicate with the person by offering them your support and (if they are verbal or otherwise communicate) asking them if they feel good.

✓ Call an ambulance if the person does not start recovering after 15 minutes.

ADHD

ADHD and autism are two distinct neurodevelopmental disorders that may share some symptoms. There are fundamental differences, and a person can have both conditions. ADHD (aka "attention deficit hyperactivity disorder") is a common neurological developmental disorder. According to
American Psychiatric Association (APA), ADHD affects about 8.4% of children and 2.5% of adults. Specifically, doctors diagnose it more often in males than females. Children with ADHD present difficulty with attention, hyperactivity, and impulse control. They may have trouble concentrating, standing still, or thinking before acting. There are three subcategories of ADHD:
- Heedless
- Hyperactive-impulsive
- Arranged

ADHD symptoms can improve as we age, and patients can gain more concentration and control over their impulses.
Sometimes it's not easy to tell the difference between autism and ADHD, especially in younger children. Here's how to distinguish the symptoms of the two conditions:

- Children with ADHD have difficulty paying attention, especially in too long intervals of time, and can be easily distracted.
- Autistic children may have limited interest. They may seem obsessed with things they appreciate and have difficulty focusing on things they don't care about. They can easily remember facts and details, and some manage to excel in mathematics, science, music, or art.

It turns out to be more immediate to spot these signs while the child performs homework.

A child with ADHD can not be able to pay attention to any topic.

An autistic child can have a high level of attention to his favorite topics, but he may not be able to engage in topics that interest him less.

Communication difficulties are mostly characteristic of autism. However, some children with ADHD also have these same difficulties but typically present themselves in different ways.

Children with ADHD can:

- Talk all the time;
- They want to have the last word;
- Ignore the influence of your words on other people;
- Interrupt others.

Autistic children can:
- Have difficulty expressing their emotions and thoughts;
- Do not use gestures to communicate;
- Have trouble maintaining eye contact;
- Fixate on a topic of conversation;
- Play differently (they may not understand turn-based or fantasy play)
- Do not initiate or respond to social interactions.

Children with ADHD can quickly get bored with a structure they find uninteresting, including that of the classroom. Without variety, they can also lose interest in activities.

In contrast, autistic children often demonstrate strong homogeneity, wanting to adhere to routines or ritualized patterns of verbal or nonverbal behavior. Changes are likely to cause upset and\or irritability.

Is there a relationship between autism and ADHD?

There are similarities between the symptoms of autism and ADHD, and you can have both conditions.

For Centers for Disease Control and Prevention (CDC) the 14% of children with ADHD in the United States also have an autism spectrum disorder. Other research places this number at 15-25%.

Researchers do not fully understand the causes of both conditions, although genetic factors likely play a role in both.

Diagnosis of ADHD is based on symptoms that have been present in the last six months. If a doctor suspects autism, they may examine your child's behavior and development in previous years.

However, in both cases, they may require the intervention of teachers and caregivers, as well as that of parents.

Your doctor also intends to rule out conditions that can cause symptoms similar to those of autism or ADHD.

These issues include:
- Hearing problems.
- Learning difficulties
- Sleep disorders

According to a study made in 2010 that looked at data from more than 2,500 autistic children in the United States, 83% of them had at least one other developmental disorder, while 10% presented at least one psychiatric disorder.

Treatment varies depending on the child, their symptoms, and the presence of other conditions.

Some treatments for autism and ADHD include:
- Behaviour therapy
- Drugs

In addition, autistic children may benefit from additional forms of therapy, depending on their needs. Some options include:
- Advice
- Educational interventions
- Occupational therapy
- Sensory integration
- Logopedic

Finally, training and education can allow parents and caregivers to manage their symptoms better.

AUTISM AND NERVOUS TIC

Nerve tics can come in several forms: clearing your throat repeatedly, for example. And while your child constantly repeats this gesture, you wonder if it is a characteristic of autism, a comorbid condition, or something else...

Some repetitive behaviours such as stereotypes (a non-functional, ritual, and rhythmic movement) are associated with autism spectrum disorders, such as when a child rhythmically shakes his hand in front of his face.

But not all repetitive movements are stereotypes. There may be more to behaviour, as there may be a connection between autism and Gilles de la Tourette syndrome. There are also some other conditions and medications that can cause tics.

For children, definitions and classification of tic conditions can be irrelevant rather the impact of behaviour on their school, social and daily lives may be their primary concern. If the world could only understand that a tic is not something they can easily stop at will and that feeling embarrassed about behaviour could actually make things worse... let's say it would be a step forward.

People who have tics describe the initial or premonitory impulse as similar to itching, an unpleasant sensation that builds up inside. Once you have a tic, you experience temporary relief.

Many people, especially children, have this kind of tic since transient tics are actually not that rare. Our idea of icts is primarily about facial contractions or shoulder jolts. Instead, there is much more to tic disorders and children with this condition often need intervention and support.

WHAT IS A TIC?

Tic disorders are neurological developmental conditions that often emerge in childhood and maybe in comorbidity with attention deficit hyperactivity disorder (ADHD), autism, or obsessive-compulsive disorder (OCD).

A tic could be described as a short-lived movement or sound that disrupts normal behaviour. Tics are involuntary movements or vocalizations, which occur suddenly and repeatedly. Although tic or behaviour is repetitive, it isn't rhythmic.

The Diagnostic & Statistical Manual of Mental Disorders includes three types of tic disorders useful for diagnosis: Tourette syndrome, Persistent disorder (also called chronic) motor or vocal tic disorder. and Temporary tic disorder. Just for classification purposes it is important to note if your autistic child's it has been presenting a tic for more or less than a year.

This article will discuss the different types of tic disorders, not to facilitate self-diagnosis, but to help alert parents of symptoms that may require further evaluation and possible diagnosis by a professional. Your child may have ADHD or other comorbidities and this could cause confusion about symptoms. This is why it is important to look for an accurate diagnosis that takes into account the child's history and coexisting conditions.

TOURETTE SYNDROME

Tourette syndrome is a complex condition of neurological development. Some criteria need to be met for a diagnosis of Tourette syndrome: for example, your child should have two or more motor icts and at least one vocal tic.

Examples of motor icts may include the following:

- Head contraction
- Blink or jolt your eyes down
- Pull out your tongue
- Shoulder stand up
- Facial grimaces
- Nose contraction

Examples of vocal tics may include:

- Clearing your throat
- To sniff
- Grunt
- Cough
- Scream

Complex vocal it could also mean that a child repeats their words or those of others. Repeating what others say is called echolalia and is a symptom of both autism and Tourette syndrome.

Another complex vocal it is a coprolaly which involves the involuntary occurrence of inappropriate or obscene vocalizations. Less than the 20% of individuals with Tourette syndrome will experience this symptom in their lifetime (Freedman, 2009).

Whether it's due to media representation or just a reflection of humanity, the behavioural act of pronouncing swearing has become Tourette's stereotype. Although it appears to be the part of Tourette disorder that most people are interested to, as it's poorly understood and more research must be done.

In addition to having more than two motor tics and at least one vocal tic, as illustrated in the examples above, the child should start showing tics before reaching the age of 18. The child should have such tics for a year and should not have taken medications that could be the cause of such (ICT) behaviour.

Although many of these symptoms are present, parents may still wonder if such symptoms can be attributed to autism or if their child has Tourette syndrome in addition to being on the spectrum. Darrow et al., study made in 2017) noticed that higher rates of autism spectrum disorder (ASD) among children with Tourette syndrome may be caused by difficulty distinguishing complex icts and OCD symptoms from autism. The authors also concluded that careful examination of the specific symptoms of autism is essential (Darrow et al., 2017). That's why an accurate (professional) diagnosis is essential.

PERSISTENT DISTURBANCE FROM MOTOR OR VOCAL TIC

Although this condition shares some diagnostic criteria with Tourette syndrome, such as onset before age 18 and persistence of tics for more than a year, multiple motor and/or vocal tics are not diagnostic prerequisites. Just a single tic or multiple motor or vocal tics (not both) would meet diagnostic criteria for constant motor or vocal TIC disorder.

Persistent motor or vocal tic disorder is a less serious condition than Tourette syndrome. Subsequent tic disorder, often described as the most common and least serious tic condition, is called transient or temporary ict disorder.

PROVISIONAL ICT DISORDERS

To meet the diagnostic criteria of the DSM-5 for a temporary tic disorder, it should occur before the child turns 18 and he should never meet the diagnostic criteria of Tourette syndrome and persistent vocal or motor icts disorder.

Many children develop a tic that then disappears without any treatment or attention. It can also cease and return for a period of time.

Do stress and anxiety aggravate icts or not?

A study by Conelea et al. (2014) discovered that the frequency of tics during the whole experiment did not grow during periods of higher heart rate, as might be expected. The doctor concluded that the suggested results (indicating that ivtdy exacerbations may not be linked to increased physiological arousal) mean that more research in this field is needed.

Stereotypes

When various tic disorders are examined, it becomes apparent how difficult the diagnosis should be, especially if conditions such as ADHD or OCD are also present. In an autistic child, icts can also be confused with stereotypes.

Stereotypes shown by autistic children can be distinguished from tics in that they are rhythmic and seem aimless. It also doesn't have the premonitory impulse that precedes a tic and subsequent relief once the ict is performed. In addition, stereotypes usually have an earlier onset than tics. Stereotypes often appear before the child reaches the age of three, while tics appear primarily when the child is about six years old.

Examples of stereotypes in autism are clapping and body rocking. When you observe some repetitive behaviour in your autistic child it can be difficult to determine whether it is a tic or stereotype; even if you ascertain that the behaviour is related to a nervous ict, you will still need a professional to determine if your child has Tourette syndrome or another tic disorder. For accurate diagnosis and early intervention, furnish your doctor with as much detail as possible about the onset and characteristics of repetitive behaviour.

HOW DOES ICT AFFECT A CHILD?

Most people who share their experience on a tic talk about a specific feeling that precedes a tic. A study by Reese et al. (2014) presented the experience of sensory phenomena (self-reported) before a tic of adolescents and adults with Tourette syndrome or chronic ict disorder.

The most commonly felt sensations preceding a tic have been described as "energy that needed an outlet," "inner feeling of excitement, and feelings of tension" (Reese et al., 2014). Most participants in this study reported that the feelings or sensations, described above, disappear after they have done or completed a ict.

It is difficult to imagine this internal accumulation, several times a day, especially for a child. A feeling of pressure, repressed energy, which can only be alleviated by a socially stigmatized ict. In addition, with this negative reinforcement the behavioural cycle continues.

Many autistic people report a need for suppressed coughing in church, for example, with eyes tearing and their throats on fire. The fact of letting the cough escape in that large, silent and sacred space was gruesome and euphoric in equal measure.

The idea of having a need that can only be alleviated through behavior that can be frowned upon must be terrifying for a child. Especially in a school environment where many children often target behaviors deemed different.

Studies have found that children with Tourette syndrome experienced more bullying, victimization and persecution than children without the condition. Other studies also discovered that children with Tourette syndrome were more likely to experience school challenges such as having to repeat a year.

Of course, Tourette syndrome is the most extreme of all tic conditions; many childhood tics are temporary or disappear without intervention after less than three months. Further encouraging news is that there is a therapeutic promise in behavioural interventions for chronic ict conditions.

ICT SUPPRESSION

One study (Kim et al., 2019) looked at tics suppression in children with recent-onset tics. The study was undertaken to determine whether the ability to suppress a ict predicted the severity of tics in the future.

The study discovered that babies who had icts for only a few months could suppress them. Suppression was particularly successful when the kids obtained a rapid reward. The study can be valuable in terms of inhibitory control over tics in the early period of onset.

POSITIVE RESULTING

Studies such as those above emphasize the importance of early intervention in conditions such as Tourette syndrome in comorbidity with autism. The study Bennett et al., 2020 detailed success when Comprehensive Behavioural Intervention for icts Disorders (CBIT) was adapted for use in young children.

Treatment and early intervention can prevent the chronic course of tic symptoms, which is why parents should never minimize the role of interfering and repetitive behaviours, thinking they are always another symptom of autism.

Chapter 6:Parenting

All the parents wants their kid to be healthy and grow up healthy; when this does not happen the birth-related family project undergoes a drastic and painful downsizing. The repercussions on parents who experience having their child diagnosed with an autism spectrum disorder affect identity, emotional and social plans and have still been poorly studied to guide the relationship of health and social service workers with parents.

The absence of medical-scientific certainty regarding the causes of the disorder fuels loss in families, The path to defining diagnostic knowledge is almost never linear and above all not immediate. In many cases some deficits or shortcomings in the child lead parents to the search for confirmations and a specialized diagnosis that is built after a period of time, sometimes imposing a late adaptation to the disability situation.

When both parents understand that they share the same concerns they realize that the problem is not the result of excessive apprehension, but that the child's difficulties are real. It can also happen that only one of the two parents realizes the child's difficulties and that he is forced not only to face his feelings with respect to the child's situation, but also to communicate to the partner what he does not perceive or does not want to perceive.

Autism is multifaceted and there are various nuances of behaviour that make each child different from others and in need of a personalized rehabilitation approach. Regardless of how the diagnosis is communicated, the resulting emotional impact is naturally very strong, in most cases it takes a period of time to deal with and process the situation. Each parent faces the situation differently; in most cases, however, the process develops gradually, passing different stages, from the initial ones where shock, denial, pain and guilt prevail, to the final ones of adaptation and activation.

Confirming the enormous suffering experienced by parents, an important American longitudinal study (Lounds Taylor and Warren, 2012) examined depressive symptoms in mothers of children diagnosed with an autism spectrum disorder. The results found that more than three-quarters of mothers (78.7%) had relevant depressive symptoms in the week following diagnosis and that 37.3% continued to report clinically significant levels 16 months after diagnosis.

Mothers show a higher level of depression than fathers. Although the couple shares high levels of stress, depressive symptoms appear more frequently in the mother. This fact is a demonstration of the different psychological condition experienced by mothers, hypothetically due to the greater involvement in care, organization and responsibility activities. For this reason, the mother may be more exposed to the difficulties of raising a child with special needs. In addition, different psychological conditions of parents are associated with self-perception within the specific parenting role.

Our research reveals that when mothers feel satisfied with their care relationship, they develop fewer psychological symptoms and that fathers have fewer when they have "limiting" interactions with their children, that is, by making rules and firm discipline. Such surveys demonstrate the importance of parents' self-perception, in addition to their psychological condition.

We highlighted a further difference in parental style in following child growth with ASD. Parenting style is represented by strategies and patterns of parents' behaviour toward their children. Our research shows how mothers of children with ASD exercise, compared to fathers, a more social behaviour with their children. This finding further supports the idea that moms and dads interact differently with babies as they grow up (Barnard & Solchany, 2002). In comparison, mothers seem to hold greater responsibility for social interaction, engaging in behaviours used by parents to engage children in visual, verbal, affective, and physical interpersonal exchanges.

As everyone's life goes on, every day, being a parent and facing one's child's disability often seems to force us to step back. Curbed by fears and anxieties that do not go away, in the darkness of solitude.

The sleepless nights after a diagnosis of a child's autism spectrum disorder, the difficult path to accepting it. The fear that the world will never treat him as you would like, the anguish for how he can feel, for what will be after us, the guilt for mistakes never made. The very long phone calls and turns of people to be able to have a support service, the cutting-edge therapies all too expensive, a teacher who is patient enough, a structure that can stimulate him, an organization that does not think only about making war with others.

Or again, legal dynamics, juvenile judges, social workers, lawyers who treat you enough, millions of phone calls to make appointments and get written reports, walls, doors slammed in your face, constantly wondering who you should turn to.

Almost impossible is to find someone who can give you what you need: valuable tips and tricks not to go wrong. And then it's hard to orient yourself: between bureaucracy, the often unsustainable costs for a family, the search for the right school, many attempts that will fail. It is above all then that you begin to feel alone.

Parenting with disabled children totally changes us. There is no denying it. The truth is that the early years take us so far away from who we were before we might no longer recognize ourselves.

You look in the mirror, with bags under your eyes, and we seem to have aged by a hundred years. Or you find yourself in a crowded room and feel completely isolated. So we wonder if we are invisible. We wonder how our world can be so different and how we can start relating to people.

We question what we know. We ask ourselves a million questions. What is our purpose? Where to find strength. In addition, one wonders why, How it happened, Why our son And not that of others.

Diagnosis calls into question the stability of our marriage, Our health, The way we are the parents of other children and Also the decision to have more children, Career and finances, relationships, but also faith.

You experience the greatest love on this earth. And at the same time one wonders how to deal with everyday difficulties. You are ashamed to be sad.

We also notice the incredible beauty that this world encloses. Almost as if we had been allowed access to a special club: full of hugs, tears of joy, anger, you find yourself celebrating for things taken for granted to others, like a single word at 8 years old, And it's great, no matter when it happens.

You learn what insensitivity means And you get out of breath the first time you touch your child. You might think you are prepared, You think you will come back with some ironic and snappy comments But you probably won't. And then spend the next sleepless nights wondering how you can live forever and change the world at the same time.

At first you feel like you're running against time, fighting against diagnosis, doing everything you can, questioning your hope . Then you find realistic acceptance and a real and strong hope. So you want time to stop, You want your child's body to stay small Because the world is kinder to children.

Diagnosing a child's autism involves a radical reorganization of family planning. Parents' ability to "resist" at the event and find meaning in everyday life is one of the strengths of the possibilities for adapting and improving life for their children. For this reason it's important to know the experience and experience of families. Families have increased the attention paid to autism through the media, favouring the spread of a collective awareness about the existence of the phenomenon itself and the overcoming of forms of prejudice towards children and parents themselves. Health and social services, being the phase of ascertaining the gradual syndrome, should structure moments of accompaniment and closeness of parents in such a way as to promote the understanding of the phenomenon, in the light of the uncertainty of the cause, which enhances the specificities and family meanings, respecting them.

McCubbin and colleagues (1996) argue that family groups seek explanations about the cause of disabilities, and although there is a fairly wide range of possible explanations, each family identifies the meanings and meaning constructions that most help them activate than the event. Families who have the ability to find shared explanations about the cause, reducing ambiguities and uncertainties, are more competent in directing their energies to functional situation management strategies. Precisely for this reason, the medical-health evaluation should be accompanied by a social evaluation and contextual support.

The promotion, already from the early stages of evaluation of the syndrome, contact and moments of dialogue with other families and associations, can represent an important support to avoid responses of desperate withdrawal into oneself and isolation, an aspect highlighted with different nuances from the family members interviewed. Alongside the necessary medical and health interventions, social support and the promotion of self-mutual aid among those who share the same situation is a fundamental support strategy that social and health service operators can immediately encourage. In addition, "network" cohesion and the sharing of objectives between social and health workers and those of the school can fuel a process that allows the needs of growing children and families to be received by providing a container that can interact in synergy, and respond in an integrated way to the needs of parents and children.

HOW TO DEAL WITH STRESS WHEN YOU HAVE AN AUTISTIC CHILD

A day in the caregiver's life of a child with autism spectrum disorder can include an infinite number of challenges and stressors. A caregiver could take their child to various appointments, support their educational needs, help them avoid sensory overload, or face an unexpected whim in public. At the end of this long day, the caregiver may feel discouraged but at the same time discover that his child cannot sleep, preventing him from getting the rest he needs.

Although parents of autistic children face many unique challenges, they are not necessarily doomed to a life of stress. Research has shown that caregivers who have and use valuable support systems and who actively solve problems (including their physical and mental health) experience far less stress than those who have no support. It's no secret that a less stressed caregiver is much more likely to raise a well-adapted and less anxious child.

Types of caregiver stress

Caregivers of autistic children face different stresses that can affect their mental, physical, social and financial well-being.

- **Psychological stress:** Meeting the needs of an autistic person can increase the risk of depression, anxiety, or other types of psychological distress of parents. Parents who don't take steps to learn the right teaching strategies and who do not receive support are likely to tend to neglect their mental health care and experience even more stress.
- **Physical stress:** Chronic stress can make parents of autistic children more vulnerable to cardiovascular, immune system and gastrointestinal problems. One study discovered that they are more likely to present higher levels of the stress hormone cortisol and a biomarker known as CRP, that is linked to a variety of physical illnesses. parents or aregivers may also suffer from increased fatigue or struggle with insomnia, especially if their child also has difficulty sleeping.
- **Social stress:** Much of society is not familiar with autism spectrum disorder, and people can blame or judge a parent when they see and misunderstand certain child problem behaviors. it can create a stigma that can lead parents to feel socially isolated. They may start avoiding public meetings or spending time with friends and family. Parents of autistic children may also be more likely to experience marital stress.

- **Financial Stress:** Some research has found that parents of autistic children can make less money or must work fewer hours than other parents. Many mothers, above all, have stopped working to be able to dedicate themselves to their child. Caregivers can also face additional expenses for therapies, medical expenses, and care in general, all of which involve an additional financial burden on the family. Some parents even risk losing their jobs if they often have to leave to take care of their child.

TIPS FOR DEALING WITH STRESS

Start with simple changes: If you have an autistic child and feel overwhelmed by all these categories of stress, sometimes starting with simple changes can make a big difference in overall functioning. Try to discover someone who allows you to get enough sleep to recharge your batteries, try exercising regularly, and plan some time for yourself.

If these activities seem unmanageable, you can focus on even smaller changes like slowing down your daily routine or drinking more water, or asking for help for simpler activities. You may be surprised at how much your stress level will decrease, and you may find that taking care of yourself also has an immediate positive impact on your child's functioning.

Focus on today's reality and not what happens if...It's easy for any parent to anxiously focus on how their child is developing, but parents of autistic children are particularly at risk of worrying excessively about their children and the challenges they may face in the future. If you're feeling stressed, ask yourself if you're focused on your child's real needs or if you're thinking too much about the longer-term future you can't handle now. Ask you, "What is my responsibility to my son today and to myself?" Can help you bring your attention back to what you can actually control.

Find a truce outside of work: For many parents of autistic children, workplace is one of the few places or the only one where they can find a break from caring for their child. Ideally, caregivers should have time and space outside of work where they can focus on their emotional and physical health, interests, and other important relationships. Sometimes fear of how your child will adapt to a new caregiver can prevent parents from seeking this support, but giving your child the opportunity to interact with other adults will benefit both you and your child.

Look around: Unsurprisingly, research has shown that parents of autistic children who access a solid support system are less likely to experience stress than those who don't or can't. Family members and close friends may have difficulty figuring out how to help, so consider giving them specific tasks when they become available, IF they become available (many relatives and friends disappear with the arrival of the diagnosis of autism). Try contacting listening groups, associations, and other community organizations, which will prove to be important additions to your support system.

Involve a professional figure: Do not underestimate the value that professional help can have in managing your stress level. If you can't or don't want to consider therapy for yourself, there are other services you can use. Consider making an appointment with your primary care physician just to make sure your physical health is good and that there are no complications that add up to stress. Disability or autism associations or your school or local ASL can also help you get in touch with support groups and assistants of autistic people. Support groups can make you feel heard, but also connect you with resources and information that can reduce the stress of parenting. If you care for an autistic child and would like to start reducing your overall level of stress, you may start by asking yourself some of the following questions:

- Are there times during the day when I can slow down, focus my thoughts and prevent worry, stress or anxiety from taking over?
- What are some significant changes, even small ones, I could make to the way I take care of my mind and body?
- Are there dysfunctional or unhealthy ways to deal with the stress I need to remove from my routine? Do I drink too much? Do I smoke too much? Do I eat badly?
- What hypothetical concerns about my child's autism hinder my stay focused on the present?

- Who did I ignore in my potential support system and who could help me instead?
- Are there any tasks I can delegate to others to reduce my stress?
- What community resources can help me manage stress, connect me to low-cost or free professional help, or provide support to my child?

Sometimes we could try to manage stress with small daily gestures. It may take a few minutes longer than our day, but taking advantage of all the options we have available can lead to a better life for both us and our child.

PARENTAL STRESS DOESN'T DISAPPEAR, BUT IT TRANSFORMS

Most parents experience stress, but for those who are raising autistic children, everyday life often brings stress with a capital S. We need to prevent our child from running away, manage their collapses, discuss with teachers, avoid images or sounds that overload the senses, and continually depend on therapists or doctors. Too often then, we do all this deprived of sleep, because so many autistic boys do not sleep or wake up in the middle of the night, and of course, we don't sleep either.

The terrible thing (let's face it) is that it doesn't end when children grow up, but on the contrary, often the stress increases or simply... it transforms.

For most parents with autistic children, stress begins at that moment when "something is wrong", we realize that our child is not talking, interacting or playing like other young children. The rest of the family says: "exaggerated", the partner adds: "let it end that way you pull it away", grandmother: "but it has nothing, let the little boy grow it".

BUT WHY ARE SOME PARENTS MORE STRESSED THAN OTHERS?

Parents who have managed to create a village around the autistic child, a network of supporters around them, experience less stress than moms whose support systems are dysfunctional.

Quite a few studies report that parents of autistic children experience more stress than parents of children with typical development, but the researchers went further by trying to understand why some parents experience more stress than others. Is this something about their children's autism type – which can fall within a mild to severe spectrum – their family circumstances or their characteristics?

They studied 283 Canadian women in the moment where their children were diagnosed with autism, and two years after diagnosis.

At the time of diagnosis, mothers whose children had the most challenging behaviour experienced more stress. But over time, those with particular adaptive strategies had less stress. Moms who were focused on getting help, solving problems, and finding meaning in their experiences have best resisted parental storms. Moms who preferred avoid their problems and emotions – suffered more stress.

People with empathetic and collaborative relatives also claim to benefit from creating a broad circle of encouragement and help. In fact, we must never think that we can do it alone, even if sometimes it is not a choice.

Parents whose stress stems primarily from their children's behavior could be taught effective ways to manage crises and other challenges. Some families would benefit from parental stays – a temporary break from care – and marriage counselling, if these are the problems. Other parents may be taught better skills to deal with autism in general, through cognitive-behavioural techniques or mindfulness training.

FINDING A LOW-COST SOLUTION TO PARENTAL STRESS

Some families don't have time and money for therapy, but one group of researchers has tested a relatively low-cost solution: parental-led support groups. For the study, some professionals taught and supervised parent-mentors to provide adult awareness or positive development.

The researchers randomly assigned parents of autistic children and other developmental disabilities to either therapy group. The group learned special breathing and relaxation techniques, meditation and other exercises to improve adaptability. Meanwhile, parents in the adult group have learned to combat concerns, conflict, and pessimism by identifying and using their strengths and abilities. Both groups of parents noticed substantial reductions in stress, depression and anxiety after six weeks of treatment.

What does awareness look like? Let's say your child is having a crisis in a store. The first step is for you to realize and accept your anxiety and frustration, then focus on responding to the crisis, without letting your thoughts go to the eyes of others and influence your decision-making.

"ACCEPTANCE" AS A PATH TO RELIEVE STRESS IN AUTISM

Another potential stress reducer is practicing acceptance, said Dr. Amy Keefer PhD, a clinical psychologist at the Kennedy Krieger Institute's Center for Autism and Related Disorders. Parents who accept their child's autism today seem to be feeling better, he said.Dr Keefer said that focusing on the present can help. "I think the parents who fare better are the ones who can celebrate every outcome and developmental improvement the moment it occurs, and who are not focused on an end result, often unattainable such as exiting the diagnosis, for example.

These parents practice being 'in the moment' against measuring progress versus an ideal outcome.'

OTHER STRATEGIES TO RELIEVE STRESS:

Positive thinking and dialogue

Positive thinking and inner dialogue increase your positive feelings. Feeling positive increases your ability to cope with stressful situations.

For example, you might have a negative thought like "People probably think I'm a bad parent." You can challenge this thought by asking yourself, "How do I know what people will think?" You could also use more positive thoughts, such as "Who cares what others think?", "I can do it," or "Stay calm."

The more you practice a positive inner dialogue, the more automatic it will become in your life. Start practicing in one situation that causes you stress, then move on to another.

Relaxation and breathing strategies

Practice some breathing exercises and muscle relaxation techniques. If you practice and use relaxation exercises as soon as you feel signs of stress, or when you are aware you are entering a situation that makes you stressed, you can definitely calm down. You can also spend some time each day relaxing, meditating, or mindfulness. Even just 10 minutes at the beginning or end of the day may be enough. This could help you sleep better and feel more positive throughout the day.

To Organize

Stress is often related to feeling that things are out of your control. Organizing is a very effective way to keep things in check, including stress levels.

You could also try to put in place some family routines. Routines help your family run your activities more efficiently and free up time for more fun things. You can change these routines for children with additional needs.

Finding time for pleasurable family activities When you have an autistic child, you may forget to carve out time for yourself. You can reduce stress levels in your family by making sure all family members, including you, have some time to do things that make them feel good . One way to do this is to convince everyone in your family to make a list of the things they love. So try to make sure everyone can do something from their list every day or every two days. Lists should contain a mix of activities that vary in cost and time.

Maintain and modify family traditions and rituals

Family traditions can give you a sense of belonging and unity. This will strengthen your family relationships, which will help you overcome times of stress. You may need to change your traditions to suit your autistic child's needs. For example, it may be less stressful to plan a camping weekend trip a little closer to home so you will spend less time in the car.

Support from family and friends

When a child is diagnosed with autism, family and friends can be a great source of practical support, if they don't abandon you of course. It is good to ask for help if you need it. It might be easy to ask an extended family member to babysit for a few hours, one night, or ask an older granddaughter or granddaughter to take your kids to the Luna park. This might even turn into a fun and repetitive activity for your kid and extended family member, and will give you some time for yourself or to do other things.

Get specific help for stress

If you or any other family member feel very stressed every day, it might be helpful to talk to a doctor. You may start by seeing your GP, who will help you make a stress management plan. And then, if necessary, hear a psychologist, maybe the same one who follows your autistic child. Raising a child with special needs often means finding yourself alone. "I understand," many say, but that's not enough. You need competent people by your side, to tell you "don't worry, you can do this: it will be fine". But even if it's hard, you should never give up, because with hard work and effort you will be able to achieve everything you want for your kid and everything will really be fine.

Chapter 7: Successful people with autism

It is normal to be afraid about the future of our child with autism, yet we must not forget that many autistic people have achieved success and fulfilled all their dreams throughout history. For inspiration, here is a list of people with autism who have had a bright future. Everything is possible.

George Orwell, Beethoven and Immanuel Kant
They had their intelligence and exceptional artistic abilities thanks to a special form of autism. This is what a study made by an Irish psychiatrist that establishes for the first time a link between autism and genius. *Michael Fitzgerald* drew up a psychological profile of a number of great musicians, writers, painters, philosophers and found that many of them had some form of autism, like *Mozart, Hans Christian Andersen, LS Lowry and Lewis Carroll.*

Daryl Hannah
The beautiful movie star like Splash, Blade Runner and Steel Magnolias – spoke, just five years ago, from her experience in the autism spectrum. As a kid, she cradled to self-soothe, and she was so shy that when she started her carreer, she refused to give interviews or even attend her own previews. Although she learned to control and live with her diagnosis, Hannah nearly left the entertainment industry to focus on other activities like environmental issues and other passions.

Temple Grandin
There may not be a living autistic person today more famous than Temple Grandin. She is The Colorado State University author and professor and she didn't start speaking until she was nearly four years old, and doctors who diagnosed her had recommended institutionalizing her.
Fortunately, his parents disagreed with them. Grandin has become a driving force in the animal sciences, was named one of TIME's 100 most influential characters, and also produced an award-winning biopic about her life. He remains an outspoken defender of the autistic community and struggles to believe that "autism characteristics can be modified and controlled."

Michelangelo Buonarroti
The artist who made the frescoes in the Sistine Chapel was probably an Asperger. Michelangelo in fact was unsociable - or rather, intractable - and immersed himself completely in work, with an almost fanatical devotion.

DAN AYKROYD

Popular comedian Dan Aykroyd had already been expelled from two different schools when he was diagnosed with mild Asperger's Syndrome as a child. Since then, Aykroyd has been honest and sincere about his experiences with the autism spectrum. The Academy Award-nominated actor and writer even talked about how his experiences with autism contributed to his character in Ghostbusters.

HANS CHRISTIAN ANDERSEN

Experts differ as to whether Hans Christian Anderson, the beloved fairy tale writer was autistic or not. Most of those who insist that he has been on the spectrum are autistic themselves, and therefore may relate to Andersen on a personal level. For example, Andersen's diary describes in detail his many unrequited love encounters for those who were, frankly, unattainable – a common personal experience, which, let's say, can affect people on the spectrum. They also cite the recurring theme of marginalized characters in his stories. Most never achieve their desired happy ends.

BENJAMIN BANNEKER

Benjamin Banneker was an African American author, surveyor, naturalist, astronomer, inventor, and farmer who lived as a free man in 18th-century America. A large amount of contemporary documents refer to Banneker's "unparalleled brilliance" and "strange methods of behaviour," which give credence to the common idea that Banneker had a form of high-functioning autism. He was known to fix some objects for a long time, until fixation led him to experience the invention of those same objects.

SUSAN BOYLE

Most of you will know Susan Boyle as the shy Scottish introvert who sold over 14 million albums after appearing in Britain's Got Talent. But even more people found Boyle stimulating when she announced that she had been diagnosed with Asperger's Syndrome, a diagnosis Boyle had said, she felt like a "relief." Boyle is still studying the autism spectrum and how it affects it, but as long as she keeps singing, people will continue to be inspired by her.

TIM BURTON

Is Hollywood director Tim Burton autistic? Her long time partner, Helena Bonham Carter, seems to think so. He once speculated that he was "possibly autistic" during an interview. While searching for an autistic character for a film, Carter argues, she had a moment of doubt and realized that much of her research was applied to Burton. Carter said "Autistic people have application and dedication. You can say something to Tim when he works and he doesn't even hear you. But i have to say that this quality also makes him a fantastic father; he has an extraordinary sense of humour and imagination. He is able to see things that other people don't see. "

HENRY CAVENDISH

Henry Cavendish is one of the most important scientists in history. A philosopher, chemist, and natural physicist, Cavendish is perhaps the most famous discoverer of hydrogen and is also thought to have been autistic. In addition to his weekly meetings at the prestigious Royal Society Club, Cavendish did everything he could to avoid public extras or social relations. In fact, he was so lonely, always communicated in writing with his servants, ordered meals with a memo left on the table, and even added a private staircase at the back of his house in order to skip the housekeeper. He also avoided eye contact and was often described by a contemporary as the "coolest and most indifferent of mortals." But he was also brilliant, although it was only after his death that fellow scientists, through his many documents, realized everything he had accomplished.

CHARLES DARWIN

Trinity College professor Michael Fitzgerald, a prominent psychiatrist, studied and published an article concluding that Charles Darwin had Asperger's syndrome. There are testimonies from Darwin's childhood that claim that he was a very quiet and isolated child, who often avoided interaction with others. Like so many others with Asperger, he looked for alternative ways of communicating, for example writing letters. He had fixations with certain topics suhc as chemistry, but he was a very visual thinker – all the traits of some autistic people.

EMILY DICKINSON

In his book Writers on the Spectrum: How Autism and Asperger's Syndrome Affected Literary Writing, academic Julie Brown includes classical poet Emily Dickinson. Brown is part of a large group that believes Dickinson showed many signs of autism: he wrote poems that were extremely unconventional for his period, was lonely, related better to children, wore almost exclusively white robes, and had a fascination for scented flowers, among other things.
Lyndall Gordon, Dickinson's biographer, insists that Dickinson's epilepsy is what makes her so lonely, but doctors are fast to point out that those with autism are much more likely to have epilepsy as well.

PAUL DIRAC

Paul Dirac has been repeatedly referred to as one of the most significant and influential physicists of the 20th century. The Cambridge professor contributed greatly to quantum mechanics and quantum electrodynamics, and even received the Nobel Prize in Physics in 1933. That Nobel, however, was almost rejected by Dirac, who was so lonely that he wanted no publicity.

Such shyness is one of the many reasons why a large number of people think Dirac may have had some form of autism. In addition to his shyness, they cite his intense concentration, extreme literal awareness, lack of empathy, and rigid patterns, among other things.

ALBERT EINSTEIN

Albert Einstein, the most famous scientist and mathematician in history, had a lot of interesting features such as trouble socializing, especially as an adult. As a child he had severe delays in language and later echolalia, or the habit of repeating sentences to himself. And, of course, Einstein was incredibly technical. Such things have led many experts to conclude that Einstein has been on the autism spectrum.

BOBBY FISCHER

Bobby Fischer, the great master and world chess champion, is said to have had Asperger's syndrome in addition to paranoid schizophrenia and obsessive-compulsive disturb. He was known to be extremely intense and did not relate well to others due to his little propensity to make friends and poor social skills. His intense focus on chess is another sign, as is his fame for not being able to deal with an unstructured environment.

BARBARA MCCLINTOCK

Barbara McClintock was a famous scientist who was very successful in studying chromosomes and how they change during the reproduction process. McClintock has long been considered autistic. He had extreme fixation on his work and was able to concentrate for long periods of time. He was also very special about what p should not wear. Remarkably lonely, she went to great lengths not to attract the attention of the limelight, McClintock hardly accepted the 1983 Nobel Prize in Physiology or Medicine, which was awarded to her for her excellent and ground-breaking work.

NIKOLA TESLA

Thanks to his main rival, Thomas Edison, who reportedly stole many of his best ideas, Nikola Tesla died poor and alone. More recently, Tesla is finally getting the recognition it deserves for many of its brilliant ideas. It is likely that the inventor was also autistic. According to time records, Tesla suffered from a lot of phobias, he was sensitive to light & sound, isolated himself and was obsessed with the number three.

LUDWIG WITTGENSTEIN

Austrian philosopher Ludwig Wittgenstein probably had autism. His most famous work, "Tractatus Logico-Philosophicus" has been often cited as a classic example of the autistic thinking process. Contemporary letters and journal entries refer to

Wittgenstein's persistent irritation, especially when it came to understanding and dealing with those around him.

What is the first step to do to help our kids become successful and self-reliant people in the future?

The first step to do is of course raise them in the way they need, love them in the way they need, develop an effective communication with them, always be there for them in a way which doesn't make them feel weak and allows them to develop their self reliance. I will guide you in the hard process of finding your own way in the world of positive parenting.

"Tailored" love

How can you start teaching an autistic child?

The autistic child only learns if guided by a well-structured, clear and predictable learning context. This, however, also applies, in principle, to adolescents and adults. Unlike other children or adolescents, the autistic child rarely learns spontaneously or incidentally or by simple imitation or by explaining to him only verbally what he needs to do.

Since its underlying difficulties are linked to the misunderstanding of the social, conventional and symbolic world of our daily reality and the relative complexities of communication, it is necessary to know how to discriminate between what is essential from what is secondary, what is abstracted from what is concrete. Therefore, in our complex world, we can only teach us simple rules, but not the most accomplished aspects, and even more difficult the emotional aspects of our behaviours. It is about knowing how to identify the fundamental priorities for a life that is as safe and autonomous as possible. Instead, a lot can be learned about concrete aspects of reality.

In general, the following recommendations apply:

- Always prepare positively and adopt a stimulating and exciting educational and educational way
- To begin with, identify a very simple goal for which it already demonstrates some attempt at understanding, interest and execution.
- Avoid verbal instructions given with very long sentences.
- Stimulate and encourage the autistic child in his areas of talent.

Don't assume that a person can't do something just because they have autism. Do not be influenced by the IQ person because it is very difficult to measure it exactly in people with autism.

- Speak slowly, clearly and specifically, also helping each other with objects.
- Be patient on time, as people with autism can take longer than others doing things.
- Use a positive approach, avoiding unpleasant comments and encouraging positive behaviours with verbal praise and physical reinforcements (caresses, compliments, "beat five, and so on").
- Never raise your voice or threaten punishment, rather help your child (for example, if you are told to sit down and your child doesn't, repeat it at least once again and, if you don't obey, take it gently and accompany them to your chair).
- Don't ask to do something, but say do it without using overly authoritative tones.
- Never allow a question asked to remain unanswered. So be patient in response times and encourage replication.
- Avoid harassing noises, loud laughter and flicker sources.
- Since children cannot fully understand and pay attention to all environmental indications announcing that a transition is about to take place (like, the time of leaving school is approaching) they must be notified when an activity must end ("in five minutes we go out, let's prepare") or another one must start ("when we finish this puzzle we will do mathematics"). Likewise, they need to be prepared if something unusual is about to happen (start a thunderstorm and warn that lightning and thunder may occur) or scary ("the bell will ring in five minutes").

Insist that an assigned task be completed, helping you with verbal reinforcements ("you're good, let me see how you do it").

- Do not suddenly block the child from the course of his routine if it is not dangerous for himself and others.
- To teach them effectively, we must first get their attention with small cunning (If the child does not look at the teacher and seems distracted, wait and, when he has crossed his gaze with you, even with a very small eye contact, it is necessary to praise him for the "beautiful look" by presenting him with a teaching activity at the same time).

Why is communication important?

I think that the first thing you should do is learn how to communicate with your kid. Many times good communication skills can solve a bunch of problems you didn't think were related to communication.

Let's make an example:

If your kid bites.

When a child bites, especially at school, social histories or positive reinforcements of appropriate behaviour do not always work, much less punishments. Or, they work in the beginning, but then the bite comes back.

What absolutely must be done is to deal with the problem upstream.

Teachers or parents often tend to refer to the bite as behaviour "that has no particular reason." There is no one who provoked it. The other child did nothing to him. So why does he bite? Sounds like a mystery.

But no, the reason is always there and most of the time it has to do with communication.

When children are two or two and a half years old, they are normally able to express their needs and can understand their feelings. An autistic child, on the other hand, becomes frustrated by his inability to find a better way to communicate.

So, he bites because he has no language skills and therefore has no other way to express himself and understand others.

Many children on the spectrum have no connection to language. There is absolutely no connection between what they feel, thought and language. These children still don't realize that language is a way to make their lives easier, a way to communicate feelings and thoughts within the outside world. This linguistic connection must therefore be taught, and it is at that point that we could find the solution. He has to be taught that connection.

Once the connection is established, it changes almost immediately. For the child it is an incredible revelation. Like, Wow!, this language thing is great! This language thing really works! And that's where I'd begin. Teaching your child the power of language is an effective way to get them to quit negative behaviours, such as: biting.

But I don't mean to teach words, so take a picture of the house and teach him to say it 8 times out of 10, but I mean teaching how to use the language, in real situations, with real context. I want the kid to realize that language can make his life much easier. No need to have tantrums or scream or bite or drag her mother to the refrigerator. He can use language in a much more efficient way to make his life better and much easier.

It is important to spend time learning what is motivating for the autistic person: it can be an activity, a reward, an environment, a game, an object. Intrinsic motivation refers precisely to motivation coming from within a person. That is, do something because you like it.

For example, the prima ballerina tries 8 hours a day because she wants to be able to perform exceptionally. In autism, motivation can instead manifest as an inner drive to perform a task or perform an activity. Your child may love cars and be highly motivated to sit by the window watching traffic or playing with their toy cars for hours. Without motivation, the learning process can be greatly slowed down or made impossible.

For this reason, you have to strive to increase motivation, first discovering what motivates your child, and then using what they like as reinforcement to learn.

It's also important to learn what's not motivating for your child, so you avoid it. Motivation is an intensive applied behaviour analysis program can initially take the form of something extrinsic, such as being rewarded with favourite food, candy, or activities. But the goal is that then this motivation goes from extrinsic to intrinsic so that a child engages in learning for personal joy and fulfilment.

Moreover, to do this you have to gradually blur the rewards and rejoice together with the child whenever he feels happy and fulfilled for a goal achieved.

Communication

Every child with autism spectrum disorders is a unique world to discover. Be wary of those who lightly utter phrases like "Autistic children must be taken like this" or "With children with autism you have to do this" because "autistic children" do not exist, but there are Anna, Michele, Giulio who, in their own way, have some of the specific cognitive-emotional, communicative, relational and behavioural.

Some children may initially be extremely difficult to understand, but if you learn to build a good relationship of mutual trust, to look at them as "children" and not as "autistic children", to discover their strengths and potential, they can offer us enormous satisfaction.

Try first of all to understand their peculiar functioning, find out what excites them, what interests them most, learn to distinguish what they do not want to do from what they cannot do, without ever justifying them if it is not appropriate, asking them for help to better understand their neurodiverse functioning and helping them understand your neurotypical functioning.

Most of the children with ASD or SPD need help in communicating and can present with non functional language skills. They are typically delayed in language acquisition and resort to younger forms of communication, such as crying, screaming, hitting, and biting. They can be echolalic and perseverative as well.

Giving children the methods to express their needs through sign language, words, PECs (picture exchange cards), or other augmentative communication is essential to support their individual strengths and help decrease their frustration.

It can help to describe what the child is doing and thinking as a "voice over" to give him the vocabulary for what he is doing and to help him learn the meaningful words in a situation. You can also encourage children to respond using the Pivotal Response Training model.

For example, when the child is fully engaged in an activity, pause the activity so that the child will request more. Depending on the child's skill level, a gesture, an approximation, a word, or a sentence are encouraged, and the child can see that by giving a response, she will get what she wants. This shows the child that communicating works.

Games that involve pointing an index finger can also be helpful because pointing is a way of attracting shared attention.

There is a lot of use of singing and chanting used in the water games. Children who don't have the words to say what they want may sing the tune. For example, a child might start to sing the tune of a song we've made up, "Going to the Pool," to let us know she is ready to go there.

There are also many moments during the water games when a form of communication is needed in order to continue the games. For example, the child must place her hand in an open palm gesture or say the word "Please" before receiving a wanted water toy. In this section you will find variety of communication tricks that are well-suited to the super strong visual skills of kids with ASD. Good and studied systems of communication like these work to keep down their frustration level. Here we will talk about visual plans like "first this, then that" constructs or like first-person stories other than transition techniques and ways to prepare the child for coming events.

Visual schedule

My most important work with children with ASD is to create methods for communication is arguably. In the United States, a highly recommended method for communication is the visual schedule, a series of pictures or photos or icons set in a row that indicate the steps to be taken in an agenda.

The level of detail you should include depends on the context and the child's needs for support in communication. To encourage literacy and develop sight words at an early age, lots of therapists think that you should include the words that describe the image. Specialists trained in the technique teach a kid to identify pictures and to comprehend the sense of sequential lists.

When the child learns how to use a visual schedule, he understands that the images tell him what comes next on the schedule, what is expected of him, and when he will be done with a task. This work should be done in preschool so that teachers and therapists can make a visual schedule at the beginning of their lessons and it will guide the kid through the time period.

A communication tool is not really useful if communication is one-way, from the therapist to the kid.

We should give the child the possibility to help us create and change the schedule for example selecting the activities on the list when is possible . For example, let your kid choose an activity from a basket with pictures of few options. Non-verbal children are not able to ask for a treat or fun activities, so when possible, offer options to those children.

When the kid becomes able at reading, you can replace the pictures with a written list.

Children with ASD have troubles with change, they like to know what to expect and often suffer from anxiety.

Anyway, they can become very rigid and so it is important to introduce some changes on a regular basis. Consider setting a "Surprise!" card on the schedule in a different place or position every day. In this way kids get habituated to change and won't feel overwhelmed when it occurs. The surprise can be something fun or a work that has to be done.

Stories

Stories are a helpful in order to give the child information that he or she doesn't pick up on his or her own. The stories can be based on topics like: school rules, social rules, expected behaviours at somebody else's house, and other things like that. Stories must be written in first person so the kid can assimilate the information easily. The topic has to be described from the child's point of view and after from a larger perspective in order to show the kid some aspects of the situation he or she is missing. They can be simple or complicated. A set of rules is a simple story, social rules in specific contexts or someone's emotional reaction to something he or she has done is a complicated story.

The key points to remember are:
• Use words that the kid can read and understand. Consider adding some pictures to the story in order to help with comprehension.
• They work best for the kid with fair-to-good cognitive and language skills. If your kid is very young or has poor reading comprehension try picture stories or video modeling.
• Use phrases like "I will try," and avoid phrases like "I will," "I must," or "I should".
• All the aspects of the story must be positive.
• Place it in a visible location and encourage the child to read the story several times a day. Remove or replace it when the lesson is assimilated.

When concepts and explanations must be communicated, along with rules, we have to create a complex story. In this story, we insert two viewpoints, one is the child's and one is ours. The child's view should be represented in an objective rendering of the situation. Our view should include big-picture information, for example social contexts, lessons to be understood, and consequences of his choices which can be hard to understand. To help your kid enjoy the story, tack on a fun or interesting introduction. End the story with an affirmation of the child's strengths so that he or she doesn't feel ashamed . Let's see a complex story.

I like candies. Yesterday mom put a bunch of candies on the table for us. I ate all the candies in 10 minutes. I did not save any for anyone else, not even her. My little sister was upset because she did had the chance to get a candy
I need to try and leave some candies so that others can enjoy treats, too. Next time mom puts out candies, I will try to take a small amount and leave the rest of candies so that my family can have some of them. In this way I will be nice to them and they can say that i am not only smart, but I am also polite.

If the kid has a favourite topic such as Star Wars, Peppa pig, planes or stuffed animals, consider writing a series of stories using the favourite topic as a theme. These stories will have an extra appeal to the child and he may "get the message" a little faster.

Transitions

Children with ASD have executive-function impairments, especially their difficulty shifting cognitively from one thought, activity or plan to another. Asking a child with ASD to transition before he is ready can produce undesirable reactions.

The therapist, teacher or parent may need to first gain her attention in order to stop her current activity. The next activity or process is explained, and the child is given time to process the information before the new activity is initiated.

Children with autism can have difficulty with transitions or sudden changes. Some children have a hard time transitioning from one activity to another or from a familiar adult to an unfamiliar one. Predictable situations are comforting, but because changes in life are inevitable, it is important to help the children deal with them. A predictable structure brings comfort, and so does the awareness that one can handle change.

As previously stated, using a picture schedule lets children know what is coming next. And consistency in the schedule means the games always begin and end in the same fashion. You can also give ample warning about what's coming up.

For example, let them know that after the obstacle course, you're going to play the blanket game.

Or when giving free time, use a timer so the children know that when the buzzer rings, free time ends and a structured activity begins.

Often, you can reduce the children's resistance to change by making sure the children know that they will return to a preferred activity.

Let's see a number of techniques which can make transitions easier.

1. Use a visual schedule
2. use a first-then board.
2. Use a visual timer to let the kid know when time has come to move to the next activity.
3. Use countdowns
4. Count down very slowly especially if the child is playing hard: "Twenty, nine-teen, eight-teen . . . three, two, one."

How to make your kid know that the activity is over:
1. Ring a bell.
2. Flick the lights.
3. create a clean-up song and sing it every time he has to stop and clean.
4. Clap hands in a rhythmic pattern that he knows.

Use an object of transition especially with locations:

1. Ask the kids to help you carry something. A heavy object helps to calm the kids, and they will enjoy the possibility to help you.

2. The child may select his or her own object of transition for example a favourite book or gadge, like a security blanket. Once arrived in the new location, the kid must "park" the object by the doorway. When it is time to change location again, the kid should take the object with him or her.

3. If the kid is reluctant to leave a location, you could choose an object you know he or she likes and suggest that he or she bring it with her.

Enjoy moving from location to location, when it is possible try to move from a location to another with a Roller skate, or riding a tricycle, or using a scooter board, or bouncing a ball to the next location.

Prepare the children

let's look at some Examples:

1. if the class is going to the zoo: let the children look at the zoo's website. Find some videos, create your own pre-trip visit. Make a list of the animals he will see. Teach the children something about them looking for information in books and online.

2. if he or she has to see a new therapist or teacher: Put a picture of this new person on your smartphone, on the wall or the refrigerator at home. Consider asking the new teacher or therapist to make a short video welcoming the kid. Play the video daily untiled or she meets them.

3. A new weekly activity: Make a video of what he or she will have to do. Put the start-date of the activity on the calendar. Create a story that explains the "when, what, where and what for" of the activity. Augment the story with pictures, especially if the child has poor reading skills.

Chapter 8: TEACHING SKILLS IN MULTIPLE STAGES THROUGH ACTIVITY ANALYSIS

Life is full of constant multi-step processes. We don't notice why we do everything automatically, but when, for example, we wear the seat belt in the car, there are several steps to take: sit down, turn slightly, pull the belt and finally slip it into the appropriate anchor.

A series of steps we take every day without thinking about it, but when we say to an autistic person for the first time: "wear your belt", the person looks at you with stunned eyes as if to say: "but what are you asking me?". That series of steps to wear the belt are precisely the analysis of the task.

What is it?

Activity analysis *(TA)* is the process of taking a complex skill such as wearing a belt, preparing a sandwich, or doing laundry and breaking it down into smaller, manageable, and achievable steps.

Why is it useful?

If a student has difficulty completing a skill in its entirety, splitting the activity into several stages can make it clear to teachers or parents where the mistake is accurately occurring. Therefore, we can use suggestions, reinforcements, and/or templates to help fill gaps. Autistic students in particular find it difficult with executive functions that regulate the ability to plan and organize thoughts, remember information, and start a business. The list of steps to take can be a quick and effective reference for learning new skills through repetition and muscle memory.

When should I use activity analysis?

Activity analysis should be used to chain a sequence of smaller steps in an attempt to perform a larger action. Many functional, self-help or professional skills fit this description. For example, these I list here are all actions that include smaller steps to complete the larger action.

- Wash the dishes
- Vacuum the vacuum cleaners
- Setting up the table
- Using your cell phone

- Cooking a meal
- Fasten your shoes
- Using the bathroom
- Doing homework

But is it just for life skills? Absolutely not! Task analysis can also be extremely helpful in breaking down the academic and social skills that have passages within it such as splitting, multi-digit multiplication, or turns during a board game. Activity Analysis can also be a great way to introduce simple game scripts for anyone learning how to properly use in-game materials. For example:

- Feeding a doll
- Playing dressing up
- Building a train track

- Playing at the restaurant
- Making sand castles
- Construction game

How to implement it?

1. Choose a specific skill

To identify the skill you'll teach, start by identifying the student's needs and the goals of their work team or family. Depending on your age or level of development, you can understand what your teaching priority is, for example: cleaning when you go to the bathroom.

2. Evaluate the student's skill level and the necessary materials or media

Start by collecting basic data on the student's ability to complete the identified skill. If you have decided to teach him how to cook, for example, consider starting by understanding if the child knows where the kitchen is, where the pots are, how the fire is lit

Similarly, if an individual's need to learn a skill is high and can perform every step, but lacks motivation, you may need to consider how to provide ample reinforcement when analyzing the activity.

3. Break down the ability

As described earlier when talking about wearing a seatbelt in the car, breaking down a skill into smaller steps can be harder than you would expect. The best way to segment information is to actually complete these steps, observe someone else doing it, and analyze the process as it occurs.

EXAMPLE OF TASK ANALYSIS:

- Brushing your teeth
- Have the necessary material
- Removes toothpaste cap
- Put the toothpaste on the toothbrush
- Closes toothpaste cap
- Wet your toothbrush (I know, it's questionable whether or not to wet your toothbrush!)
- Brush surfaces to the left at the bottom
- Brush surfaces right at the bottom
- Brush surfaces right at the top
- Brush on the left bottom surface
- Low front surface brush
- Brush the front surfaces high
- Rinse your toothbrush
- Rinse your mouth
- Dry your mouth

- Put the toothbrush in place

Of course, when writing a task analysis, there is room for flexibility. There are those who wet their toothbrush before putting toothpaste, for example. There are those who put salt in pasta water before pouring pasta so you could write your version slightly differently: this is where customization comes into play.

4. Determine the completeness of the activity analysis

The best way to make sure you've developed a comprehensive task analysis is for someone else to perform the steps exactly as you wrote them. Then you will see if something has been left out and you can review the steps as needed.

5. Develop a teaching plan

Depending on the complexity of the student's skill and basic data, the teacher should determine the best way to teach it: can the student manage the analysis of activities in its entirety, should some of the steps be taught in stages or use anterograde or retrograde chaining?

For students who are very gratified by the final product (example: cooking), start with the last steps (retrograde chaining) and end with the positive experience of how to get there.

The way Activity Analysis is presented should take into account the student's style and learning skills. Some may need images of each step, others may have the passages written, and still others may benefit from a video demonstration of the activity before completing it. Steps should be simple but comprehensive and efficient in communicating the process to the student.

6. Implement and monitor progress

When collecting data for task analysis, it is necessary to assiduously check the progress of competence to identify steps that could be difficult for the student. Isolating these difficulties allows the teacher to practice with the child in any step independently (if possible or applicable). In addition, the checklist should include a section outlining a student's level of application to complete the skill. Since the goal is always for students to be as independent as possible, this will also help guide future education.

Therefore, whether it's wearing a seat belt, fastening your shoes, cooking a dough or making a sandwich, remember that life is full of many steps that make up a broader action. Finding a way to effectively break down these steps and teach gaps can help students gain valuable skills, a higher quality of life, and self-confidence.

Chapter 9: 10 Strategies to Encourage Language in Autistic Children

1. **Minimize direct questions.** Often and with the best intentions, parents believe they stimulate language acquisition in their children by asking them a lot of questions. Try to avoid these questions as much as possible. When one of you talks to your child, try listening and remember to reduce direct questions.

2. **Comment on the actions.** Let yourself be guided by the child, observe what he does and comment on the progress of the actions, acting as a model of what could be his internal dialogue. Questions and orders generally do not facilitate language development, while these comments can help you more easily

3. **Stimulate communication.** Parents can encourage spontaneous language by paying attention to what is happening and trying to stimulate communication. To this end, it is preferable not to anticipate every need of your child, but to wait for him to ask for what he needs

4. **Use facial gestures and expressions abundantly.** To support language acquisition it is essential to use exaggerated facial expressions and emphatic gestures. Adult movement and gestures can foster recourse to speech. Don't be rigid. Resort to acting. Capture the child's attention and present the meaning of some words that may not be clear to him with a visual illustration of what you mean.

5. **Use eye contact.** Ocular contact. Looking at the person you talk to is a fundamental aspect of communication. Look the baby in the eye and encourage him to do the same. "Look at me" is the easiest indication to make.

6. **Be a model** that means, provide the child with an example of what he should say. It is preferable to focus on presenting appropriate expressions and phrases, rather than correcting errors. Feeling constantly corrected is depressing for anyone. Modeling is a positive way of acting, while continuous corrections give the impression that you are more interested in how your child is communicating more than what it means - absolutely to avoid.

7. **Simplify.** When you are a model or commenting on a child's activity, or are talking to him, shorten your sentences, that is, reduce the complexity of your language. For example, if your child does not yet use words, speak to him as much as possible with sentences composed of single words, while if he is almost at the level of two-word sentences, reduce the length of your sentences by two words as much as possible.

8. **Exaggerate intonation**, volume, and tone of voice. It is essential to capture the attention of children who have spontaneous communication problems. Pitch, volume, and tone of voice, if varied, can help with this. It is no coincidence that children's songs and nursery rhymes are an excellent tool to stimulate early linguistic development: they are in fact repetitive and rhythmic. Try singing a little song and let the baby complete a verse.

9. **Strengthened.** To increase spontaneous language, it is critical that you respond and strengthen your child's spontaneous productions. Don't ignore his attempts to communicate, whether verbal or nonverbal. Respond, with words or not, but respond, thus reinforcing his effort to speak and teaching them that there is an advantage to speaking.

10.   **Make this fun!** Try to have fun, talk in a pleasant tone of voice, smile, help your child associate communication with warmth, affection and joy, try to stay relaxed. Why should the child want to communicate, if it's not a fun thing?. Be playful, imaginative and creative.

Communication with your No-verbal kid

These children struggle to refer to others to communicate, indeed they do not feel the need for it and do not understand the reason for this type of contact with other people. So for these children there is a double difficulty: not only must more effective communication methods be learned, but above all, the basic idea of communication has not yet been reached (Volkmar, 2004); because knowing how to communicate is more than being able to speak or put words correctly, it is the ability to let someone know that you want something, to tell a fact, to describe one action and to recognize the presence of the other. All this can be verbally or nonverbally, through gestures, through the use of signs or by indicating an image or a written word.

In order to foster real progress in communication, the very function of communication should be considered more important than form or structure. Too often autistics are led to the correct production of certain sounds, words, signs, even a "complete phrase" without them having any idea of intentionality (Volkamr, 2004). Therefore, any intervention should promote the communicative initiative in these children, facilitating the assumption of the role of issuer as well as that of receiver.

There are many important aspects that nonverbal children should acquire to be better communicators, and in particular:

Understand the cause and effect

Understanding cause-and-effect relationships is related to whether or not the child recognizes that their behavior can have a clear effect on others and their surroundings. In communication, if the child does not understand this type of relationship, he will have difficulty asking for help to reach an object or to communicate his needs. Without this type of reasoning, the child cannot request certain behaviors or objects from others, which instead constitutes one of the first communicative acts of typical development. It is therefore important to have activities for these children that provide for each cause to have its effect, so that a minimum communication exchange is formed.

Want to communicate

Often children who do not use verbal language, manifest little willingness to communicate with another person, since one of their main difficulties is the inability to relate to others in a conventional way. They often do not notice their presence or show particular interest in them. One of the reasons this occurs relates to the poor understanding of cause-and-effect links described above. If the child does not understand that someone else can help him, or if he does not understand that his actions can produce the effect of achieving something, he will not feel a strong need to relate to others. Parents often anticipate and respond too quickly to the needs of these children; they give the child everything they need, without waiting for him to communicate with them.

Communication exchanges should be scheduled in which to require the child to interact with others.

Someone to communicate with

Often adults dealing with nonverbal autistic children take on the role of initiators of communicative exchange while the child is left with the task of responding. When the child's needs are met even before he can communicate with them, the child is deprived of his communicative partner. After some such exchanges the child expects to be guided towards the behavior that leads him to get what he wants, without striving to take the initiative of the request.

Something to communicate about

If the autistic child does not have something to communicate about, he will not communicate.

The recommendation is to let the child establish the object of communication; the child should take the lead and direct the communicative interaction. So it would be better to start from objects or actions that the child likes, in order to have something interesting as an object of communication that stimulates him to communicate. Once communication has been started, the operator can work on extending the vocabulary.

A means of communication

For the child who has not acquired verbal language use, learning to speak may not be the best or preferred way to communicate. Extensive research has shown that although children with autism have strong difficulties learning to speak, they are able to communicate more easily when using alternative systems, such as gestures, sign language, image and pictogram exchange, written word communication schemes, and computer aids. It is important for the operator to start from what the child knows how to do and make sense of those gestures, postures and signs, in order to then expand communication skills with other alternative systems, which use multiple variables. We know that these types of children have considerable difficulties in managing variables and communication has many and must be introduced to the child very gradually. Studies have shown spontaneous increases in the use of speech or vocalizations that are typically observed in about a third or half of those individuals who do not speak and who learn to express themselves through the use of other modalities. Therefore, the use of non-verbal communication or alternative communications does not inhibit verbal language, on the contrary it favors it.

The use of signs as a communication system has many strengths but also some weaknesses.

One of the main strengths is that in the early stages of communication the signs can be devised by the therapist and coupled with the appropriate reinforcement. The first exchanges can be difficult because the child needs to learn the relationship of the sign with an object or action, but this is a first step to starting a first communication. Signs can be used in any context and at any time, can express the baby's need fast enough, and can be easily sequenced to get a sentence. Signs are often conceived in such a way as to resemble the object or action associated with them, in such a way as to facilitate the autistic child, who is very attached to material reality and the world of the concrete.

The limit of this communication system is in its effectiveness: to be an excellent partner in sign language you have to be good at understanding them and you have to be practical about them; moreover, to communicate the child must recover from his memory the appropriate sign for the context in which he finds himself. Therefore, the child must not have neuropsychological problems associated.

Another means of communication is through objects. Children with autism often use objects spontaneously to communicate, but instead of giving the object to another person, they put it close to the desired thing.

A step forward will be when the child begins to touch the desired object directly. The subsequent evolution, but very difficult to see in autistics, is made when the child begins to move the gaze between the desired object and the person close, especially if the gaze is accompanied by a movement of the hand towards his goal and / or change in the orientation of the body.

So it is important for the child to learn to give the object to a person, because this helps them understand that people can be the means to achieve a desired end.

Yet another means of communication can be images and pictograms and this type of strategy is called PECS (Picture Exchange Communication System). This system offers functional and immediate communication. Initially the operator observes and decides which elements or objects are best to facilitate communication in the environment surrounding the child. Subsequently, the child is taught to associate an image with the appropriate element. The child is required to take an image and place it tone of the parents or a therapist, who exchanges it for the object he gives to the child; the figures must be placed on a panel on which Velcro is attached, from which the child must detach the image before giving it to the operator.

For all this it is necessary that there is a good cognitive development of the child, which supports him in the realization of this request; in fact, the child must associate the meaning of the image with the right figure and know that this will bring a change in the behavior of others.

There are two variables (meaning and meaning) that children with severe autism fail to manage and that leads them to use easier and more tangible means, such as gestures or objects. In addition, the use of an image has as a prerequisite a certain level of mental representation, which is one of the deficits of autistic disorder. This communication system has insufficient expressive power with less tangible communication functions, such as emotional expression. Instead, it achieves good results if this system is used to refer to the sphere of the concrete, as objects and actions.

A good cognitive level, but also good motor skills, is necessary for the IT media, but the positive side of these means is that they arouse a lot of motivation in children and therefore favor the initiative of their use in communication.

Above were explained the most used systems to allow an autistic child to better integrate into an interactive situation and the choice of a certain system does not necessarily exclude the introduction of a later, indeed for many children more systems are used for more effective communication depending on the context. It is important that the selected system is suitable for the communication profile for the individual in question.

You should adapt to what the child proposes, to have a motivating and interesting starting point for it, so that he can solicit attention and joint action. In addition, the most effective interactions are those in which the child is close to his communication partner, so the therapist must gradually reduce proxemics towards him. It is also important to seek eye contact in order to share an experience. It is advisable to enter their space with kindness, observe their behavior for a moment in silence and, at that point, transmit a message. How to convey a message?

The verbal and nonverbal components of communication need to be emphasized to increase the likelihood of the child extracting the meaning of the message. Enthined intonations, facial expressions, and gestures make the message clearer. The pace must be slowed down so that nonverbal suggestions are fixed in space and time, as if it were a slow motion movie. In addition, if you want to accompany nonverbal communication with words, you have to send clear, simple messages and speak very calmly. Breaks proved useful after sending a message. The break gives the child time to integrate information and respond, that is, to organize and find an answer.

To facilitate the input of the message it is necessary to structure space and time, as already mentioned, to make the actions and words of that context predictable and clear.

It is necessary to structure the environment in such a way that it is characterized by high predictability and in it modify the routine that has been established over time; modifying objects, events, not respecting shifts in a game or pretending to forget to share objects, violation of the function of objects, hiding them or making them inaccessible. Researchers have found that children communicate more frequently during unexpected or destabilizing events than during simple play. In addition, the unexpected event of holding back and not sharing objects increases attempts at communication. It is also effective to put the child waiting during an interaction, to see if this behavior arouses something in him.

In summary, in the predictability of the environment, unexpected or suspenseful events favor communication.

Promoting Communication in Echoic Autistic Children

Echolalia should be considered as a dynamic and integral component of the child's communicative functioning rather than an isolated and dysfunctional behavior, or at least not always. To assess whether it is interactive or non-interactive echolalia, it is necessary to take into account the previous situations and conditions that may have caused the echolalia and whether nonverbal behavior has been associated with it. In short, it is necessary to evaluate whether the echolalia is contextualized or it is only the repetition of a unit of language. Such considerations suggest that for many children with autism echolalia is a verbal strategy to support and compensate, which can be used for a variety of social and cognitive purposes and which plays a significant role in the child's transition from automatic to more generative forms of language production.

For these children it is important to make a careful evaluation of all the sentences produced and contextual variables and this will allow to make various hypotheses about the nature of the child's communication system; at this stage the detailed stories of parents about the child's activities and his verbal production in different contexts are also important.

Research have suggested that echolalia is more likely to occur in some specific environmental and interaction conditions often as a compensatory medium of communication. It has been noted that the incidence of echolalia is highest when children are required to participate in unfamiliar and challenging activities, during unstructured periods of time, during highly managerial interactions. Difficulties in language comprehension and social situations are associated with a higher production of echolalia.

It is not easy for the operator to evaluate the communicative intention of schoolboys, because repetition could be done in a specific context and can be interpreted as a request.

In other cases communicative behavior can be seen by the interlocutor as having a communicative function without the child having the intention of either transmitting any particular message or interacting verbally with a person.

In addition, a child's echolalia could be a non-interactive labeling behavior that the child was "practicing."

The communicative intent underlying echolalia does not seem to be an all-or-nothing formulation, but rather seems to be part of a progression ranging from the absence of intention (reflective, automatic, devoid of purpose awareness) to clear intentionality, in which communicative behaviors are coordinated and directed to others in an attempt to achieve a purpose.

Later stages of the evolution of echolalia supported by therapeutic treatment:

- Initially the child produces sentences without awareness and are usually accompanied by non-finalized activities, in which they do not pay attention to the presence or absence of an interlocutor.
- Subsequently he will use an echolalia learned elsewhere in a more generalized way, understanding that his verbal production will allow a behavioral change in his interlocutor. At this stage the child then begins to be aware of the purpose he wants to achieve and to use the communication methods he knows to achieve him.
- Subsequently, the autistic child will be able to formulate a simple coordinated plan to achieve a purpose: he uses objects of intermediation or the composition of motor and / or vocal behaviors and directs actions towards another person, as shown by body orientation, gaze or waiting for a response.
- The next step is that the child uses an alternative strategy that is directed towards another person following at least one failed attempt to achieve a purpose.
- Finally, the highest step is reflection on the means, success or failure of a plan to achieve a goal; often little seen in autistic children, because it provides for a high cognitive and communicative level.

Intervention strategies can be direct or indirect

Indirectly, the space can be structured in such a way as to decrease the level of confusion or disorganization on the part of the child, which causes non-directive school production.

These children should speak slowly, with simple and short sentences and possibly talk about concrete events, perhaps concerning the activity in progress, because school sentences are produced more when the child does not understand the adult's sentences; it sometimes happens that the level of understanding of the child is overestimated by the communicative partner. And it is also very important not to have a managerial style of communication, that is, not to overinvest the child with verbal requests, but rather to allow him to control the center and direction of the verbal exchange most of the time.

The adult should allow periods of silence and listening before the start of another sentence and the majority of sentences should be unbinding (e.g. reflective questions, requests to report, positive or confirmation answers and comments). This communication style, compared to the managerial one, decreases the frequency of those productions.

As for direct strategies, you should try to promote school sentences especially if they are used for communicative purposes, through the emphasizing of the child's school sentence and environmental references, demonstrating through verbal expressions that the school communicative act has been understood and responding contingently to the child's intention.

Offer the child systematic modifications that serve to reduce, replace or expand the parts that make up the repeated sentence, in order to promote progress in language processing and creativity. A development from this point of view is detectable through mitigated echolalia, that is, it is a beginning of linguistic elaboration that involves the modification, through omissions or additions, of pure echolalia.

For those children who show resistance in this type of treatment and their language productions remain strongly unconventional, with little evidence of communicative intent, nonverbal Alternative Augmented Communication strategies can be useful as an alternative means of efficient and conventional communication, reducing, on the one hand, school models and replacing, on the other, difficult verbal behaviors. Finally, those strategies can be useful for verbal language acquisition by helping young children transition nonverbal to verbal (even if echoic) systems, or by assisting some children in the transition from the stage of non-interactive language to that of generative language.

Promoting Communication in Verbal Autistic Children

Children with autism with higher skills possess a basic language system and need specific pragmatic intervention, should improve the effectiveness of communication in all its aspects. With these children we must assume that the form and linguistic content (syntax and semantics) must be directly linked to the pragmatic function (requests, proposals, etc.) and the social context.

Also in these cases it is necessary to take into account the unique profile of the child which is fundamental for the success of any intervention plan aimed at enhancing the effectiveness of language for communication purposes. The language profile, unique to each child, depends on the link between linguistic and social knowledge, which is reflected in the child's use to interact with other people. The area of pragmatics, long recognized as a deficit in autism, is therefore under discussion.

Assuming the perspective of the other is the aspect of pragmatics that concerns children's ability to understand that others have views that may differ from their own. There are three main areas of perspective assumption: the perceptual area, which concerns the child's ability to understand that others can perceive things differently. The cognitive one, which concerns the child's ability to understand that others may have different ideas and intentions from his or her own; and the linguistic area, concerning the child's ability to adapt the form, content, and communicative purpose of the sentence to meet the needs of the situation and/or interlocutor. The notion of taking perspective is critical to the ability to understand the relationship between external conditions and inner mental states; many authors have speculated that a deficit at that level would have a profoundly negative impact on the child's ability to give meaning to the social world.

A common mistake made by those seeking to improve the communication of these children, is to focus on the lexical elements, form and structure of language separately from problems in social cognition. Consequently, if the child's communication competence is to be improved, intervention strategies must be aimed at strengthening the child's social knowledge.

In addition, these children, in addition to real this difficulty towards abstract social information, show the phenomenon of hyper selectiveness of the stimulus, which leads the child to focus his attention around a specific aspect of a larger structure; and this cognitive process is also transferred to the linguistic area, leading the child to have a lack of flexibility in expressive language.

You should evaluate in verbal children, as has already been said for non-verbal children, the communicative intention and, then, also the syntax, that is, the ability of the child to identify the structural dimensions of language and to apply the rules of word combination, in order to convey a meaning; semantics must be evaluated, that is, the personal dictionary of the In addition, the therapist must evaluate the understanding of the lexicon and the ability to process specific verbal information in the presence or absence of suggestions

He must also evaluate whether communication is a dynamic event that takes place in a given context, which by its nature transforms the message into something qualitatively different from the mere sum of its static parts. Finally, the non-verbal aspects (proxemics, gestures, mimicry and postures), the alternation of shifts and the assumption of the point of view must be evaluated.

Treatment for these children, as well as nonverbal and school children, involves the use of tangible environmental supports, which offer an ideal framework with respect to their needs, because they can help stabilize an ephemeral social world; they can increase the salience of socially derived information so as to make it more relevant. They can help children derive more information from their environment; they can help children conform their behaviors to more conventional standards and their use is consistent with their cognitive style. To allow the child to monitor the events and activities of the day, non-linguistic supports can be introduced, such as a pattern of the day, made up of visual symbols, so that it helps the child develop an understanding of time intervals and get an idea of the succession of environmental sequences. Symbols indicating change can be introduced during the daily time, to allow the child with autism to understand that something unexpected will take the place of some activity that is usually part of the pattern of his day.

In addition, the outline of the day offers an ideal frame of reference, to be able to discuss past, present and future events and simulate questions and conversations related to the activities of the day. In the construction of these supports it is important to take into account the visual preferences of the child, in order to motivate them and make them more active in the interaction. For example, for a child who has not understood the concept of alternating shifts, you can use a colored object or of interest to him, which signals the turn of the two interlocutors, putting it in front of the person who deserves the shift.

Non-linguistic supports must be combined with linguistic supports by the therapist, so that information on social and emotional reality is highlighted so that it can become more meaningful for the child.

Too often there is too much attention to pushing children with autism to respond to situations appropriately, without the slightest regard for them having any understanding of the situation or event they need to respond to. In itself it is difficult to generate suitable answers without the slightest understanding of the situation and it is even more difficult for autistic children. As a result, it is important to increase the child's understanding of environmental and behavioral information, in order to promote a "bond of meaning" between observed behavior and appropriate responses to it.

Ways to report the environment can be: highlighting social information (e.g. "Look Thomas is greeting you, will you greet him too?"), emphasizing emotional information (e.g. "Mary got hurt. Look, she's crying. You can tell Maria that you're sorry"), highlight anticipatory information (e.g. "Watch Luca is about to throw the ball"), structure comment information (e.g. "Watch Bob is playing with the toy car"), encode feelings and reactions (e.g. "Luca is very angry because Maria took the ball"), and ultimately encourage taking the point of view.

The use of linguistic and non-linguistic supports therefore allow the child to adapt their verbal and non-verbal behavior to the demands of the environment and, in addition, help the child with autism reduce anxiety in unfamiliar situations.

Children with autism, who have high lexical skills, however, have difficulties in pragmatics: they tend to use communication functions for instrumental rather than social purposes, that is, related to the satisfaction of needs rather than social interaction; moreover, they cannot adapt their language according to the context in which they find themselves.

Situations can be designed for these children and opportunities can be created to expand their use of language with various people in various contexts. The idea is to move from a similar family situation to another through an unfamiliar situation. For example, if a child usually makes requests that have food as their object, while they tend to wait when it comes to other objects, it would be appropriate to extend the requests to a variety of objects in multiple contexts and with different people, before paying attention to more "social" requests such as those for assistance, information and attention.

Once the child has mastered this type of requests more related to the material aspect, other skills can be developed in him, which allow him to have greater control over his life, such as asking for help in difficult situations. The development of pragmatics in these children is important to restore the balance between the individual and the environment, and consequently this contributes to increasing the child's sense of well-being.

These children are also called passive interlocutors, that is, they tend to respond to requests, without ever taking the initiative of starting a communication; the therapist to promote this type of communication can restructure the space, violating routines or posing obstacles., so that the child is in a position to start an interaction, asking for help, in order to carry out a task.

For these children who have a good lexical and syntactic basis, but fall into pragmatic abilities, it is useful to design with them skits of daily life through play, so that the child is provided with functional communicative patterns for social interaction. You can structure games with the characters in the little house or make scenes that take place in the kitchen, in order to recreate a familiar setting situation, in which the child can exercise his pragmatic functions. Once the child has acquired these skills within this environment, their new communication knowledge can be expanded to less familiar situations. This is possible if the child has a high capacity for mental representation and generalization of concepts.

Another activity that can be done with these children is reading a book. This type of activity allows the child to acquire new vocabulary, but above all to listen to and acquire communication exchanges, which the child can take as an example for a future play or daily activity. In addition, the therapist can dramatize these stories through the use of puppets or dolls. This approach has many advantages.

- First, three-dimensional visual supports are more concrete (and probably more interesting) than the one-dimensional images of a book.
- Second, telling a story in this way allows the adult to slow down the pace, use repetitions, and simplify language input to meet the individual needs of these children.

- Third, this allows the child to identify with the characters and develop the ability to change point of view.

Since communication cannot exist in isolation, but is rather included in the context of interpersonal events and relationships that help define and shape it, the success of communicative and linguistic efforts is directly linked to variables that exist outside the child's domain of experience and control. When there is a failure in this process, this should be interpreted with a phenomenon involving two people and requiring a solution involving both. This type of orientation encourages adult interlocutors to examine factors that may have contributed to failure on their part, for example, saying sentences that are too long, or waiting for an insufficient amount of time to adapt to the child's processing skills.

It also directs attention to other factors that do not come directly from the child, such as excessive stimulation by the environment.

The advantage of this type of orientation is that it is a multidimensional approach focused on a variety of possible factors, in contrast to unilateral attention focused solely on the child. This overall perspective promotes a mental attitude on the part of adults, which encourages them to modify and/or adjust their teaching strategies and interaction style according to the needs of children with autism, thereby increasing the chances of success in their use of language for interactions.

Chapter 10: ERROR-FREE LEARNING

Error-free learning is an educational strategy that allows children to exercise skills with confidence. Ensures that students always respond correctly, building their trust and increasing their knowledge at the same time. When error-free choice is provided on spreadsheets or hands-on activities, it reduces the need to solicit a student verbally and thus reduces the chance of a student relying on your suggestions!

Error-free learning is an antecedent Applied Behaviour Analysis intervention. An antecedent intervention is something you do before the student completes the assignment or shows the behaviour you expect. This method of teaching skills minimizes opportunities for error. It also increases the frequency with which the child encounters reinforcement. Minimizing mistakes also reduces the likelihood of the child engaging in challenging behaviours.

Teachers use suggestions to help the student respond correctly. The teacher then systematically fades suggestions to promote an independent response.

When a teacher first introduces a new skill acquisition goal, they use the fewest suggestions. For example, if you decide to error-freely teach your child to clap their hands when they say "clap your hands," you start immediately using a full physical tip. This allows the student to clap their hands successfully due to that complete physical solicitation.

Students are often easily frustrated when learning a new skill. They may also stumble when you practice with an old man he hasn't mastered yet. Error-free learning takes away that frustration. It can also build student trust. Repetition in error-free learning activities has been shown to increase student success even when the error-free prompt (help) is faded later.

Like with any other skill, we want to decrease support over time. When we fade suggestions, we increase student independence. We always aim for 100% independence with any skill! Error-free prompts should be systematically removed until a student is able to respond correctly on their own.

Error-free learning not only reduces frustration, but can also create motivation. We are all motivated when we do something right. Increasing this motivation and enjoying a task can really be helpful for students' learning and reducing behaviours.

Almost all students can benefit from using this strategy.

• Students who easily feel frustrated with new assignments
• Those who do not retain information for a longer period of time
• Students who require high levels of suggestions to succeed would all benefit from this teaching strategy

Basic skill learning is a great starting point for error-free learning! There are many basic skills we want our students to learn. When we work on these, we can provide students with the best opportunities for success. Students get exposure to the materials and content they need for the rest of their lives.

I suggest you talk about this method with teachers or tutors if you think that your kid would learn better with it but also to practice it at home. It can be very useful also in order to teach your kid something without the risk of making home a place of frustration and discomfort for him.

What to do when a crisis occurs

At first glance the sudden crises of some autistic people appear unpredictable and explosive, which often leads parents to understandably avoid comparisons or make requests that could aggravate the mood of the bambino. The good news is that we own a lot of research to support the usage of strategies based on the principles of A.B.A. to help solve the mystery surrounding a kid's behaviour and to develop treatment plans that can successfully reduce these difficult behaviours.

There are *3 key concepts*:

• <u>Behaviours are learned.</u> This is not to say that a parent has decided to teach their child to beat others, for example, but rather the child has learned that beating "works" to satisfy a desire or need. Classic example: A child is screaming in front of the supermarket checkout because he wants candy. His mother can initially say no, but when the child keeps screaming and ends up throwing himself on the ground, the parent will finally give him candy. This choice makes sense right now because it interrupts behaviour, the child is now happy and no longer has whims in public. But this could cause problems in the future because the baby has learn that screaming becomes candy. The good news is that if a kid has learned to beat others, whine, or whims, they can also learn to behave in a new and more appropriate way.

• <u>Behaviours are forms of communication.</u> Autistic children often have difficulty communicating: they may have a hard time telling you what annoys them or they may not have a good way to ask for something they want. Even children who are verbal enough may have difficulty "using words" when they get frustrated or angry. Autistic children, whose communication skills are limited, can learn that their behaviours communicate their desires very effectively. So when your child engages in problem behaviour, an important question to ask is, "What is that my child is trying to communicate through this behaviour?" A whim might say, "This is too difficult." Screaming could mean, "Leave me alone." Hitting might communicate, "This is mine. Return it." .

• <u>Behaviours perform a function</u>. A child can take action to escape or avoid a situation or request. For example, a child who has realized that he is entering the gym to play sports, could beat another student in class to "escape" the terrible noise he hears in the gym. A child can also engage in problematic behaviour to attract attention. For example, a kid might bang his head because he has learned that this will quickly attract his father's attention when he speaks on the phone. A child can learn that his behaviour gets him what he wants. For example, a child can scream loudly when his mother turns off the TV because he learned that screaming the mother turns TV back on so as not to hear him screaming while his little sister sleeps. Finally, some children engage in some behaviours because they are pleasurable to the child or are "automatically" rewarding. For example, a child can drum their hands because they find it pleasant to do when excited. We often consider these behaviours as motivated by factors such as sensory input, reduced internal anxiety, or perhaps simply pleasing the child.

When it comes to managing challenging behaviours, the starting point will always be to try to understand the purpose or "function" of your child's behaviour.
For example, a child in the classroom starts screaming while deciding to do a job with the class (crop and draw) the teacher decides to take the child out of class, to the library for example, because he annoys his classmates. This child creates a disorder because he is trying to escape work in class.
Although the teacher's consequence is logical, it will not be effective in reducing behaviour in the future because the child managed to escape work in class and succeeded by screaming. Take the same behaviour and response as the teacher, but this time the function of the child's behaviours is to attract the attention of his classmates. In this case, the teacher's solution to remove it from the classroom could help decrease disruptive behaviour because it targets the correct function of the child's problem behaviour: seeking attention. This is why it's so important not to focus only on behaviour when thinking about how to handle the problem behaviour.
It is more useful to aim for the function of behaviour!
Now that we know that behaviours always have a function, all that remains is to work to understand what function it is and with what strategy to manage the child's behaviours. You therefore need to create a serious work plan based on data collection, always keeping in mind that any new strategy may take some time to work as your child or student is learning new behaviour! Your child will learn to accept rules when they see you respond the same way each time.

5 STEPS TO TACKLING AGGRESSION IN AUTISTIC KID

You feel overwhelmed by your child's aggression but traditional parenting strategies don't work.
You know that your child's aggression is not his fault, but you also care about the safety of other children or those with whom your child takes it.
Not to mention the relentless concern of all of us parents with disabled children: what will our autistic child's future look like if he can't control aggression.
Now I explain, with the utmost simplicity, some fundamental steps to put into practice to manage your child's aggression. also securing the people around them, respecting everyone and ensuring that your child's needs are met.

STEP ONE: REMOVE YOUR NEGATIVE ASSUMPTIONS

Before you can really manage your child's aggression, you need to test your assumptions.
To recognize and correct your assumptions, first start by listing any thoughts you might have about your child's aggression.
"He's just violent, He just wants to hurt the people around him, He wants to terrorize his brothers, he's offensive."
Leave on paper all the thoughts you wouldn't dare say out loud. Now take every thought and remove the judgment.

Words like violent and offensive are totally full of our ideas. Making assumptions about our child's motivations, what he wants, or why he's aggressive simply remains an absolutely aside assumption before we can handle aggression.

STEP TWO: MANAGE AGGRESSION WHEN IT HAPPENS

Ultimately, we want to stop aggression before it happens, of course, but until then we need a plan for how to handle aggression when it happens.

To do this, think specifically about what your autistic child's "aggression" looks like.

- Does he hit?
- Does he start the fight?
- Does he scratch?
- Does he push?
- Does he Pull your hair?
- Does be Spit?

You need to be as specific as possible because the plan for a child who scratches may be completely different from the plan for a child who spits.

Now that you're clear what he does, in particular, you'll ask yourself: How can I protect them and others when the problem happens?

Do I block my son on the ground with an act of restraint? I don't know if he would be safe with such an action. Don't do anything while kicking me until it hurts me? This is also not sure.

The three best ways to protect people during the assault are:
- Separate by removing other people from the aggressive child
- Push back by adding a physical barrier around the other person
- Redirect by directing aggression to an object rather than a person

THIRD STEP: FIND THE REAL CAUSE OF AGGRESSION

Now that you have a plan on how to protect everyone during aggression, you can start to find out why aggression happens.

Because remember, aggression never happens without a reason.

In addition, before I delve deeper into how to find that reason, I want to clarify one thing. Just because aggression has a reason doesn't mean aggression is justified. Recognizing the reason for aggression does not mean you accept it.

That said, how do you find out the reason for aggression if your child can't tell you? You have to look at and make written patterns.

Start paying attention to when your child tends to be aggressive and take the assumption that they "get out of nowhere" out of your mind.

Look for patterns like the time of day, sensory environment, where he was, the people involved, or even the day of the week.

When you make these patterns, you start getting clues about what's actually causing aggression.

If we remember that aggressive, behaviour is communicating something we can look at the patterns we are compiling with a new lens.

So look at the notes you took and ask yourself: how about this? Could it trigger the aggression of my autistic child?

STEP FOUR: SOLVING THE REAL PROBLEM (REMEMBER: IT'S NOT AGGRESSION)

Now you can solve the real problem! We might think the problem is aggression, but in reality it's just the consequence of whatever's triggering it.

So this step is about creating a trigger plan you identified and then solving the real problem, allowing us to avoid aggression.

This plan will vary depending on what is causing your child's aggression. In general, you'll want a plan that avoids, welcomes, or manages your child's triggers. A plan that avoids a trigger could include avoiding certain situations that lead to aggression.

A plan to adapt could include adding a tool or strategy that helps your child overcome situations that lead to aggression.

Moreover, a plan to manage triggering could include changing your approach to a situation that typically leads to aggression.

STEP FIVE: REASSESS AS YOU PROCEED

You now have a plan on how you will handle aggression when it happens and a plan to solve the real problem and avoid aggression altogether.

But we're not done yet. You see, there are many things that can get in the way of our perfect plan. We may not be right about the real cause. Our plan to solve the problem could make the problem worse. We may find that our plan is not practical. Our son may not like the plan we put in place. All of this means you'll need to revaluate this process as you progress.

But you don't have to be discouraged!!. Every time you create and try a "not really right" plan to avoid aggressive behaviour, you get one step closer to discovering the perfect plan for your autistic child.

It can take some time to do it exactly the right way and you may feel frustrated or discouraged along the way.

But in the end you will succeed and the satisfaction will be really immense.

Chapter 11: A space and a time for a new alliance with the Autistic Child

In normal development, the age of two is a critical period for the social regulatory function exercised by parents. The child begins to move; his ability to touch objects, understand them and find them interesting dramatically increase; however, the ability to understand dangers or needs beyond the immediate moment does not increase as quickly. His emotions are now organized into precise desires and wills.

For the majority of parents this is a period of fatigue, since right now personal and educational limits prevent the socialization function from being carried out adequately, paving the way for future disorders or difficulties of the child in the relationship with others. However, we are talking about normal difficulties, with "normal" children, so parents, to exercise this function, can always count on the baggage of inter subjectivity.

By having this social heritage shared with the child at their disposal, they can in fact try to teach him appropriate social behaviors and to put limits on excessive or dangerous behavior. All this is possible thanks to the fact that it is absolutely natural for the child to refer to the parent as a source of vital and interesting experiences; he understands what the parent refers to in encouraging or limiting, why both have a common feeling about what is good and what is not. In this relationship, therefore, a lot of energy, patience, good humor, expressiveness and firmness are needed, but always and in any case it must develop on the basis of skills already present in the child.

Even the child with social difficulties develops, often with extreme energy and competence, the journey, the race and he too develops desires and rejections. But in this relationship there is no possibility of mediation built on socially shared meanings and lacks the possibility of using behavioral tools, such as punishment, and it is not possible to motivate the child by rewarding him. Parents can't always understand what the child wants or doesn't want, because he doesn't always know how to show or indicate: after all, he doesn't even know what needs to do it. Parents are therefore unable to share with him a single emotion, a feeling: look for the mother only if she is hungry or if she wants to swing or jump; some social skills and contact actions, in fact, are activated only if linked to her desire or interest. Parents can only continue to try to gain a mutual relationship, even if with obvious failures.

To meet the needs of these parents there are programs, provided in many treatment centers, which allow a better understanding by the parent of their child's problems, so as to meet them by working together in reducing socializing difficulties. The educational strategies, which will be proposed below, allow parents to rediscover at least in part that alliance, which of course should be created between child and parent. Most children find it important to have a place to place their personal affections and special tools, as well as a clearly delimited area in which to carry out an activity; this is especially true for autistic children who tend to enter into distress for every slightest change in the environment or routine. The structure is used to compensate for an autistic child's difficulties in organizing and understanding their reality. By establishing positive routines through structured education, both parents and caregivers can take advantage of this child's need and help them develop better learning skills and patterns.

The organization of physical space

Careful organization of the physical space in which to ask the child to play is considered a necessary element to facilitate interaction. It is necessary to study the space accurately so that it is clarifying for the child: the place chosen and the ways in which it is prepared will tell the child how to behave. Especially between the ages of two and six to seven, he receives messages more from things than words, and you have to be careful not to send him misleading ones.

The structure of the place prepared for the activity can be very simple, but it must be well visualized, that is, the elements that compose it must be very clear and visible to the child. The place must be protected and in a confined space.

It is very important, therefore, that physical space is:

- visually identifiable
- circumscribed, defined with visible boundaries
- essential: that is, endowed with what you need
- comfortable and comfortable

Above all, it must not contain elements of distraction and attraction, which can disturb the child's attention from the proposed activity.

The organization of physical space is therefore a necessary tool to communicate clearly to the child where they play, what they play with, and can also serve to communicate when they start and when they end.

Following the principles described, the structure of the space must be organized in a personalized way tailored to the specific needs of each child.

The structuring of time

Games require the adult to offer them a lot of attention, patience, dedication and commitment; to the child, they require involvement in an area that is very difficult for him. For this, it is necessary to practice them for a fairly short time, predetermining their duration.

The time aspect of the structure requires decisions about how long the game must last, how to communicate to the child the beginning and end of it, how to respond to behaviors of the child that seem to indicate that he wants to stop or wants to continue. It is much better to define a short playing time, repeating maybe two or three times the game sequence. If play with the child works and if you see that he responds, it is good to try to move forward, risking protracting the game until the baby begins to show signs of fatigue and behave unpleasantly.

Therefore, for a while you can try to continue, but you should never insist excessively: you can offer him another game or you can continue the adult to play; it can simply happen that it is a "day no" and that the operator cannot motivate the child for the time he had set himself.

Over time, you can gradually increase the duration of the game, always considering the child's feedback.

To communicate to the child the beginning or end of an activity it is useful to build rituals, such as shoes that take off at the beginning and put back at the end.

It can happen that the child wants to continue playing beyond the set time, at this point on the part of the adult it takes a bit of elasticity.

Predictability and repetition

The children we care for benefit from predictable and repeated situations in the same way for a long time. It is therefore important that the game is always presented in the same place, more or less at the same time or, better, with the same succession over the other actions of the day, and that it has a ritual of beginning and end.

Individual activities can be repeated in the same way for a long time: this will help the child learn and pay attention to the social elements of the game. It is very important to accept, indeed to encourage the possibility that some of these games become real rituals.

When a play routine is well established, variations can then be introduced, always preserving the ritual form as a spare card in case the child manifests crises of distress, signs of fatigue or to conclude the session.

The child needs to be introduced to a change at a time. To bring about changes in the child's action you can vary the material, maintaining the same routine, or you can maintain the same material and vary routine activity.

In all this it is important to consider the pleasure of the child in rediscovering a new activity and perceiving his state of well-being in carrying out that activity together with the reference adult, in such a way as to create a relational situation that favors good learning for the child.

The cure for motivation

Motivation problems often encounter many autistic children. They can be problems of poor motivation in general or, more likely, in cases of this disorder, these can be bizarreness and restrictions in motivation: the child gets excited beyond measure and seeks only certain experiences with extreme energy, remaining distant, cold and indifferent to others.

The majority of the activities that arouse in the normal developmental child at least a little interest are not motivating for the autistic child.

This problem can largely be summed up in the concept of lack or scarcity of social motivation. If an activity interests the child, well; otherwise, social mediation does not lead him to take an interest in things that are shown to him, that are asked to do, or that are simply done before his eyes.

All this makes the education process a slow and difficult process. The use of artificial motivators, such as praise and rewards, which is also useful for helping the child with typical development to learn the fundamental elements of autonomy, in cases of autism is instead problematic and has a slower and more difficult effect.

Therefore, you don't have to think that what is motivating for the adult or other children should be motivating for the child.

Motivation consists of several aspects:

- What you understand is motivating.
- What you are able to do is motivating. If you know that thing at least a little, you try more willingly.

- What responds to one's emotional and perceptual style is motivating: autistic children mainly prefer the visual channel and, therefore, are interested in shapes, colors, moving objects, lights and repetitive movements. They are often very physical: they climb, run, jump and love open spaces.

It is important that the objects and activities that are prepared and offered to the child speak for themselves to his motivation, without the need for the presentation of the adult. In this way, the operator can join the child's activities, sharing them, and therefore can teach him skills in the social field, then trying to expand his capacity for motivation towards something that is proposed to him.

Autistic children may have particular repulsions or discomfort towards certain environmental stimuli, which can be of any kind; it is therefore important not to mix motivating stimuli with repelling stimuli in treatment with these children.

HOW TO DEAL WITH BATHROOM OR SHOWER PROBLEMS

The issue of shower or bathing is a delicate matter for autistic people and, often, hygiene time becomes a nightmare.

The shower, like the dentist, involves the sensory processing system, where autistic people often have several difficulties and are stressed by several, too many inputs.

That's why we should not insist on showering or bathing with extreme perfection, but focusing on the quality of the bathroom, even if it doesn't last long. Showering, therefore, especially if the autistic person demonstrates intolerance and terror, must be done in the shortest possible time.

First of all, prioritize the main parts to wash: face, armpits, penis/vagina, butt, feet. Everything else, while the water falls on the body, washes itself. Also take into account the following aspects:

Water temperature (I marked hot water with a red ribbon and cold water with a blue one)

- Bathroom lights or mirrors that reflect lights (must be too intrusive)
- The slipperiness of the surface in the tub (non-slip mats can be used)
- The smell of soap (not too strong)
- Room temperature (some people don't like the cold you feel once you get out of the shower or while bathing)
- Water or shampoo over the eyes (swimming eyelets can be used, for example)
- The sound of water (if you take a bath you could prepare the room first, fill the tub before and when the room is totally quiet and warm let your child in)

Add some strategies like:

- Once you have identified the average time you spend in the tub or shower, add a timer for the person to see how much time is missing at the end
- A bath grab bar, if the person has balance problems for slipperiness
- Use a combination of conditioner and shampoo to speed up your hair washing time, or use dry shampoo. Obviously the hair should not be washed every day
- Attach an anti-fog mirror to the shower so that the person is seen while washing
- A visual sequence to remember the parts of the body to be washed and make the person more autonomous while bathing
- A demo video (to be seen together first). Videos work well.
- Introduce the shower into the calendar of the day
- Talk to your son or daughter often about bathing time through a social story.
- Add a favorite toy if your child is small and make bath time fun. You can also "bathe" for your favorite animal or character.
- Always try to shower or bath at the same time and day (habit always helps states of anxiety)

Chapter 12: Tools and games

In the first year of life sensory and motor play allows the child to get to know his body and the world around him. Put hands, feet or objects in your mouth, shake and move arms and legs, research, grab, shake, manipulate.

The game later becomes combinatorial, that is, the child experiments and tries to relate two or more objects, initially randomly and then voluntarily. This is how functional play is acquired: the child shows that he has learned the social meaning of objects and their functional relationship (eg: spoon / dish, brush / hair).

Initially, it will be oriented only towards the object (for example, the child will take a pot, put the spoon on it and turn it, pretending to cook); only later will he be able to orient the game towards himself (so he will pretend to eat from that pot), towards a puppet (e.g.: he will eat the doll) and, finally, towards others).

This begins to build an exchange not only with the object, but also with the other. Around 18 months the child is usually ready to develop the real game of pretending (symbolic game), which demonstrates the ability to build mental representations of the meaning of the object, regardless of the actual function. Gradually the object comes to life in the hands of the child who makes him talk, walk, play with him. The theory of mind begins to emerge, that is, the understanding of one's own and others' mental states. From 2/3 years old the child begins to imitate first and then to seek peers for play. From the age of 4, the growing interest in cooperative play will reflect the affective and social development of the child.

Play in children with Autism Spectrum Disorder does not always emerge as described above; often the child may have remained at a stage of development earlier than his age. Symbolic play, if present, can also be repetitive and not spontaneous. You may lack pleasure in the shared game. This, however, does not mean that play is not important for these children,rather they have a different way of playing or interests than those of others. Such interests can sometimes exaggeratedly absorb their attention.

It is therefore useful to understand what is motivating for the child. Hooking up to this allows you to use the game (in all its forms) as a means of bringing out social interaction skills.

In particular, the game allows you to work on what are called prerequisites of primary inter subjectivity, namely orientation and activation towards a stimulus; interest in the human face and its expression, alternation of shifts and the ability to integrate different sensory modalities (eg visual and auditory); and secondary inter-subjectivity, characterized by joint attention, imitation, joint emotion, joint intention.

Through these skills it will then be possible to build the relationship with the child with Autism Spectrum Disorder and through it work towards acquiring other skills, such as language, or towards enhancing cognitive abilities. In addition, intervening by stimulating play will reduce restrictive and stereotypical interests and behaviors, thus expanding the activities in which the child may be interested and from which he can derive pleasure.

The game sections in an educational and rehabilitation sense must first be organized in physical space and structured over time. This means that the child must be able to visually identify where they are played: it must be a circumscribed, distractor-free, comfortable and comfortable space. It can be a carpet, a room. In addition, time can be marked by rituals and must take into account the child's attentive resources, in order to prevent moments of fatigue and / or any problem behaviors.

To ensure that the gaming activity is motivating, it is good to start from the level of development of the child, from what he can understand and is able to do, taking into account what his interests are. In particular, in children with Autism Spectrum Disorder, sensory (shapes, colors, moving objects), auditory (songs, nursery rhymes, onomatopoeic sounds) or physical (climbing, running, swirling) can be motivating. This is a first step in creating a comfortable environment and starting to weave the plots of the relationship.

The game allows us to build a social routine: if the child likes sensorimotor activities, such as tickling or chasing each other, these can be used to create an exchange with the adult. In these cases, the adult is a source of pleasure, since it is the one who physically tickles or chases the child. The latter will try to continue the activity and the adult will be able to attach himself to this desire to promote joint attention through, for example, the research and exchange of looks, and to create in the child the need to communicate with looks, gestures, sounds, smiles.

The repetition of this game will also allow a sharing of positive emotions born from the pleasure not only of receiving but also of tickling. An essential assumption is that the adult has fun with the child!

Here's how seemingly simple activities represent valuable opportunities to promote a positive relationship and communication with each other. The goal will then be to favor a semi-structured game: if on the one hand you will have to follow the motivation of the child, on the other the therapist or parent will have to insert variations, always having clear the objectives for which you are using that game. The balance between novelty and repetition will allow you to enrich the playful repertoire, passing from a senso-motor game to a functional game, up to symbolic game and, finally, to a social game.

Among the opportunities that the game offers is that of being able to generalize activities and objectives in different contexts given the ease, for teachers and parents, of having opportunities to play with the child. Parents will also be able to feel an active part of therapy, experiencing a sense of effectiveness and gratification. On the one hand, in fact, they will be able to learn more functional game strategies from the comparison with the therapist, on the other, being "experts" of their children, they will be able to offer many suggestions to the therapist. The game will help rediscover to moms and dads the flow of positive emotions, which are sometimes missing and often needed.

Within a more extensive treatment program, the game-centered intervention therefore allows you to promote the development of socio-relational, communication and cognitive skills, respecting the needs, times, methods of learning and individual characteristics of each child!

Increase the use of the gaze: to look, to be looked at, to look at one thing together.

The tricks to take into account to achieve these changes are: doing the activity with interesting objects for the children; asking them to look at you or the object or action that takes place; telling him: "Good! What beautiful eyes! How good you looked at me!" Even if the look was short and fleeting; emphasize actions with voice and gestures, sending clear and precise messages.
It can also be helpful for the therapist to try to point well to the child a position that facilitates him to look at him or look at the object, or that organizes positions that help him stand still instead of running around the room. To do this, it may be enough to tell the child to stand still, or it may be necessary for the therapist to hold him, for example by firmly but calmly putting one hand on his leg, or the two hands on his pelvis. It is important to try to understand if the child receives a message from all this, even in a long time, or if it is a compulsion for him, so much so that, instead of correctly interpreting the exhortation: "Stop and look", he understands that, if he wants to obtain freedom, he must be able to wriggle. It is clear that in these cases you should come up with other ways to interact.

Shift exchanges

To teach a child to take an action by swapping the turn, it is necessary that they first know and appreciate this action. Before proposing a shift, the therapist then has to do the action many times until she notices that the child knows and researches it; or she lets the child do it for a long time alone and, subsequently, inserts with the shift gradually. Also in this case speed and timing are necessary, so that the child does not lose interest in the game.

Indicate and follow the indication

For many children with autism, the indication is a point of arrival, while normally already very young children are able to indicate or respond to the indication.
At first, the therapist can indicate by touching the object with his finger, then he indicates it from a greater distance; the indication will be accompanied by other redundant elements, such as sound exclamations, physical guidance of the child's behavior.

On the contrary, to stimulate this action in him, the therapist can initially accept that he stretches out his hand towards the object; without insisting excessively, he can evolve this gesture into an indication with his finger.

Share an emotion

To get the child to share emotion, a considerable emphasis is needed, but expressed in ways that do not cause discomfort in him: the therapist must therefore smile, laugh, express suspense with behavior in careful harmony with the child.
The way to carry out this task is to choose games that can really please the therapist too, and follow indications of time and place that can give him calm and tranquility. And, it is important to carry out activities that certainly provoke strong pleasant emotions in the child, such as movement games and with music.

Materials and 9 games for non-verbal children

1. **Soap Bubble Games:** The function of this game is to watch, watch together, exchange looks, smiles and vocalizations. It is a very simple game, in which the therapist stands in front of the child, asking him to stand still, to look at the bubbles, then to look him in the face while they make bubbles. The therapist should describe the characteristics of bubbles: "look at how beautiful...big...small...of so many colors are", to keep the child's attention alive. Since children really like bubbles, they can be useful to promote communicative acts: for example, the therapist, when he is sure that the child looks with interest, can take breaks in which the game remains suspended and wait for the child for a communicative act, even minimal, before filming it.

2. **Balloon games:** This game has the function of shared attention and emotional tuning. Both of these abilities can be stimulated by the sound of the balloon swollen, increasing the volume of the balloon and its color itself. All of these are fun-creating situations, which can be shared with the therapist. To stimulate eye contact, the therapist can approach the swollen balloon to the baby's face and, looking through the transparency of the balloon, the face can be observed; in this way a child interested in the sensation derived from contact with that material to approach the exchange of gaze is helped. Again, interruption of play can stimulate a request from the child, remembering, however, that many children need longer time to do this.

3. **Ball games:** this game in addition to having the function of joint attention, also involves imitation and exchange of turns. The therapist sitting on the ground with the child, with outstretched and open legs, begins to spin the ball in

different ways, asking the child to look at it together and point to it. Once the ball is stopped, the therapist can ask the child (verbally or nonverbally) to try. In this game the therapist must be very timely and willing to change the mode of carrying out according to the child's answers, without ever forgetting the goal. Swapping the ball is one of the first social games, so finding that your child doesn't send it back to the therapist can cause discomfort and disappointment. In this game it is useful to have a large number of balls to always find new ways to continue the game, even if the exchange does not take place properly.

4. **Voice games:** The therapist sits with the baby near or in his arms and pays attention to his voice issues. If the child does not speak, the therapist resumes in sounds and repeats them for a long time in the same way, with the same intonation, the same duration and the same volume. Next, introduce some variables, changing modulation or volume to create some sort of dialogue. A variation of this interaction sequence can be done by singing a little song to the child, rocking or hopping him: the child is asked to repeat short sentences or words from the song. This game is useful for promoting voice exchange, attention to each other's face and the exchange of looks.

5. **Contact Games:** These games can be made from different materials, such as mattresses, towels, fabrics, inflatable balloons and balloons. You can go from the simple game of discovering the baby's belly and pretending to eat it, to the game of clapping his hands against his, adjusting the pressure according to the baby's response. Another game may be to have the baby lie on a big inflatable balloon; the therapist rocks him with light pressure and after a while he makes him fall gently on the floor or on himself, warning him: "Now I'll drop you." Contact games allow you to work on the exchange of looks, on the exchange of voice and on the creation of an alternation in the time of exchange.

6. **Movement games:** these are games that can be performed with mats, trampolines and large pillows. They are games that can be modified according to the interests and needs of children and promote emotional activation and synchronization, joint emotion, joint intention, trust and attachment, synchronization of kinesthetic sensations with tactile, auditory and visual sensations.

7. **Games with toy cars and other semi-moving objects:** the therapist equips herself it a number of toy cars and stands next to the child. He moves the cars on the floor one at a time, looking at where they stop. She asks the child to look with her where the cars go, where they stop, how they run if they are fast, slow etc. the therapist takes care of the attention times, so that the child looks with her every time a toy car is thrown. Then he can ask the child to take turns,

emphasizing the game with gestures and voice. Alternatively, the therapist can place the child in front of her, throwing toy cars at him and emphasizing the fact that the object has arrived near the foot or any other part of the body. Later, she can ask the baby to raise it back and if he does not do so spontaneously, she can teach him the necessary movement, if necessary by guiding his hand. A child who loves these games can also benefit from them for communication; as with other games, the communicative function of the request can be encouraged by the organization of situations in which the child is stimulated to ask for the departure of a toy car, to say or indicate which toy car he wants to move. These games, therefore, stimulate imitation and joint attention.

8. **Construction games:** at the table, near or in front of the child, with a box full of objects, the therapist begins to classify the objects and, subsequently, will ask the child to do the same; he will observe his way of classifying and accept it, commenting on the criterion he uses and giving few verbal or gestural indications to share a certain type of classification. In construction games there is a strong interest on the part of the child that also stimulates him to play alone. It is therefore the active function of regulator and custodian of materials that gives the adult an important role, both in the social aspect and to move later to the exchange of messages. With these games the therapist can in fact help the child first understand his end-game message and then produce it spontaneously. It can also handle the material in such a way as to make it necessary for the child to express some form of request.

9. **Nursery rhymes:** nursery rhymes known to the therapist can be used; words are not important, they count the sound of the voice, the predictability-surprise repetition scheme, physical activation, the change of position and rhythm. With these games you favor tuning of intention, emotion and attention thanks to the repeated synchrony of auditory, tactile, proprioceptive and kinesthetic sensations in predictable patterns.

Materials and 6 games for verbal children

1. **Games with toy cars:** even in the case of children with high-functioning autism, the game of toy cars is useful to promote communication skills and to reduce problem behaviors, such as schooling or motor stereotypes. A path and / or a simple story can be structured, so that the child can focus on an activity and can inhibit finalistic behaviors. With this game, in addition to favoring the development of symbolic or representative capacity, action is also taken on the communicative aspects: the child is required to have a functional language inherent in the activity carried out, thus reducing school production. Selective, sustained and joint attention is also enhanced.

2. **Play with the little house and the characters:** this type of game has as a prerequisite representative ability and has as its strengths the possibility of expanding the creativity of the child. this game is suitable for children with verbal autism, who are quite competent in communication. With this game we intervene on prosody, tone, on the ability to maintain a triangulation between activity and adult for a long time and, above all, allows you to stimulate a creative language and reduce repetition language. In addition, the child is allowed to know, through play, situations inherent in reality and, therefore, the development of behavior patterns appropriate to different contexts and a better examination of reality is encouraged.

3. **Table drawings:** with this activity, the child can be asked to graphically represent his life experience or an activity just carried out in therapy; in such a way that the child can verbally rework the lived experience, under the guidance of the therapist, and can understand the temporal scanning of events. In addition, drawing can be a tool to promote more functional communication suitable for the context.

4. **Reading stories:** Reading short stories is useful for fostering sustained and joint attention. It is important to emphasize and gesticulate during the story, to keep the attention of the little one alive. Once the story is over, the child is required to tell it, helping with thoughtful questions and phrases. This type of work helps to develop a creative and less automatic and repetitive language.

5. **Structured and boxed games:** These are for example the game of checkers, Memory and goose play. These activities are useful to promote the relationship with peers and to allow the child to better organize his free moments.

6. **Developing talents:** we try to promote the development of those skills, to which these children are brought and in which they manifest greater flexibility of thinking, control and expression of their self, giving space to the creative side of being autistic, instead of paying attention only to their limits. Talents offer a positive view of Autistic Disorder, as they allow the child to perfect their strengths and make them a starting situation with which to achieve the right balance with themselves and overcome the communication difficulties that are connected with the disorder.

How the Games Address Specific Characteristics of Children with ASD and SPD

Many kids who suffer from the autism spectrum and\or with Sensory Processing Disorders can be often overwhelmed or anxious and utilize defensiveness as a method of protecting themselves. A social situation which can be normal to us can be very stressful for them, maybe because they don't know what can happen next or what is expected from them. Their systems can be put on high alert by irritating sounds, smells, textures, uncomfortable lighting, or loud noises. They find themselves in a state of perpetual fear, they are easily distracted and unable to stay calm. It is vital to understand what is stressing them and solve it.

Giving the kid a picture schedule that shows what will be happening next can reduce their fear.

Other activities in the games which will calm your kid are:

- Wrapping the kid up in a large and soft blanket
- Paying mummy with bandages around the arms and legs
- Wearing weighted items
- Massaging with lotion hands, foots, ears or back
- Slow back-and-forth motion, for example swinging.
- Aquatic therapy

In your games keep a predictable schedule, but also include new games for variety. Give the children free moments when they can play quietly alone or with another kid under adult supervision.

Kids on the autism spectrum often have different interests from typical kids, such as lining up objects according to size or other interests that typically are directed around objects and not people. Even if it's fine for kids to have their preferences, if we want these children to enjoy socializing, they need to develop the readiness to participate. Because we don't want to stress our kid, we should find a balance and a compromise. It is important that other than activities preferred by the children you include new ones which will expand their interests making them more social.

If your kid wants to repeat an activity, give him or her extra time to do this if thaw kid is not using this activity as a way to avoid other things or people. If he or she is doing so, then give what they want to do as a reward for trying another activity in which he or she is less interested.

Your kid can be frustrated by his or her inability to communicate his or her needs; a lot of stress, can easily result in an unexpected crisis. For sure, every child is different, but there are some common things that can cause stress. For example, pay attention to the Environment because it can affect the children's sensory systems, and they won't be able to understand or communicate that. Some factors are: irritating noises; unpleasant smells; and uncomfortable textures and sights.

It's useful to give the kid calming input frequently, rather than waiting until the crisis come.

Also encourage your kid to say what they need if they can or by imitating words.
Examples of games you should try

1. Baseball with a balloon

Balloons attract attention, are light and easy to play with. Let's play baseball with a balloon. The balloon moves slowly so that your kid can more easily hit it.

GOALS

Coordination of eyes and hands, roles learning, concentration and modulation, Motor planning, awareness of space, Vestibular stimulation

MATERIALS

You just need some Newspaper sections, Tape and
Balloons

SETUP

Make newspaper sticks by rolling up sections of them and taping them.

DIRECTIONS

you or another adult have to throw a balloon toward the child with the bat. Let the child to hit the balloon or ask someone else to stand behind the kid and physically prompt him on timing. Then, encourage the other players to try to catch the balloon. Have kids take turns being pitcher, batter, catcher, and fielders.

WHAT IS BEING LEARNED

• Coordination of movements and timing to hit the balloon. They will see the results of their movements and will be able to modify their actions in order to get the desired consequence.
• Roles. Somebody throws, another bats, and others catch.
• Balance and spatial awareness because they run while looking up to catch the balloon, and at the same time they are trying not to bash into others.

MODIFICATIONS

• Some youngsters can have problems following the balloon to catch it or can get distracted or lose interest. In this case they require verbal signals to stay on task.
• Children who have difficulty with timing and eye-hand coordination will need hand-over-hand assistance.

2. Ride on a Ship

Unpredictable movements can furnish many opportunities for fun and motor skill development.

GOALS

Tolerating the unpredictable, acquiring the ability to pretend to play, Boosting language skills

MATERIALS

Large box
Optional: pictures of a ship

SETUP

Place the opened box on the floor.

DIRECTIONS

Tell the children that it is time for a boat ride and let them sit inside the box.

Sing what is happening, for example: "oh-oh. There's a storm. Hold on," as you start swinging the box back and forth or, "Oh, there are big waves!" and you rock a little harder.

VARIATIONS
1. you can pretend the box is a train, a bus or a car. Use your fantasy.

WHAT IS BEING LEARNED
• The unpredictable. They are learning that sometimes they have no control over what happens and shouldn't be afraid
• They are learning the meaning of fast and slow, stop and go and in and out, in order to make them learn better try to say these words while doing the activity.
• They are comprehending how to play pretend and use their imagination so that inanimate objects become other things.

MODIFICATIONS
• Begin the rocking slowly to catch how it is accepted. If the kids seem to enjoy it, increase the rocking.
• Use a smaller box if a large one swings too much .
• If one kid seems uncomfortable, before he or she has a crisis, pretend that the boat has arrived at a port and that he or she needs to disembark. After, create a pretend stop and see if he or she wants to get back on. Or stimulate the youngster to say, "Stop!" or position his or her hand out to gesture "stop," offering him or her some control over the action.
• For kids who are new at pretending and using their imaginations, show them a picture of a ship.
• if a youngster has gravitational insecurity and requires stability or tactile pressure, include an adult in the box to hold him.
• if a child is hypersensitive to touch, put him or her in the boat by himself or herself for a few sessions before the others.

3. "I'm Here!"

It is hard for many kids with autism to learn to answer to being called by name, to call others, and to welcome others. with this game, you can practice in a more relaxing situation.

GOALS
Recognition of names
Social reaction
Auditory and visual stimulus
Improving language skills

MATERIALS
Large box or large piece of material, like sarong or curtain

SETUP
Establish the large box or hang the curtain in order to block off one part of the space. An adult should hide behind the box or curtain and the children should sit facing the curtain or box.

DIRECTIONS

An adult in the group should call out to the person behind the box or curtain. The name should be called with a melodic inflection: "Maria, where aaaaare you?" Then she appears and says, "I'm here!" Encourage the kids to clap and smile and welcome the person.

Accomplish this with several individuals to furnish a model and then let each youngster take a turn.

VARIATIONS

1. you can also hide stuffed animals behind the box and call out, for example, "Giraffe, where aaaaare you?" and then carry the animal in front of the box and say, "hello!"
2. Use a book of animal pictures and call out each animal. For example "Frog, Where aaaaare you?" then oper the page in which you will find the picture of the frog and say hi or kiss the picture. You can also have a kid look through the book and ask him to find the picture.

WHAT IS BEING LEARNED

• Kids are learning a way of greeting by saying, "Hello" or "Hi" when somebody appears. It is also an opportunity to practice.
• Having the group give a exciting cheer when your kid appears has the beautiful benefit of making him or her feel seen, admired, and loved.

MODIFICATIONS

• For the kids who are easy to distract, have the person behind the curtain greet the youngster with a hug or firm touch or ask the person to dance or wear a funny hat.
• If your kid is confused about the rules of the game, go behind the curtain ot the box with them when it's their turn. Encourage the kid saying, for example, "Wow, that's your name. They want you. Let's go!" Then press the child to appear.
• If your kid or another player reacts badly to sudden noises, use the sign language for applause instead of clapping.

4. Leap the Shoes

Make the game easy with just a few shoes or challenging with a pile of shoes.

GOALS

Accepting being the centre of attention, Altering movements to leap more extended distances and more elevated heights.

MATERIALS

Shoes

SETUP

Line the youngsters up, then put one shoe in front of the first kid. Keep other shoes where it's easy to reach them.

DIRECTIONS

Invite the youngsters to leap over the shoe. For the following turn, add another shoe and so on, until the line is too long to jump over.

Then, modify the game by creating a pile of shoes in the centre of the floor. Now, ask the kids to jump up over the height of the pile and take a running start.

To increase the excitement while someone is playing, encourage the others to slap hands or cheer the player in any other way.

VARIATIONS
1. Use different things instead of shoes.
2. Pile cartons in a tower or wall and let the kids run and kick it down. Children can take turns piling the cartons back up.

WHAT IS BEING LEARNED
• On the motoric level, youngsters understand how much power they need to utilize in order to jump off the ground. They understand to predict at which point they need to take off in order to make the jump. This understanding teaches them self-regulation.
• Youngsters are learning to take turns and to be the centre of attention, feeling very noticed and special.

MODIFICATIONS
• Some kids will require one or two grown-ups or other youngsters to run with them to give them the feeling of how fast to run and when to jump.
• Some youngsters will perch the pile rather than leap over it or jump beside it. They may be lacking in power and coordination. Let these kids have some extra practice on other days with smaller piles.

5. Stop and Go

This game allows train the capacity to stop and start action quickly, other than how to respond to a warning as important as "Stop!"

GOALS
Motor management
Following instruction
Imitation
Moving with others
Vestibular, auditory, visual, and proprioceptive stimulus

MATERIALS
Optional: stop signal, green and red fabrics, a bell

SETUP
Kids and adults, standing in a line, are holding hands. The leader (one adult), is facing the line.

DIRECTIONS
The leader says, "Go" and starts to walk backward while everyone else moves forward at a normal speed. The leader then says, "Stop" and everyone must stop instantly. The leader persists with these calls while altering the amount of time spent walking or stopping.
 Since you are holding hands, youngsters can feel the suddenness of the actions.

VARIATIONS
1. The speed of the action can also be changed depending on how fast the leader can run backward!

2. Extremely slow motion is also amusing.
3. Play this game in sand at the seaside for a further level of challenge.

WHAT IS BEING LEARNED
● Listen to recommendations, observe what others are doing, and emulate them.
● Control their bodies ably by starting and stopping on cue.
● Being parts of a group and in sync with others.
● If you perform this play at the beach, you will improve their capacity to balance and stimulate their vestibular systems.

MODIFICATIONS
● Some kids may require further verbal or auditory signals ,like having the other adults repeat "Go" or "Let's go!" after the leader.
● Youngsters who react more to visual signals may do better if a red bandanna is waved or a stop sign is kept up when it is time to stop, and a green bandanna or sign is employed when it is time to go.
● Youngsters who are more autonomous can be authorized to play without having their hands held.

6. Target Games

The eye-hand coordination needed for throwing is one of the most basic motor skills. For youngsters with ASD, who mostly need to understand how to transfer their learning from one activity to many, throwing games can be done in a variety of ways. And doing this game with others can boost the fun, and the excitement.

GOALS
Improving eye-hand coordination, increasing muscle control, Reaching goals, Cognition of others, Visual, proprioceptive, and vestibular stimulus

MATERIALS
Containers, for example open cardboard containers, plastic containers, or buckets. Things to throw, like balls, beanbags, and so on.
SETUP
Place a few containers on the floor and have some objects to throw near you.

DIRECTIONS
Maintain each child standing in front of a target, or you could have all the youngsters sit in a circle with the target in the center. Give each youngster in turn something to throw, and have them throw it into the target of their choice.
Make the game easier or harder just by changing the distance between the thrower and the targets.

VARIATIONS
1. Utilize socks as balls and buckets as containers.
2. Utilize bean bags or ping pong balls and containers of different sizes.
3. Use balls and paper targets on the wall.

WHAT IS BEING LEARNED

• Youngsters are realizing that it is required to look at an object in order to be capable of throwing it. They are understanding the importance of letting their eyes direct their hands, so eye-hand coordination.
• how to manage and grade their muscle strength to accomplish specific physical goals like throwing farther, higher, or harder.

MODIFICATIONS
• Some youngsters can only throw by walking up to the target and dropping it because they haven't understood yet how to use their arms to project. Assist them by maintaining them at a short distance from the object and, utilizing hand-over-hand, direct their hands through the throwing movement. Tell your kid to open his or her hand when he or she has to throw.
• Some youngsters look in directions other than where they are throwing. Tell them where to look."

6. Cereal Box Puzzles

Cereal and cracker boxes can be utilized to create an instant puzzle. This is a good habit to recycle, reuse, and educate.

GOALS
Noticing elements of a whole, Visual stimulus, Spatial understanding, Improving fine motor control

MATERIALS
Cereal boxes
Scissor

SETUP
Clip the front and back of the box. Cut each side in half, creating two large rectangles. Create a few sets of puzzles so each youngster in the party can have one.

DIRECTIONS
Show kids how the parts can be put together in order to make a whole picture again and let them try it providing assistance just if needed. when the kids have accomplished the assignment for a few times, let them trade puzzles with another kid.

VARIATIONS
1. After the youngsters have learned this game ,you can cut the halves in half again so that there ending up with 4 halves.
2. Cut the box side with a diagonal cut to have two triangular halves instead of rectangular.
3. When the youngsters are prepared for an added challenge, cut the parts in abstract shapes. If your kid needs help with this kind of puzzle, lay the puzzle on a piece of paper and trace each piece.
4. You can also create a puzzle using pictures from a magazine.

WHAT IS BEING LEARNED
• Puzzles motivate kids to catch similarities.

• When youngsters try more than one puzzle, they are comprehending to transfer their learning from one experience to a comparable one.
• By trading puzzles with other players, they are learning that sharing enlarges your experience.

MODIFICATIONS
• For kids with motoric difficulties lay down a nonslip mat so the puzzle pieces will stay placed while the other parts are being added.
• To Assist Youngsters in the Understanding of The Concept of putting pieces together in order to make a whole, let them see the picture on the whole side of the box before the cutting or let them help you cut the box.

7. Drawing Faces

Some youngsters have problems reading expressions. We can improve their awareness of somebody else's feelings by drawing smiling faces and other uncomplicated versions of emotions .

GOALS
Understanding of emotion, training reading facial expressions

MATERIALS
Pens
some paper

SETUP
Keep one adult working with each child.

DIRECTIONS
The adult in each team has to draw an essential smiley face, tell the kid that it is an happy face and smile. Encourage the kid to copy the adult's drawing and do what he or she has done.
Do the same with every facial expression linked to feelings you can think of.

VARIATIONS
1. Invite The Children To assume Which feeling you are experiencing by your expression and posture. Invite the youngsters to take turns modeling an expression or a posture for the others players to identify.

WHAT IS BEING LEARNED
• read facial expressions and body language in order to be better at understanding social situations.

MODIFICATIONS
• For youngsters who doesn't have yet enough hand control to draw, do the drawing hand-over-hand.
• If the youngster cannot read facial expressions yet, exaggerate them.
• For youngsters who need it, add a sensory input making them feel your sad (happy, scared, OK) face with their fingers.

Chapter 13: HOW TO TEACH THE CHILD TO PLAY ALONE

Playing alone, as a child, is the basis of what will then be the free time of our teenage and adult children.

If you don't teach a child solo play, over time he will become more and more dependent on us and when the end of high school comes, and our child will have more free time, he will not know how to use it or simply totally depend on us to have fun.In addition to learning social play skills (fundamental to language and interaction), it is essential that autistic children learn to play alone.

Your kid needs to learn to do independent activities! This is crucial for brain development. By learning more independent activities, your child will be less bored, engaged in less destructive and/or non-functional behaviour, and will have less tendency to engage in overly repetitive behaviours.

You need time for yourself. You also need time to clean, wash dishes, sit down, have coffee, and the list goes on and on… You can't and shouldn't occupy every moment of your child's time. Especially when your child grows up (aged 4 and up), it is important that you learn how to occupy time in a fun and functional way!

HOW TO TEACH AN AUTISTIC CHILD TO PLAY ALONE

ENRICH YOUR ENVIRONMENT

In order to teach your child to play alone, you will need to organize the space. Start by creating a corner dedicated to games or pastimes. It can be a box, a basket, any container with games inside. Or, you could do as I do: I have a specific place at home, on a shelf for example, where the kid knows where to find it.

ORGANIZE EACH BOX OR BASKET FOR ACTIVITY

Each box or basket should contain an activity.

CREATE A LIST OF POSSIBLE ACTIVITIES TO BE CARRIED OUT DURING YOUR FREE TIME

Attack the list in a prominent place, so that the kid sees it, and at a specific time, he watches it and chooses what he wants to do. These activities have been agreed with the kid listening to his desires. Everything it takes to accomplish these activities, the kid should know perfectly well where to find it.

LABEL EACH BOX OR TRASH WITH A CLEAR PHOTO SHOWING THE ACTIVITY INSIDE.

This photo will allow the child to choose the activity they want to do and store the activity once completed.

TEACH YOUR CHILD FIRST TO INTERACT WITH MATERIALS BY SETTING UP A SCHEDULE.

This means that before you can expect your little one to pick up a basket of toys and games appropriately on their own, you'll need to spend time teaching the function of those materials on the floor or at the table in a scheduled play/work session. Prepare a box with 6-7 toys inside. Set aside 5-10 minutes and show your child how to use toys in a fun and appropriate way.

SHOW YOUR CHILD WHAT YOU EXPECT FROM THEIR INDEPENDENT GAME

Your kid will be excited to learn about independent play as it opens up a new world of possibilities. However, it may not seem like that at first. Your youngster may resist being shown how to play independently and functionally.

He or she might try to leave the situation when you're showing steps toward functional independent play. This may discourage you, but no, you always have to move forward with your goal.

Don't worry, soon it will be easier and more rewarding for both you and your child. In the meantime, just keep going. Keep showing what you really mean by functional and independent play.

REWARD YOUR CHILD WITH PRAISES AND REWARDS!

When your child starts playing independently, be sure to pay attention! Do a lot of praise. Step into your child's play space (bedroom, living room, etc.) and tell your child what great work they're doing playing alone.

This is very important even if your kid does not speak.

When teaching an autistic child to play alone, it's really important to teach skills step by step and offer plenty of quality reinforcements!

Remember: Just because a child doesn't talk, doesn't mean they can't hear you and understand what you're saying. Autistic children often have difficulty expressing themselves verbally, but have a high level of receptive understanding. Do a lot of verbal praise. It will certainly make you and your little one feel great!

HOW TO WORK ON FLEXIBILITY AND TOLERANCE

Struggling with rigidity is part of the diagnostic criteria for autism:

- Limited and repetitive patterns of behaviours, interests or activity, manifested by at least two of the following:

- Inflexible adherence to habits, routines or ritualized patterns of verbal or nonverbal behaviours (p. E.g., Extreme anguish over small changes, difficulties with transitions, rigid thought patterns, greeting rituals, need to take the same path or eat the same food every day).

HOWEVER, WHAT IS RIGIDITY?

Rigidity is an inflexibility, an inability to tolerate change or unexpected events, at various levels of difficulty.

Many of our children, almost all of us, struggle with this problem on a daily basis, and all this can have a negative impact on life. Issues related to rigidity can affect school day, social relationships/bonds, home life, change, community integration, and professional/work success (for older people).

Some examples may include:

- Difficulty tolerating a teacher change
- Difficulty staying calm if something breaks down, loses power or the battery runs low
- Difficulty staying calm if mom or dad pass in front of a favorite place, but they don't come in
- Insistence on the same routine every day, Monday to Sunday
- I refuse to change eating habits, narrow clothing choices, etc.
- Difficulty sleeping if you are traveling away from home or if your bedtime routine is different

Since stiffness is a key feature of autism, treatment or intervention on it needs to be approached carefully. The goal shouldn't be to turn an inflexible person into a flexible person. The goal is to help the person adapt to an ever-changing world that will NOT remain constant and to increase the person's adaptability to accept what they cannot control.

To some extent, we're all creatures of habit. We buy a certain brand of makeup, brush our teeth a certain way, try to park in the exact same place when we go to the supermarket or work, we always sit in a certain place when we are in class at school, etc.

But, This becomes a problem when the reaction to the interrupted routine becomes explosion, aggression, self-harm, etc. For example, I have a specific restaurants where I order the same thing every time I go. If one day I were to order a dish and it wasn't available, I would be disappointed, annoyed... I could also get up and go eat somewhere else. But I wouldn't become a danger to myself or others and I wouldn't persevere on that nuisance for hours or days.

The **ABA** provides many strategies for teaching flexibility and tolerance to change. Let's discuss some of them:

What are we teaching? This should be priority #1, and it's really important. We can't just take away established patterns and rituals from our kids, we need to identify replacement behaviours first. This could include teaching the possibility of request ("I'd like the red cup"), or learning to wait ("we're passing by the park now, but we're going there in the afternoon"), to self-manage anger and disappointment ("I see you're angry. Let's take our deep breaths, okay? ") And/or to fix the problem ("Oh no, the tablet battery is low. Shall we put him in charge?").

Have we ruled out underlying problems? It is not uncommon for autism to occur in conjunction with other diagnoses. Is the student just "rigid" or is it an Obsessive Compulsive Disorder? Or are you struggling with an undiagnosed anxiety disorder?

Introduce changes intentionally and systematically. I know so many families who try to get around this problem by avoiding changing things in their child's environment, giving in to rituals, even moving away from all people and places to prevent their child from getting nervous. I know this seems like the easiest way to handle this problem, but it will actually make things worse. It is almost a lie against the child to act as if nothing in their environment needs to change. This is not real life. We need to help the child by introducing small intentional changes (it starts super small) and then helping him tolerate that change. **Speaking of tolerating.**

Help your child develop an "action plan" when they know they can get nervous. It has to be a very specific plan, so there is no general recipe for everyone. What is more important is to teach an adequate strategy for reducing escalation. For example: when there is an alternate teacher at school, always inform the child. (if possible). Talk about how you feel about this change. Empathize with her anguish and don't minimize it. Engage in action steps such as rhythm, compression of a stress ball, deep breathing with your eyes closed. Remind the child that there is always an alternative to changing things. For example: "I know you're angry that Master Mario isn't here today. It's disappointing. We can go to the corridor and take a break, and when we come back let me know if you want to do math or English first. Okay? ".

I referred to "Empathy". I know that it can be frustrating and stressful when your child/student explodes for a shifted seat, a different colour plate for breakfast, or a music video on TV you don't see. Let's be very honest, most of us don't like unexpected and unsolicited changes. It makes us angry & we feel annoyed. That "relationship" is empathy. Put yourself in the child's shoes and treat him as you would like to be treated if you were so upset and agitated.

FOOD, A REAL CHALLENGE

There is a quote from Anthelme Brillat-Savarin that says, "Tell me what you eat and I'll tell you who you are." which means, you are what you eat

I want to show you how our children's nutrition can affect their overall functioning.

Do you ever feel that your child's whims are going over the line? If you answered "Yes" to this question, you are not alone.

A parents of kids on the spectrum commonly complain of outbursts of anger. These "whims" could lead you to isolate yourself because you never know when crises could occur, screams.... You may wonder why these collapses and struggle to find an answer. Did you know that the processed foods you feed your child could be part of the cause of these behaviours? Processed foods can be the culprit you've long overlooked. This article shows three reasons why processed foods should be taken into account when managing outbursts of anger in the autistic child.

PROCESSED FOODS CONTAIN EXCESS SUGAR

Processed foods are known to contain excess sugar. This sugar can have a really negative impact on your kid's behaviours. When youngsters have tantrums, it could therefore be the result of instability in blood insulin levels. Unbalanced insulin levels, however, aren't the only problem with the child following a high-sugar diet.

Sugar can weaken your kid's immune system, making it difficult for them to fight infections and making them more susceptible to several diseases. Sugar can also be the cause of hyperactivity and low concentration for your kid. A study which was published in 2018, The Hidden Dangers of Fast and Processed Food, found that there may be a link between processed food and the destruction of brain cells, lowering intelligence. Candy and sugary baked goods can even stimulate the brain so as to be addictive, which can lead to more serious illness. This is actually a great reason to start investigating on the number of processed foods you are providing your autistic child.

PROCESSED FOODS CONTAIN ARTIFICIAL DYES

Artificial staining is another ingredient contained in processed foods. These synthetic ingredients can be harmful to your baby's health and at the root of whims. Food colourings are found in so many foods. Red #40 is one of the most widely used artificial dyes, but it is not the only one linked to children's behavioural problems. Dr Benjamin Feingold was one of the first doctors who linked food colourings to many children's behavioural problems. His diet recommends eliminating artificial dyes and other additives found in foods. Removing processed foods will, at the end, result in the removal of artificial dyes, which could contribute to the baby's whims.

PROCESSED FOODS CONTAIN MSG

MSG is also known as monosodium glutamate. MSG is a flavour enhancer found in processed foods such as fast food, snacks, condiments and frozen meals. MSG can harm your child's health and be the root of whims. MSG acts as an excitotoxin that can damage neurons, which in turn can affect your child's ability to regulate. When your child consumes processed foods containing MSG, they may experience a reaction that causes many negative behaviours such as outbursts of anger, hyperactivity, and lack of concentration.

MITIGATE BEHAVIORS PROBLEM

So what can you do to minimize your child's problem behaviours?

Check food labels and try to stay away from foods with listed ingredients you don't understand

Watch your child search for clues to see what foods they might react negatively to and create a journal to track behaviours

Switch to a diet richer in healthy nutrients and minimize the number of processed foods your child is consuming

It is essential to understand that targeting minimally processed foods is the best way to eat. Our Mediterranean diet offers extraordinary ideas for carrying out a diet rich in minerals, carbohydrates and healthy proteins.

Starting to review your child's diet, eliminating excess processed foods, and understanding the root of their whims is the first step in helping them achieve a better quality of life.

Inquiring about the most dangerous additives is always helpful. Nutrition (now more than proven) conditions people's behaviours, so, with effort and stubbornness, we try to eliminate junk foods and try to introduce healthy foods into our children's diet.

ABOUT MANIAS AND OBSESSIVE DISORDERS

According to a 2015 study that monitored the medical records of nearly 3.4 million people in Denmark over 18 years, autistic people are twice as likely to also have Obsessive Compulsive Disorder.

Obsessions and compulsions can affect anyone: it is common to worry about leaving the gas on or anxiously rummaging through a bag in search of keys. "They're really part of the normal experience," says Ailsa Russell, a clinical psychologist at the University of Bath in the UK. The majority of people find ways to dismiss those unpleasant thoughts and move on. Among people with obsessive compulsive disorder, however, such concerns accumulate over time and disrupt daily functioning.

A crucial distinction, noted by the 2015 analysis, is that obsessions trigger compulsions but not autism traits. Another is that people with obsessive compulsive disorder cannot exchange the specific rituals they need, says Roma Vasa, who is the director of psychiatric services at the Kennedy Krieger Institute in Baltimore, Maryland: "but they need to do things a certain way, otherwise they feel very anxious and uncomfortable." In contrast, autistic people often have a repertoire of repetitive behaviours to choose from. "They're just looking for something that's relaxing; they're not looking for a particular behaviours," says Jeremy Veenstra Vander Weele, a professor of psychiatry at Columbia University.

These shared traits make autism and obsessive compulsive disorder difficult to distinguish. Even in the eye of an experienced physician, the compulsions of obsessive compulsive disorder may resemble the "identity insistence" or repetitive behaviours that many autistic people exhibit, including touching, ordering objects, and traveling the same route all the time. Untangling the two requires careful work.

It is essential that, as parents, educators and careers, we realize how much anxiety obsessions create, how frequent they are, how much they tardy social life, in order to intervene in the most suitable way for our children.

Autism and technology to learn

Technology is, nowadays, a part of our daily lives and that of children and young people who are familiar with computer and technological tools and programs.

The same goes for those on the autism spectrum: technology can influence the cognitive, linguistic and social development of children and teens on the spectrum and can become an ally for learning, communicating and interacting with new ways.

What happens when a child has learning disabilities or has a basic learning skills disorder and beyond? In the case of autism, as in other cases of learning disabilities, computer use appears to foster the development of visual-spatial skills, attention, responsiveness, and the ability to identify details.

The role of the computer

The computer creates an explicit, clear and structured communicative context thanks to the use of visual stimuli and written language:

The learning environment does not depend on social mediation, is highly predictable and takes advantage of visual skills that are one of the strengths of people with autism

The language of the PC and the responses it provides have no emotional nuances, intonation, timbre, accent, nonverbal language and other characteristics that can complicate communication: for example, a person with autism can better understand the voice of a speech synthesis that produces a stable auditory stimulus and without particular inflection

The computer "does not get angry" and, in the face of errors, does not use irony or express disapproval: interaction and communication are facilitated precisely by the "neutrality" of the computer.

The advantages of the computer are obvious, but using the computer discontinuously or without a precise goal can produce poor results or not produce any at all.

Any approach that considers the use of technology as a tool to promote learning and communication must take into account the individual learning characteristics of the student, characteristics to be successfully enhanced and exploited with the use of customizable software and inserted into a complex, organized and articulated psychoeducational design.

The role of the adult to achieve learning goals

Those who follow the student – parent, school worker, educator, teacher, reference specialist – and educate him to use technology must be flexible and propose various and different educational activities, structured and well organized, and work on the autonomy of use of computers and software.

In this way, the student:

- Accumulate technical knowledge
- Learn actively?
- Improves his self-esteem and psychological well-being
- Can reduce stereotypes thanks to new and different possibilities, knowledge and experience

Finally, adult support and work in small peer groups are useful for avoiding social isolation and allow technology to be used as a bridge and a tool for communication and sharing.

Areas of intervention in autism with the use of technology

The technology used methodically and the most suitable tools and software for children and young people with autism can positively intervene in multiple areas:

- Emotional affective area
- Cognitive area (cognitive)
- Teaching area and study method
- Autonomies area
- Communication and language area
- Social area

Emotional affective area

Recognizing and managing emotions is a fundamental objective in an affective-emotional path in autism and concerns:

- Knowing how to understand and communicate your emotions
- Possess strategies to self-regulate
- Knowing how to read the emotions of others and adapt your behaviours accordingly

Cognitive area

How does a person with autism process information? The ability and possible difficulty in doing so involves several aspects:

Attention

To work with both children with hyper selective or hypo selective attention (which can affect learning) and stimulate selective attention that allows you to economize the information coming from the environment and focus on processing the required information, for example during the study.

Memory

Memory as a skill can use external media, for example provided by the environment, or internal media such as mental strategies that facilitate memorization.

A method known and reproposable within a program designed to work with autistic children and young people is the method of descending suggestions, with progressive cards that present a stimulus from which elements are gradually removed to be recalled by heart, for example a kitchen with many objects that are hidden: the indications provided to help memorize can concern the position, size and orientation of hidden objects.

Executive functions of office

Executive functions are about the ability to solve problems, plan, use flexible strategies, keep information controlled and filter relevant data, perform multiple actions in parallel.

Some aspects and areas to be strengthened that can benefit from intervention with the help of technology and that also directly involve school learning are:

- The ability to categorize information, from concrete ones such as the characteristics of some objects to the most abstract ones, for example semantic
- The perceptual organization
- Language, grammar, verbal functions
- Concentration tests such as arithmetic reasoning and memory of numerical facts

To promote the achievement of autonomy starting from even the simplest daily actions that due to deficits of attention, communication and executive functions are not learned with the same spontaneity as their peers: examples are actions such as brushing their teeth, using the toilet, dressing and teeing shoes, eating and drinking. In these cases, task analysis can help with the breakdown of complex action into simple actions and the organization and visual analysis of the materials to be used to perform a task: technology helps the teaching of different daily skills with the use of images, visual prompts that add the advantage of not depending on the presence of a person who instructs ("self-education").

A child with autism can have more or less profound difficulties when it comes to socializing, and they need to learn what other children learn by experiencing: interpreting other people's behaviours, understanding and respecting social rules and conventions, developing problem-solving skills, and even learning to play with others. In this case, for example, a software can help set up:

- Personalized and modifiable social stories that display expected social behaviours and the motivations underlying them, reflection activities on social rules and those to be respected in contexts related to the daily life of the child

- Problem solving task boards to adequately deal with situations of different types, calibrated and customized on the child's difficulties and strengths
- Sequences of events and behaviours to follow to be able to play together with others, also planned to stimulate flexibility and the ability to respond to unexpected situations and behaviours.

3 EASY WAYS TO EXERCISE

Physical activity is and must be an important part of everyone's life and well-being. Experts agree that children under 18 should do a minimum of 60 minutes of physical activity each day. Adults should have at least 30 minutes of physical activity five days a week. Recent studies have revealed, however, that people choose television or an electronic device instead of going out and exercising. Unfortunately, it can sometimes be difficult for people with autism spectrum disorder to participate in physical activity.

How can we improve these statistics?

With the diagnosis of autism spectrum disorder come various social and cognitive barriers. Many autistic people have difficulties in social situations. They may have difficulty communicating their own needs or understanding the expressions of others. A trip to the gym, participation in team sports or even a walk in the park can be an overwhelming task. They may also have difficulty processing instructions or understanding abstract concepts. The act of running on a treadmill or attending a group exercise class can easily overload the senses.

So what can we actually do to alleviate some of these obstacles?

The first step to facilitating a new business is familiarity. Everything gets easier when we know what to expect. For example, imagine you're in school and your teacher comes in and tells everyone that there's a test in five minutes and that you're the only one supporting it. You don't know what the test covers, how long it lasts, and why you're the only one who supports it. Would you be nervous, anxious or worried? Would you be able to focus on studying for those five minutes before the test, without knowing what you should study? Well, most people on the spectrum face this same scenario with almost every new activity in their lives. Now compare your thinking process and emotions if you knew exactly what topics your test would cover, and you spent a considerable amount of time studying days earlier, so you feel prepared.

Would you feel less nervous, anxious or worried? Probably yes!

So, we follow this same concept when we introduce new physical activity to our children or alumni into the spectrum. If you are planning a simple walk in the neighbourhood or a visit to the park, plan it in advance. Talk to the person involved about which path you want to take and when you want to do it.

If it comes to going, for example to the park, talk about the children playing there and maybe even take a short walk to the park.

Indicate all the great things you could do those days. If you have decided to go to the gym, take a tour of the structure first and indicate the different equipment you can use.

These actions help figure out what to expect when it's time to do them. Be sure to include the exact dates you plan to participate in these activities. Enter the agreed days in the visual calendar.

TAKE A TEST TOUR

The easiest way of facilitating a new activity is practice. Taking a test run to the park or gym helps people on the spectrum feel comfortable with the idea of doing something new. Your practice run may be limited to wandering around the parking lot or a short walk in the playground.

The goal is to find positive responses from our autistic child or student. It might help to add positive comments while doing a test run. For example, while you are taking a tour of the park it emphasizes all the fun and fantastic things that children can participate in. Take time to sit on a swing and show how much fun it can be. First visits to your new business should be full of positive experiences and comments.

TAKE A LITTLE SPEECH BEFORE TAKING THE WALK

Conversations can go a long way. Whenever possible, talk about your next release and come up with a plan together. If your visit is to the gym talk before, during and after what you will do. Talk about the things you see and how excited you are to do them. What are you going to wear? It is useful because conversation can create excitement with the right comments and approach.

In addition to creating excitement, these conversations can also help develop a plan and structure for your visit. Be fully prepared to repeat each step more than once when needed because every individual react in a different way.

Take your time to introduce a new event or activity to increase success. Stay positive and supportive during this process. It takes time to implement rituals and events into someone's daily routine, but it's worth it.

PROACTIVE STRATEGIES TO REDUCE PROBLEMATIC BEHAVIORS BEFORE THEY OCCUR

What is the absolute best way to deal with problematic behaviours? Anticipate it! Procedures and routines coupled with pre-correction strategies are evidence-based interventions to support autistic students. Instead of quietly waiting for a challenge to arise and react to it, use proactive strategies to reduce opportunities for negative behaviours to occur. When uploading lessons anticipating teaching expectations, students know exactly how to behave in the environment, and through repetition, for sure they will be more likely to perform the skill without additional suggestions or support.

What is a routine?

It is called routine a set of procedures for managing items like appeal, delivering tasks, or starting a verification period. The routine could also outline what students should do when there are small interruptions in education, like how to ask to use the bathroom or when moving to different areas of the school. These procedures are not only for students, but can also exist for teaching staff. Members of the teaching group often have specific procedures to attract students' attention, distribute documents, and publish lesson goals.

Why do it? Routines and procedures help make the school environment predictable and safe, which can help reduce stress and anxiety in what is already a complex environment for autistic students. The classroom in particular can be incredibly overwhelming when it comes to moving, in social situations & sensory inputs, all while trying to learn! Some established routines allow students to know what to expect and what is expected of them, and as a result, they are more likely to follow procedures. In addition, adding a structure to your environment increases students' feeling of safety. As we already know through Maslow's hierarchy, students must meet their basic needs before they are ready to engage with learning.

How should I do that? The key to establishing a routine is to have a plan. There are more routines to consider during a school day. There are transition routines between activities inside and outside the classroom, switching to leisure activities once work is complete, bathroom routines, going out into the environment (for things like throwing away trash, tempering pencils and procuring material), and emergency transitions such as a fire drill.

There are also routines designed just for the teacher and routines that only students perform.

1. Have a plan:

It's helpful to start thinking about a detailed list of how you would actually like your student's behaviour to be. Think about where you want the material you use to be stored and whether there are certain times that are appropriate or not to follow the routine. For example, if you see that the lesson is continuously interrupted because so many students temper pencils, set a time to temper pencils: before starting the lesson, for example, or after recreation.

2.Practice:

So, make a plan to teach the class routine and practice, practice, practice. Depending on students' routine and needs, you could create visual support with the included steps, preferably an illustrated list, with images If you're not sure how to start with, consider where students have the most difficulty, where there are more behaviour issues—sometimes the reason is because there are no clear procedures.

Pre-correction

What is it? Pre-correction is a proactive strategy that consists of providing a verbal, gestural, or visual suggestion just before a predicted problem behaviours. It can be given to an entire class, a small group or a single student. It focuses on using positive language so that the autistic student knows what they should do and, just like routines and procedures, allows staff to reduce the likelihood of negative behaviour occurring in the first place.

Why do it? Tackling the problem before it occurs allows you to focus on prevention rather than responding to negative behaviours. If the data indicate that the autistic student has difficulties in a specific context, routine or activity, pre-correction, coupled with other interventions such as using social histories, can be a positive way to teach a skill rather than trying to intervene after negative behaviour has already occurred.

How should I do that? The part about pre-correction is that you can do it at any time. If I'm going to ask the whole class a question, I might raise my hand as a hint to say, "If you know the answer, raise your hand." However, there may be times in your classroom when you need a more explicit teaching model.

1.Identify key moments

Start by looking for times of day when a problem behaviour is most likely to occur, after already adapting and teaching a routine or procedure to the class.

2.State expectations

Processing many steps can be overwhelming for autistic students. When expressing expectations, keep directions short and concise. Pairing your lens with some sort of gesture or visual signal could also help ensure students understand what is expected of them. It might sound like, "to stand in line, remember to walk in a straight line, in silence, and with proper posture."

3.Role-playing

One strategy you should consider in pre-correction to teach is the "super student" model. Research shows that autistic students respond more effectively to imitating typical neuro peers. After expressing the expectation, you might say, "Before lining up, Roberto will show us how to walk in line properly." If a peer model is not available & the autistic student has problems with a particular skill, you could practice with him first and then mate it with a typical neuro student for classroom demonstration, or they could do so independently.

When using any of these strategies to proactively address classroom behaviours, it's critical to provide reinforcement to students. This will help increase the likelihood of students continuing to behave the way you predicted. Whether it's a positive and formal behavioural support system or behaviours-specific praise like "I like how you waited your shift in line today," giving some sort of recognition is a key to helping make your class work successfully.

Chapter 14: Adolescence

Why is adolescence so complicated?

After adults, adolescence is a difficult and problem-rich time. What are the most common false myths and characteristics of this phase of change? Adolescence begins at age 12 and ends around age 24. That's right! Many people believe that this life phase begins around the age of 14 and ends around 18, but is actually much more extensive.

A common feature of many families is the conflict between parents and children during this phase of life. On the one hand, parents are not satisfied with their child's "wrong companions," academic achievement, or behaviours. The teenage son is described as short-tempered, impulsive, moody, and unresentful of the rules. On the other hand, the boy feels distant parents, sometimes controlling, anxious, overly in demand. Precisely because of obstacles like these, adolescence is often a difficult time.

4 false myths about adolescence

1. Hormones make the teenager "get out of your mind." Although there is an increase in some hormones, it is the brain changes that occur that have a greater weight on behaviours. In particular, different brain structures and functions are maturing through real remodelling.

2. Adolescence is just a difficult and annoying phase. As we will see, some features can be a strength. Likewise, they can be cultivated positively within the parent-child relationship.

3. To grow up, my son must immediately become autonomous. It's great now! In reality, the transition to autonomy is gradual and does not happen at any moment. In other words, your child still needs you and your support.

4. My son has become disobedient, I have to be stricter. In reality, the attitude of the "I command, you obey" type is the most frequent reason for conflicts between parents and adolescent children. Although it is necessary to maintain some rules firmly, the figure of the father-master has several risks. In fact, often maintaining the status quo of the authoritarian parent increases the rift in the parent-child relationship.

Dan Siegel, an expert in interpersonal biology, described **4 key characteristics** of adolescence that make this moment as full of opportunities.

1. Search for news. In adolescence there is a drive to live new experiences, with greater intensity and involvement. However, increased risk appetite, excessive impulsivity, or minimizing negative consequences can become problematic.

2. Social involvement. Relations with peers are becoming increasingly important. Some adolescents are much more inclined to equals than others who maintain a sufficiently stable bond with the family. Certainly adolescents who totally move away from their parents show more risky behaviours, such as substance use. In this regard, we consider that social relationships are the beating heart of the quality of our lives. This can be helpful in building a social identity.

3. More intense emotions. If well managed, emotions motivate and guide our actions, thus being an essential source of vitality. Instead, when they become excessively intense or lasting, they can be an obstacle. Especially during this stage of life, managing emotions such as anger is crucial.

4. Creativity. Flowering of ideas, uncommon ways of coping with life. Thanks to the development of abstract reasoning, in adolescence, the first questions about the meaning of life emerge. This can turn into an identity crisis, accompanied by strong stress and a sense of bewilderment. However, creativity if well channelled, can lead to the realization of musical, scientific and technological works. This quality allows you to cultivate a vast number of expressions of yourself.

Puberty brings with it numerous changes, involving the hormonal and endocrine system, body fat distribution, skeleton, muscles, reproductive organs, and sexual characteristics. In everyday life the boys notice the first pimples, the weight gain, the change in body shapes, the body hair ... Inevitably these transformations have an impact on the psycho-emotional sphere of the adolescent, going to influence his self-esteem, now struggling with the confrontation with the outside world, with aesthetic canons and peers. From a relational point of view, physical appearance plays a crucial role in popularity, its role within the group of friends, and its way of relating to others. Adolescent changes involve not only the body, but also the psychological, emotional and cognitive spheres. Intellectual and metacognitive abilities (the ability to reflect on one's internal states) are refined, and the adolescent begins to wonder "***Who am I? Who do I want to become? What adult will I be? Who would I like to look like?***"
These questions are about self-perception, the identity dimension as well as, once again, self-esteem.
To find answers to these questions, the teenager begins to explore the world with increasing autonomy, starting the path of separation-identification from the family. Here the parental function is called to carry out a new task: to guarantee the presence, support, and safety necessary for the adolescent to be able to explore new horizons, accepting the movements of estrangement and rapprochements that characterize this evolutionary phase of the children.
Playing this new role is not easy... it requires a lot of effort to hold different thrusts together. On the one hand, you have the desire to protect their children from the dangers they may encounter, on the other the feeling of feeling rejected as reference figures. How to do it?
There is no perfect parent recipe, but you can keep a few aspects in mind. First of all, give importance to the evolution of the parent-child relationship. The boy, who today seems so different from the child he was, carries with him the baggage of relational and emotional experiences made during the previous stages of life. Investing carefully

in a harmonious parent-child relationship already in childhood, learning about and enhancing the personal aspects of your growing child, is an element not to be underestimated.

It is also important that every mom and dad takes the time to self-observe, trying to understand what their parenting style is.

- Am I authoritarian?
- Am I too permissive?
- Am I usually running, busy, distant and uninterested in what concerns my son?

Spending time thinking about your attitude can prove critical to making a significant change in your relationship with the adolescent first-hand. In addition, we do not lose sight of important concepts such as availability and containment at this stage. It is in fact important to put yourself in a position of listening and understanding, while maintaining attention to positive rules, which do not make the teenager feel alone and without references.

The ability to compromise is a valuable ability. In fact, it allows the parent to maintain fixed points, aimed at the protection and education of children, at the same time gives the adolescent the opportunity to feel more involved in the decisions that are made. The boy will thus be able to feel that his needs are being heard, valued and that it is worth considering his point of view.

These are just some of the precautions on which it is good to dwell in the face of a complex period such as that of adolescence.

They certainly don't solve everything that happens in a family at this time nor can they be a solution "to all evil." The point I would like to share, however, is that it takes time to listen to yourself and your children, dedicating yourself to a reflection that does not only aim to find limits and difficulties, but that brings to light the resources and strengths of the two parents in their individuality and as a parenting couple, of their adolescent child and the attachment relationship that binds them.

People with autism tend to take a self-closing mental attitude and direct out unified if not monolithic (monotropism) attention. Being monotropic in a polytropic world – that is, in a world where people use multiple communication channels, face very different tasks and can divide their attention between multiple different interests – can give rise to numerous problems.

Despite their closure and their apparent disinterest in the people around them, people with autism show a great need to be with others, but they must be satisfied in a structured and adequate way.

Autism cannot be adapted to the conditions of normal sociability. If anything, it is the world that must adapt to this way of being, respecting its unique characteristics, the enigmatic and paradoxical request it makes. Interaction of people with autism requires suitable settings.

Perhaps it is difficult to think that many of the internal conflicts and problems of autistic adolescents are, after all, made of the same paste as those of all adolescents. Thus, autistic adolescents, like all adolescents, also need to break away from the family unit, despite having it as a reference, have friendships and places where you can have fun and cultivate your interests.

Support to provide to autistic adolescents should result in helping build and use the grips needed to climb the difficult but fascinating growth wall (the same as their peers), making them get as high as possible.

Sexuality seen by autistic teens

Physically in puberty children quickly change physical appearance, sexual characteristics and develop sexual desires. On a cognitive level they develop the skills to form abstract concepts and ideas of identity in relation to the environment and society in which they live, and ideas and concepts of feelings as well as perceptions of others.

Unfortunately, autistic subjects due to the non-ability to form abstract concepts, during puberty tend to continue to adopt and behave with skills mostly based on the senses and perceptions, so they tend to interpret others and the environment through the senses.

Autistic subjects also often lack the ability to enter and interact with peers during puberty.

The ability to relate to peers helps the development of the sense of self in relation to others and constitutes the transition, the transformation from the position of child to young independent adult.

The lack of social inclusion of autistic children, and the general disinterest in creating relationships with others also favor the period of sexual experimentation that non-autistic adolescents tend to have or at least seek.

Lacking skills, social concepts, and experimentation with peers, autistic adolescents manifest sexual desires almost exclusively through masturbation and/or inadequate sexual attitudes.

For example, autistic adolescents can practice masturbation in public or seek physical contact with others inappropriately and not considered acceptable by society.

Unfortunately, we cannot think of teaching our children about sex education and we cannot try to encourage experimentation with peers, but what we can do is teach them certain appropriate sexual behaviours.

Always keeping in mind the human right our children have to express their sexual desires.

We must all (family members and teachers) focus on teaching practical methods, appropriate sexual behaviours that are accepted by the environment around us and the society in which we live.

First, both we parents and professionals need to change behaviours toward the boy.

Let me explain better:

Considering that the boy does not go through that period of cognitive transition and social development that other adolescents go through in puberty, it is clear that the autistic boy continues to perceive himself in relation to others as he has always done, that is, as a child.

It is the adults who see him grow up and physically change and see the transformation from child to teenager. Therefore all the kisses, hugs, cuddles that were appropriate from both parents, family members, therapists, teachers etc. are no longer adequate.

In other words, our behaviours towards the autistic boy must be the pattern of behaviours he must follow to learn to behave appropriately and acceptable during puberty and one day also as an adult.

Having said that, parents and family members will naturally continue to behave affectionately, but they too will have to have in mind that certain affections expressed in the past no longer represent an educational model for the boy. Keep in mind that the period of childhood is a fairly short period in the course of a person's life, (about 7% / of life) most of life is lived as adults; if you want the boy to behave properly as an adult in the future, you have to start teaching him now.

Therapists and teachers will need to change their relational attitude towards your child. The kisses, hugs will be gradually removed. Only occasionally, for example at the end of a session, or when the boy has worked very well can therapists give him a kiss or hug. Or if it proves to be sad etc., a comfort hug is appropriate.

The "good baby, good child," etc., will have to be replaced with other verbal reinforcements: good, very good, you are a champion, you worked well, or, give me a 5, etc. The physical contact so far expressed with kisses and kisses will need to be replaced with a slight pat on the shoulder, an expression of contentment associated with adequate verbal reinforcement.

Teach the boy what kind he belongs to. For example, this can be taught with play, starting at home, inviting perhaps all therapists and family and / or friends to the sessions. Saying all the males on this side of the room and the females on the other side of the room. Helping the boy physically put himself on the side of the males. You can also start small team games, with males versus females.

This type of teaching can certainly be practiced in school.

Teach the boy the typical characteristics of males and typical of females, for example, males shaving, females take care of their nails, to promote the formation of the concept of diversity and identity.

When you are at the restaurant, pool or other public place and your child must use the bathroom emphasized on recognizing the correct bathroom for males and females.

Teach body parts by saying the correct terms for sexual organs and their functions.

The expression of sexual desires through masturbation can become a problem for example, he can try to touch his genitals or practice masturbation in public, so he must be taught that certain acts are normal but are private.

When your child expresses his sexual desires inappropriate acts, parents and therapists must never demonstrate attitudes or behaviours of disapproval because this can only increase his frustration and anxiety. Whenever your child touches his genitals, parents and therapists will have to accompany him to the bathroom or his room and tell him that if he wants he can touch himself there.

This is in order for the boy to understand that his desires are normal and acceptable but are private. In the future you could also set times when your child can go to the bathroom or his room, to strengthen the sense of privacy in him.

There are other inadequate behaviours related to masturbation for example excessive masturbation, which can be due to a compulsive attitude and a failure to achieve satisfaction.

We all belong to a gender, regardless of our abilities, disabilities, pathologies. Sexuality is part of the life of each of us, it includes the biological, psychological, social, emotional sphere and values of each of us. Sexuality starts with us and extends to our relationships with others. Like any peer, autistic adolescents too must learn to manage their feelings in a refined way, inhibiting some of them, stalling over others, moderating their impulsivity, expressing something without unbalancing themselves too much.

Like many other skills and knowledge, those related to the affective sphere and sexuality must also be learned systematically by autistic adolescents, that is, learned in an individualized, structured way and based on concrete educational strategies, which reduce the use of verbal language as much as possible.

On the contrary, visual media, such as photographs, illustrations, videos (you can find them also on YouTube or you can make them with your computer) can be of great use. The modalities of education must be adapted not to the age of age but to the real development of people (it should not be forgotten that those with autistic disorders often present developmental delays), to their interests, motivations and specific needs. In addition to being considered shameful, sexuality in disability is treated not as a legitimate expression but as problematic behaviours, without considering that the problematic aspect is that related to the system of social rules in which the person with severe difficulties is immersed, on which no one has been able to pass on the correct information.

The task of families and specialist services is expressed in this regard. First of all, they must prepare autistic adolescent individuals for the physiological changes that will take place in their body. In addition, they must be taught the discernment between the public and private spheres, and how certain actions such as genital self-stimulation are to be carried out only in a condition of intimacy that can only be found in an intimate and private context. Difficulty of relationship, empathy towards other subjects, understanding the situation can lead to an inadequate understanding of what is public is what is strictly private, this could hesitate, in some subjects in performing acts of masturbation in inadequate contexts.

Offering autistic girls, women, boys and men knowledge about sexuality and opportunities to make friends and improve communication and social skills as much as possible will reduce the likelihood of them being abused or sexual exploitation. Regardless of what parents can expect, autistic adolescents with severe difficulties will need to be educated to understand their menstrual cycle that will be repeated on a monthly basis, should be trained on sex education and sexually transmitted diseases. Another problem found is that children and adolescents diagnosed with autism spectrum disorder are at an increased risk for emotional, physical & sexual abuse. Depending on the severity level of autism, these people may need assistance in daily activities, which may include the fact that their bodies are touched by adults to meet their personal needs. However, often these guys are not educated about the prevention of sexual abuse, and it is precisely this that puts them in a condition of greater risk. ***Autistics are not eternal children.*** They will get excited, touch each other, and they will also do so in public, if they are not prepared to handle the drives. This is why it is important to teach him how to do it from an early age.

Looking at each other and touching each other's face in the mirror, recognizing oneself in photographs are useful pastimes to stimulate self-perception: the autistic child must feel like an "other" individual by parents and educators. But above all to prevent them from being sexually abused in the future, it is essential to teach them right away to say 'no' and respect their rejection.

The third step? Draw the circles of knowledge on a sheet. A real scheme to make together and that he must always carry with him to understand who, among friends, acquaintances and close relatives can be close to him and who cannot. The same can be done to teach how to recognize and respect the emotions of others, drawing the 6 most common feelings (happy, sad, angry, scared, surprised and disgusted) on as many cards to associate with family members throughout the day.

Enforcing rules at home is just as important: before entering the bedroom you have to knock and wait for permission. It is a private place, the only one where you can masturbate. It is forbidden to use nicknames to indicate the penis or vagina: call them by the right name. It will avoid confusion.

Ban on movies like Butch Cassidy or Fifty Shades of Grey. Certain films represent relationships in terms of power, with seduction games that are difficult for an autistic person to understand, who might learn that you can win over a person aggressively. To prevent them from masturbating spontaneously in public, then, you need to understand what excites them (it can be nail polish on their nails, a naked chest at sea) and create a book of clippings with these figures. The boy or girl may have time scheduled to look at the book in his room with the door closed and masturbate. The secret to understanding what triggers excitement? Have a very open mind and do not neglect any details.

SEXUALITY MANAGEMENT IN HIGH-FUNCTIONING AUTISTICS

Just like typical neurons, individuals with autism spectrum disorders show the full range of sexual behaviours. However, due to the main symptoms of the disorder, including deficits in social skills, sensory hypo and hypersensitivity, and repetitive behaviours, some autistic individuals may develop quantitatively above-average or non-regulatory sexual behaviours and interests.

Autistic individuals appear to have more hypersexual and paraphilic fantasies and behaviours than general population studies suggest. However, this inconsistency is mainly driven by observations from autistic males. This could be due to the fact that autistic women are usually more socially adapted and show less autistic symptoms. Many studies suggest that autistic individuals seek sexual and romantic relationships similar to the typical normal population and have the full spectrum of sexual experiences and behaviours. However, there are still many stereotypes and social beliefs about autistic individuals, which refer to them as uninterested in social and romantic relationships and as asexual.

Most of the research that has existed so far has focused on men, and few studies have addressed gender-specific issues regarding social, emotional, and cognitive domains, and even fewer studies exist that examine sexuality independently in autistic men and women. The few clinical observations and the small set of systematic studies indicate that autistic women may have less pronounced social and communication deficits and have special interests more compatible with the interests of their peer groups. Furthermore, autistic women seem to apply coping strategies, such as imitating the social skills of their typical normal peers, thus being more socially discreet. As for sexuality-related problems, autistic women appear to have poorer levels of overall sexual functioning, feel less well in sexual relationships than autistic men, and are also at greater risk of becoming victims of sexual assault or abuse.

Autistic males have been found to engage more in solitary sexual activities, and have a greater desire for sexual and romantic relationships; however, evidence has shown that autistic women, despite having a lower sexual desire, engage in dyadic relationships more often.

Although autistic individuals seek sexual experiences and relationships, the development and maintenance of romantic and sexual relationships are strongly influenced by deficits in social and communication skills and difficulties in understanding nonverbal or subtle interaction signals and mentalization (meaning being able to understand one's own and the mental states of others, for example, the emotions, desires, cognitions experienced by such individuals. In addition, many autistic individuals do not receive sex education that takes their behavioural peculiarities into account, and are less likely to obtain information about sexuality from social sources.

Another point to consider are narrow and repetitive interests, which may be non-sexual in childhood, but which can turn into sexualized and sexual behaviours in adulthood. In addition, frequently reported sensory sensitivities can lead to an overreaction or insufficient reaction to sensory stimuli in the context of sexual experience. In hypersensitive individuals, soft physical touches can be experienced as unpleasant; on the other hand, hypersensitive individuals may have trouble getting excited and orgasm through sexual behaviours. Taken together, the main symptoms of autism combined with limited sexual knowledge and less ease of romantic and sexual experiences could predispose some autistic individuals to develop challenging or problematic sexual behaviours, as hypersexual and paraphilic behaviours.

For the proposed eleventh edition of the International Classification of Diseases (ICD-11), the following definition for the diagnosis of compulsive sexual behaviours is being considered:

Compulsive sexual behaviours disorder is characterized by persistent and repetitive sexual impulses that are experienced as irresistible or uncontrollable, leading to repetitive sexual behaviours, along with additional indicators such as sexual activities that become a central focus of the individual's life to the point of neglecting even health and personal care as well as other activities, unsuccessful efforts to control or reduce sexual behaviours or continue engaging in repetitive sexual behaviours despite adverse consequences (e.g., relationship interruption, work consequences as well as negative impact on health). The individual k experiences increased tension or affective arousal immediately before sexual activity and after relief or dissipation of tension.

As for paraphilias, the DSM-5 now distinguishes between paraphilias and paraphilic disorders, thus aiming at a de-stigmatization of non-regulatory sexual interests and behaviours that do not cause discomfort or impairment to the individual or harm others. In DSM-5, paraphilias are defined as "any intense and persistent sexual interest other than sexual interest in genital stimulation or preparatory caressing with phenotypically normal, physically mature, consenting human partners" (see Box 1 for a list of paraphilic disorders included in the DSM-5).

Although the proposed criteria for paraphilic disorders in ICD-11 resemble those of DSM-5, one of the main differences between these two diagnostic manuals is the removal of paraphilic disorders diagnosed primarily on the basis of consenting behaviours that are not in themselves associated with functional discomfort or impairment. This led to the exclusion from ICD-11 of fetishism, sexual masochism and disguised disorder, behaviours that were reported in autistic individuals.

WHAT CAN WE PARENTS DO?

As we have read so far, autistic adolescents develop sexually in the same way as other adolescents but may need additional help to develop the social skills and understanding that accompany sexual development.

Your kid will be more or less interested in sex and sexuality, just like other children of the same age. Your child may also develop romantic relationships, which may or may not be sexual.

Some teens are attracted to people of the opposite sex, some are attracted to people of the same sex, and some are bisexual. Sexual attraction and sexual identity are not the same thing. Young people attracted to the same sex may or may not identify as gay, lesbian or bisexual. They could identify as heterosexual.

Your child's sexuality may be different from yours or your expectations. But if you can accept your kid's sexuality, you've earned so much on the path to their healthy development and your relationship with your child.

Many autistic teens may have difficulty understanding sexual feelings in themselves and others.

You can develop your child's understanding by helping them break down sexual feelings into thoughts, bodily sensations, and behaviours. For example, if your youngster is sexually attracted to someone, they may have:

- **Thoughts**: thinking a lot about the person
- **Bodily sensations** – tingling sensation in the stomach or erections when close to the person
- **Behaviour**: try to find ways to stay close to the person.

You could use social stories or visual media to talk to your child about sexual feelings. It can also be difficult for autistic teens to express sexual feelings. If your child finds this difficult, they may be more likely to do inappropriate or risky things or enter into unhealthy relationships.

These ideas can help:

Practice social interactions with your child using role-playing play. For example, you could play a role-playing game by talking to someone at the park or party or asking to go to the movies. You can also simulate what to do if the person answers "yes" or "no" to the request to go to the movies.

Set some clear rules on how to invite someone to an appointment. For example, 'You can ask someone out once. If he says he's not free, you can ask him again. If he tells you no again, even if he gives you an excuse, you shouldn't ask again.

Set limits on appropriate behaviours. For example, chasing someone around or contacting them online often isn't good.

An individual's sexual orientation has to do with romantic or sexual attraction. It is different from their gender identity, which is a person's sense of who they are: male, female, both or neither.

When your autistic child goes through puberty and learns about sexual feelings, you'll need to talk to him about sexual relationships.

It's very important for your child to know that sexual intercourse is a normal part of life, but your child doesn't have to have sex if they don't want to. She doesn't have to have sex to be popular or because her peers say she should.

Your child also needs to know other people's sexual cues. When your child knows how to interpret other people's sexual cues, they can increase their confidence, protect themselves, and avoid harming others unintentionally.

Explaining sexual cues can help. For example, "somebody might be interested in having sex if they kissed you or touched you and then invited you to their bedroom. If you desire to have sex with this person, you must always ask for their consent. You don't have to do anything the other person doesn't want to do."

You and your child can get sexuality and sexual health advice from your GP, for example. You can also tell your kid that they can ask you anything. But if you think your child may feel more comfortable talking to someone else about it, a brother, friend, or other family member might also be an option.

CONSENSUS AND SAFETY FOR AUTISTIC TEENAGERS

In any intimate sexual situation, the most important things for your child are consent and security:

Consent means your child needs to feel good for any kind of sexual activity. The other person also has to agree.

Your kid has the right to say **"no".** All young people must have the right to control what happens to their bodies and your youngster should never feel compelled to do something that doesn't seem right to them.

Safety means that the experience is *respectful and not violent.*

Autistic people may be vulnerable to sexual abuse because they don't always recognize when something is wrong. So you may have to explicitly teach your child the difference between good touch and bad touch.

For example, good touch is something friends and family could do to prove they care for each other. These touches could include a handshake for greeting, hug, or kiss. A bad touch is something that makes you feel wrong or uncomfortable, like a stranger asking you for a kiss.

You may also need to explain that a touch could be a positive touch for one person, but the same touch could be a negative touch for someone else. For example, a person might like tickling (it's a nice touch), while someone else might not like tickling (it's a bad touch). Or it's okay to say goodbye to a dear friend or family member if you see them on the street, but it's not okay to kiss a stranger.

You will probably have to re-read these directions many times with your child. Try to be patient with your child and yourself. It might be helpful to share experiences and get support from other parents. You could try support groups online or in person.

New studies

According to a recent scientific study, adults with autism say, three times more than their neuro typical peers, that their sexual orientation cannot be described and identified through the labels "hetero-", "homo-" or "bisexual."

This study, conducted in Sweden, is based on a sample of more than 47,000 adults. The results indicate that among people with autistic traits, about one in five individuals is not reflected in any of these standard categories that define sexual orientation.

The conclusions therefore suggest that the scientific community, researchers, doctors, therapists, and psychologists should be open-minded when discussing sexuality with people with autism.

"These traditional categories don't work," says researcher Kyriaki Kosidou of the Karolinska Institute. "Addressing sexuality issues is important in clinical settings, but our results show that we need to think outside the box; we need to think innovatively." Several studies have also confirmed that sexual orientations that are usually represented as a lower percentage in the population have higher numbers among people with autism. This year, for example, some Australian scientists were able to say that almost 70% of individuals with autism, compared to 30% of neurotypical adults, reported not being heterosexual.

"This the new research provides further evidence of the link between neurodiversity and diversity of sexual orientation," says John Strang who is the director of the gender and autism program at the National Health System in Washington. "Studies like this encourage people with autism to listen more closely to their experience than their sexual orientation."

Returning to the first article we cited, Kosidou and his colleagues analyzed data from 47,456 Swedish adults, who filled out various public health questionnaires between 2002 & 2014. Among the surveys was a 10-item questionnaire called "AQ-10" that highlights traits associated with autism, such as difficulties in social interaction & communication. Adults who obtained a score above a given threshold were classified as people with autistic traits.

Participants also had to answer a question asking whether they considered themselves heterosexual, homosexual, bisexual, or "none of the previous ones."

From this analysis, more than 3,000 respondents, about 7.5% of the total sample, showed traits associated with autism. Of these individuals, 77% reported being heterosexual; those who had no autistic traits indicated 89.5% of cases to be heterosexual.

The group associated with autistic characteristics, moreover, was particularly inclined to say that none of the labels listed corresponded to their sexual orientation: 19.1% selected the item "none of the previous ones", compared to 6.8% of participants without autism traits.

People with autistic characteristics who were interviewed indicated, to a slightly greater extent than the normo-typic sample, that they were bisexual: 2.5% of them said they were; 2.1% of adults without autism traits gave the same response. The results of this study appeared on October 30, 2017 in the Journal of Autism and Developmental Disorders.

"Everyone who works with people on the spectrum should be wider-minded in discussing sexuality and sexual orientation," Kosidou says.

No one yet knows what connection there may be between autism characteristics and sexual orientation. Biological factors could be part of this link. Exposure to some high levels of male sex hormones in utero, for example, is known to increase both the chances of autistic traits and unconventional sexual orientations.

It is also possible that people with autistic traits are less interested in adhering to social norms that affect sexual orientation, compared to most neuro typical people. People with autism, therefore, may be more likely to experience or reveal non-standard sexual orientations.

"Features like being direct, honest, and very concrete, which are so common among people with autism, could lead them to more honestly describe their sexuality, albeit outside of conventional categories," Strang says.

Uncommon sexual orientations can thus present additional challenges for people with autism or who have autistic traits. Some of these individuals experience stigmatization and discrimination both for their autism-related behaviours and their sexual orientation.

"Sometimes it feels like you have to out twice," says Jeroen Dewinter, a clinical psychologist at the GGzE Center for Child & Adolescent Psychiatry in the Netherlands, who hasn't been involved in the research, but has been dealing with teens with autism for a long time. Next step is, Dewinter says, is to conduct qualitative research with teens and adults with autism to better understand how they live and describe their sexuality, whatever it is.

Autistic teenagers: the challenge of families

In the past there was the erroneous conception that autism was caused by the inadequacy of parental care and the affective coldness of mothers. In The Empty Fortress, Bruno Bettelheim (1967) called mothers of autistic mothers refrigerators and children similar to empty fortresses, a widely outdated concept.

Children with autism spectrum disorders often pose significant behavioural challenges for their parents and other family members. In fact, when a child is diagnosed with autism spectrum disorder, intervention on the family environment is indispensable: the whole situation needs adequate restructuring and re-composition. Giving proper skills to parents is a way to expand the quality and availability of services for autistic children and adolescents.

Parental inclusion as treatment providers for their children is now considered an essential component of intervention in autism. The importance of the role of parents as collaborators and mediators in interaction was introduced by Eric Shopper in 1960, who showed that parents who show higher levels of synchronization and contingent responses during interaction have children with autism spectrum disorders who develop superior communication skills.

Research conducted in recent decades in the field of developmental psychology and psychopathology has also highlighted the central role of parenting relationships in the development of the child.

In addition, the importance of the quality of interaction with parents for the psychic development of children. Parental-mediated intervention programs are recommended in children with autism spectrum disorders but also in cases of autistic adolescents, as they are interventions that can improve social communication and problem behaviours, help families interact with their children, promote the development and increase of parental satisfaction, their empowerment and emotional well-being.

Interventions in which work is done on the interaction between parents and children with an autism spectrum disorder allow parents to have constant support and favour the modification of the methods of relational approach by parents, in line with the "atypical" characteristics of the child, to live and relate to him.

The purpose is not to impart new techniques to the parent for how to relate to the child but rather to expand the skills which he already possesses. In this sense, one of the main functions of the therapist is to show the parent, through their interaction with the child, how they are successful and those doomed to failure . In addition, parents who pose as providers of the intervention to their children often report reduced feelings of depression, stress, a greater sense of empowerment and optimism about their ability to influence their child's development.

When the child begins to grow up, all the fears about what will happen when they are gone there originate in the parents. Imagining your child with autism, adult, autonomous, able to lead a normal and independent life is certainly not easy for a parent; it is a goal that the parent often imagines as unattainable, if not purely utopian.

The particular pervasiveness of the symptomatic triad and the chronic trend of the pathological picture habitually determine disability conditions in adulthood, with serious limitations in autonomies and social life. Currently, a very high percentage (60 to 90%) of children with autism become adults who are not self-sufficient and continue to need lifelong care.

Considering the limitation of autonomies and the need for continued care for low-functioning autistic adolescents, it is important that families take action right away to understand what is best for him and his future. For some families, even the achievement of basic autonomies (autonomous nutrition, personal hygiene, etc., can be enormous achievements, etc.), others may see work for the child impossible, due to the absence of language, intellectual disability, excessive stereotypes or obsessive rituals.

Temple Grandin, a(professor at Colorado State University), known for her work as a livestock equipment designer, is an autistic woman who described herself in her famous book Thinking in Images and other testimonies of my autistic life. Temple reports that when someone talks to her she immediately translates words into images. The autistic boy can seem strange in society, some of his obsessive behaviors can be bizarre in the eyes of others. But, the extreme selectivity of the interests and their so particular skills (maniacs for calendars and schedules, above-average cataloguing skills, excellent visual memory with attention to detail, musical skills, mathematical skills, interest in animal species) should be valued to ensure that they can become an occupation for them. It is essential to look into the perspective of a Project of adult life, coming out of the stereotypes of child-sick and son-children, and not seeing the family of origin as the only place and only resource for the future life of the child.

It is important to welcome the stereotypes and narrow interests of autistic adolescents and treat them as hooking opportunities, bridges. Often the interests of autistic teenagers are abstruse and far from reality (memorizing the phone book or counting toothpicks in containers), but in some cases, however, we find elements that allow us to share many things. It is then a matter of trying to broaden the field of interest, in the sense of enriching it or making it as mutual, interactive or shared as possible.

Chapter 15: Emotionality in autism: the causes of aggressive behaviors and self-harm

One of the basic emotions is anger. We are well aware that we are angry with our boss following an unfair rebuke, with mom not giving us chocolate etc. and we may react with aggressive behavior that manifests the anger we feel (slamming the door, screaming, etc.). The roots of the feeling of anger can be traced back to the adaptive function it has: it is a defense to survive in the environment in which you live. Aggression is one of the possible behavioral reactions to anger, with which the individual responds to internal and external stimuli. For some children or adolescents with autism, however, it may not be so easy to recognize their emotional states, and therefore may not recognize the signs and why they happen to get angry and show aggressive behavior.

What causes aggression?

Aggression can have different causes such as frustration, anxiety, agitation, fear, or confusion. More specifically, children with autism live with high levels of anxiety, as sometimes their routine can be disrupted by some unexpected events. This leads to an easier expression of aggression. The social interaction and the resulting stress also give rise to feelings of frustration or anger in them.

Fueling such feelings of frustration and anger, there are difficulties in understanding the behaviors of others, as well as expressing their emotions.

Also not to be underestimated are the communication difficulties on the part of the child. In fact, the child may not be able to tell his mother that he has a stomach pain, that he is thirsty, that he feels cold or that he does not like pasta and beans and that therefore would lead him to a feeling of frustration.

In general, aggression can manifest itself in very different ways.

How does it manifest?

Aggression can manifest itself:

- **In verbal form.** Through the use of words and phrases that can insult, offend or hurt oneself or the other. For example, use swearing, threats, or shouting.

- **In physical or non-verbal form through motor activities.** For example, throwing objects, spitting, trying to bite or scratch, kicking, slapping or punching at yourself, each other, or objects in the outside environment.

In fact, we talk about hetero directed aggression when behaviors are aimed at objects or other people and self-directed aggression when assaulting oneself. In addition, other demonstrations are related to oppositional behavior in which the child or boy persists in rejecting any request made.

Often, in Autism bursts of anger and aggressive behavior can manifest themselves with screams, tears, self-harm (beating, biting hands). This also happens in public places (for example in a supermarket, a shop, etc.), last even hours and be very difficult to contain.

For this, they can be one of the most difficult issues for parents and family members to manage.

What to do? The importance of the reference socio-health network

Generally, aggressive behaviors in children or teens with Autism take time to develop and stay stable, becoming increasingly frequent and intense. Although outbursts of anger also "communicate" something, they could over time become violent behaviors and be dangerous for both others but especially for the child or boy himself.

Therefore, it is of fundamental importance to intervene immediately, turning to your social and health reference network and keeping it always informed.

Together you can work on how best to manage these behaviors, in particular on which strategies to use and possibly on which alternative behaviors to propose.

All negative experiences, lived by human beings, such as stress, trauma and deprivation, especially affective but also material, cause, on a psychological level, alterations and dysfunctions, which stimulate intense feelings and behaviors of rebellion and bitterness, towards both individuals, who are somehow believed to have been or are the cause of their suffering, and towards life and the world in general This is especially true in the case of young children, who live in a very limited and restricted reality. When these little ones suffer suffering, they project their aggression not only onto their parents and family members but also onto the whole world.

Therefore, one of the causes of aggression, present in normal children and in subjects who have psychological disorders, is caused by the suffering they have suffered, for various environmental causes: excessive limitations or frustrations of their desires and needs, injustices suffered, poor presence of parents and their physical and / or emotional estrangement, insertion outside the family nest at an early age or in the absence

In these, and in many other cases in which the child's living environment is not appropriate to his needs, aggressive manifestations signal the situation of discomfort and suffering in which the subject finds himself, but also the need that he feels in trying to obtain, through his behavior, a retaliation and revenge for what he has suffered.

The subjective element is important in aggressive reactions. Therefore the same action can be experienced differently based on personality characteristics and experiences of the moment.

The severity of the aggressive reaction is in proportion to the degree of motivation and emotional investment present but is also in proportion to a person's resilient abilities. There are therefore men and women who are able to resist frustration more easily, finding in themselves new and different ways more creative to achieve their goals, despite obstacles and, other people, who fall and depress or react aggressively following even minimal frustrations.

In children with autism spectrum disorders, aggression arises from the severe suffering present in their soul due to the anxieties, phobias, anxieties and fears to which they have been constantly subjected, since they have closed in on themselves. In that condition of extreme defense, any solicitation coming from the outside world but also from the internal one, has frequently been perceived as a serious threat to one's own safety or life.

Moreover, since the most frequent solicitations come precisely from human beings who ask, demand and stimulate to do or not to do certain actions or behaviors, thus putting them in serious difficulty, since these behaviors accentuate their anxieties and fears, the greatest aggression they feel is towards them but can be expressed towards everything and everyone. This aggression does not always explode and manifest. It is contained and frozen in children who have a higher degree of autism and therefore closure. It is as if, in this particular condition, this fundamental defensive drive is also sterilized, in order to avoid the unleashing of destructive actions and annihilation by the surrounding world. Indeed, in some cases, in order to protect himself, the child assumes an apparent conciliatory and smiling behavior.

On the contrary, aggression manifests itself more frequently in children with mild autism, as they still maintain some connection to the outside world, or is evident in children who have a severe form of autism, as their condition improves. In the latter case, when their emotions begin to thaw they can finally manifest on the outside the anger they hatched inside. In practice, the rebirth to the life of the autistic child begins precisely with the unlocking of aggression.

Aggressive manifestations turn to objects that are slammed on the walls or on the ground in an attempt to destroy them or on clothes that are torn. However, it can also manifest towards parents, family members, workers and teachers, when they insist on some request, that they fear it may worsen their inner suffering, or towards all people who, with their anxious, blaming, irritating behavior, cause their exasperation.

Even simply being physically approached can trigger the aggression of these children. Williams explains very well one of the causes that stimulated her aggressive reaction: "They were people who out of selfishness stole my sense of peace and security that, unlike them, I couldn't find in their version of 'daily life'".

Self-aggression

When the child turns aggression towards himself he bites his hands, arms or tongue, bangs his head to the wall, punches and slaps on his face or legs, scratches his arms. These manifestations of self-harm that deeply disturb you, can have various causes.

By uncovering the frustrations suffered on themselves, these children can bring out at least some of the aggression, without however incurring punishment.

Self-aggression can manifest the need for and pursuit of sensory stimulation. Finally, it could be an atonement, linked to guilt towards a good person towards whom the subject has presented unsuitable behavior.

Since the self or hetero aggressiveness present in the soul of children with autism symptoms cannot be erased, it is necessary to manage it in the most appropriate way with various precautions, so that it is gradually eliminated from their soul.

When these aggressive manifestations turn to objects, it is good not only to let it do it, without manifesting amazement, bewilderment or disapproval at all, but rather it is appropriate to help him get rid of the long-repressed aggression, which stifles his psychological development, offering him other objects on which to vent his negative and destructive emotions.

If, on the other hand, his need to vent aggression is aimed at some adult person, it is usually the mother, grandmother or a teacher, more rarely the father, even in this case these manifestations should not be repressed but transformed into a pleasant game in which to participate together. A game in which the adult and the child enjoy fighting, using harmless tools, such as fluffy pillows. In this way this negative emotion can be fully expressed without any guilt or frustration in the child.

As for self-aggression, this will tend to disappear rapidly as the child begins to have full confidence in parents, family members and adults in general who are committed to implementing Self-Managed Free Play daily with the child. The only game loved and desired by these children, because it lacks any advice, indication or worse of impositions or constraints. It is therefore good not to intervene violently or neutering, blocking the child's arms or hands.

Self-injurious behavior must instead be prevented by avoiding giving rise to crises of anger caused by some of our requests or incongruous behaviors in the child. If, despite all our efforts, it should manifest itself, we will use the strength of our affectionate, serene and tender closeness to regress self-injurious behavior.

HOW TO TEACH AN AUTISTIC PERSON TO MAKE FRIENDS

Children on the autism spectrum often tend to focus on the "details" of communication, and get lost in the overall "plot." This can make them bullied at school because of their unusual behavior, language, interests, and a tendency to tell others what to do. Their reduced ability to properly perceive and respond to nonverbal cues can lead to conflict or being ignored by others. Children with Asperger's syndrome can be extremely literal and have difficulty interpreting and responding to sarcasm or jokes. A child or adolescent with Asperger's syndrome is always puzzled by the abrupt ways he's treated, unaware of what he's done wrong. Children on the autistic spectrum, especially mild ones, often want to be sociable, but it is difficult for them to make friends. This can lead to antisocial behavior, particularly in adolescence. It is at this stage of their lives that they risk being drawn into unsuitable and inappropriate friendships and social groups. Learning how to create appropriate friendships can minimize these problems, reduce bullying, and lead to better relationships even with people who are not on the autism spectrum. The sooner you teach these skills, the better.

SOCIAL SKILLS ARE COMPLEX & HARD TO LEARNING

Non-autistic people sometimes how complex social skills are & how long it takes to learn them. Tony Attwood, a world-renowned autism expert, lists some essential skills children need to make friends:

* Know how to get into other children's activities
* Know how to welcome other children in their games or activities
* Recognize when and how to help others and how to seek help from others
* Compliment at the right time and know how to respond to compliments
* Know the right time and way to criticize
* Be able to accept and manage criticism from others
* Welcome the ideas and suggestions of others in an activity
* Give and receive in a conversation or activity
* Manage disagreement with compromise instead of aggression or emotional outbursts
* Recognize and understand the opinions of others
* Understanding facial expressions and body language
* Empathize with others in situations, both positive and negative
* Appropriate behavior and comments to be alone or disrupt interaction.

Typical normal children usually learn all these social skills unconsciously and intuitively by observing and interacting with their surroundings.
 In contrast, the autistic child is focused on the "details" instead of the general "plot": therefore, they need to learn these social skills in a different, more concrete way. We can help them learn to make friends through place and assimilation.

PLACE- CHANGE THE ENVIRONMENT

The place involves changing the child's physical or social environment to encourage positive social interactions.

INVITE FRIENDS HOME

Encourage friendships by inviting more children to the house.

Remember that they do not necessarily have to make friends with children of their age or gender. You could ask your child's teacher if there are children at school with whom there is empathy. You can then arrange for potential friends to come to your home to make a specific game. Your child will be more relaxed in the home environment and will be better able to work on appropriate social interactions.

ACTIVITIES THAT ENCOURAGE SOCIAL INTERACTION

It could help that your child frequents supervised activities such as after-school care, holiday care, Scouts, or a sport, where attention to an adult's supervised activities can reduce problems of poor social interaction. This is especially useful if the activity focuses on a particular interest of the child.

MENTORS PEER

Peer mentors are peer counselors and have been shown to be an effective strategy for children on the autism spectrum. A similar age classmate who interacts positively with the child is chosen as a mentor. The difficulties of Autism Spectrum Disorders are explained to the peer mentor in an age-appropriate manner, so that the mentor can help learn appropriate communication skills. Teachers and parents can lead the mentor among equals, so that social skills are learned in the natural environment – among other children.

Sensitization

Raising awareness among others about autism spectrum disorders is critical. Parents can explain their child's autism characteristics to the teacher who in turn will explain it to the children in the class.

When meeting other families, it can also help explain your child's autism spectrum disorder in the hope that parents and their children respond in an understandable way to any inappropriate behavior or communication from the child.

CONNECTION WITH CHILDREN WHO HAVE SIMILAR INTERESTS OR WHO FALL WITHIN THE SPECTRUM

Often these wonderful children have special interests and passions that few other children will appreciate. Parents can use the parent support group or the local autism/Asperger's association to find other children with a similar interest, be it spiders, dolls or cartoon characters. They often find it much easier to relate to each other than to non-autistic children, especially if they share common interests.

ASSIMILATION- DEVELOPING YOUR CHILD'S SOCIAL SKILLS

The place predicts changes in the environment. Assimilation, on the other hand, focuses on changes in your baby. In a way, the place offers your child the opportunity to make friends: assimilation gives your child the social skills to encourage friendship. Theory of mind holds that individuals on the autism spectrum have difficulty interacting socially with other people because they can't understand that other people think differently. Children may therefore not understand and get angry if someone does not know the answer to a specific question. The autistic child may appear self-centred, eccentric or indifferent because he has difficulty anticipating what others will say or do in a variety of situations. But there are many strategies to help him develop his social skills in this area.

IMAGES TO LEARN FACIAL EXPRESSIONS AND BODY LANGUAGE

Parents can use images that show a variety of emotions in faces and body language. This can help your child interpret visual cues when someone gets angry, bored, saddened, frustrated, or happy. The next step could be using a video camera to record someone showing these emotions and helping the child recognize the signals.

LEARN TO ASK QUESTIONS

Children with autism or Asperger's syndrome often don't grasp "give and receive" in conversations They can be very talkative and come to dominate a conversation by talking only about their interests. A crucial skill they must learn is listening to others: they must realize that other children have their own interests. An example is to create a Q&A game, in which parents and children alternate by asking questions about each other & providing a short answer. This can explain to the child that a good conversation is where both people can talk the same way.

Another tip is to make a game where you ask questions. For example, you can play a game where your child is a famous journalist or interviewer. At first, you can give your child a list of easy-to-ask questions like age, work, school, or hobby to suit the person they're interviewing. Over time, you can encourage your child to "interview" others at school or neighborhood and generalize these new listening and discussion skills in all areas of their lives.

SOCIAL STORIES

Is developed by Carol Gray: as an effective tool to help children on the spectrum learn many skills, including communication skills. Stories are short, can be supported with visual images, and contain ideal phrases and structures to encourage new skills. An example is:

"Knowing how to listen"
It's very important to look at people & stop what I'm doing when they have something to tell me.

Sometimes adults tell me very important things I need to know.
If I don't look and listen, I might miss something important and anger the grown-ups.
I know it's bad to keep doing what I'm doing when adults want me to listen.
I will listen to the grown-ups when they talk to me.

ROLE PLAYING GAMES

Role-playing games can give your child time to learn general social skills. The parent must interpret typical situations where the child may have problems: starting a conversation, joining another child's activities, or inviting another child to play. In real life, this can be difficult for the child as it takes time to interpret facial expression, understand body language, and understand appropriate responses.

A role-playing game gives the child plenty of time to work through these processes and hopefully increase speed and social skills with practice. If the family has a video camera, it can be helpful to record these role-playing games. Many children with autism or Asperger's syndrome learn more effectively visually, so reviewing role-playing in video can be an excellent way to show the child what they did well or analyze what didn't go so well. Remember to be very encouraging & supportive when reviewing the footage! You can also lock frames in relevant parts to give your child time to analyze facial expressions or body language.

HELPING THE CHILD CHOOSE FRIENDS

Children with autism or Asperger's syndrome appear to have a one-dimensional view of their own personality or that of others. When asked about themselves or other children, they tend to make descriptions of height, age, or appearance. If personality is described, it will tend to simply focus on whether someone is "beautiful" or not. Non-autistic children are usually ready to intuitively learn the personalities of others. They take in the inclination of other children to be chatty, bad in class, friendly, manipulative or angry. Often do not know how to grasp these signals and may try to form friendships with children that are not suitable for them.

One visual way parents can help their child identify other children's personality traits is to convince the child to select an animal they believe represents someone's personality. Parents can play a constructive role in their children's lives by encouraging them to analyze the personalities of others so they can choose more appropriate friends as they get older.

Adults on the autism spectrum continue to struggle with many of these problems.

Empathy

Making friends for an autistic child can be very difficult, so developing empathy in children with autism is really a major challenge. For an autistic child, in fact, it is very difficult to put himself in the shoes of the other, understand the internal mental states of others & understand the intentions and purpose of the actions of others. The area that suffers most from this deficit is the social one, they are children who struggle to understand the emotions of others and feel empathy.

Mental states cannot be seen or grasped concretely, yet humans are sure that mental states exist and that they play a central role in their lives. It is precisely these internal states that push people to pursue certain goals, which guide them in the choices of their appropriate actions and allow them to achieve complex goals.

The attribution of mental states allows for a causal understanding without which the most common social interactions would not be possible.

We can transmit empathic capacity to our children only if in turn we have been respected and listened to, if we have felt welcomed into our feelings and needs as children, if we have not been denied consolation, acceptance and sweetness.
Consequently, the indispensable first step for our children to be empathetic is to resolve our "emotional sufferings."

They learn from what we do not from what we tell them to do, with regard to empathy this is doubly true. The example we give them will allow our children to learn that people are able to understand others, put themselves in their shoes, be moved and live feelings without judging.

Your attitudes and your way of speaking to others will be what will most make your children understand the correct way to behave and relate to others and this also applies when there are conflicts and differences of opinion.

If when we are children instead of receiving acceptance we are repressed or ignored with growth our self-esteem will be damaged. Surely from this article you realize that simply being an empathetic parent with your children is the best way to help them develop this ability. To help children understand others we must first help them understand themselves and this is a process that begins with allowing our children to express their needs and feelings (even negative ones!).

In order to recognize the emotions of others and identify with them, it is essential to know how to recognize your own.

This is why the points explained above are very important, if parents value the emotions of their children he will learn that his emotions are important and will not deny them.

From early childhood we can help them express emotions and name and identify them. "you are happy!, you are angry, you are afraid.." the situations of everyday life give us many opportunities to work on emotions and to talk about.

THE HIDDEN LINK BETWEEN AUTISM AND ADDICTION

Repetition is an important part of an autistic person's day. The researchers found that this love of repetition extends to addictive behaviors.

A person might smoke a cigarette, but then they need many more. The same concept could apply to drinking or using harder drugs. Because repetition is so ingrained in the mind, addiction takes hold very quickly. For this reason, autistic people are more likely to be affected by addiction.

There are similarities in how autistic and drug addicts use repetitive behaviors to cope with emotional problems, as well as their impulsivity & compulsions. The 2 conditions affect some of the same regions of the brain & involve a few of the equally genes. It is hoped that a new area of research will help improve the treatment of autism and the treatment and prevention of addiction.

For much of the 20th century, many of those diagnosed with autism were in the most severe part of the spectrum. In this largely nonverbal population, alcohol and drug addiction seemed unlikely. In 1994, when the "Diagnostic & Statistical Manual of Mental Disorders" added Asperger's as a category, extended to people who had much more access to alcohol and other medications. However, for years, the assumption remained that addiction was a concern that the autism community could safely ignore. Some studies suggest that Asperger's syndrome is not linked to an increased risk of addiction, as people who have this disorder do not tend to look for unusual experiences. They seem to appreciate predictable, measurable, and programmable things, so they wouldn't appreciate the strange visions and sounds that a drug use or glass of alcohol might offer.

But there are some people who struggle so much with their inner world, who may be tempted to smooth out their limits with drugs or drinks. If these people go to a party, they might drink to fit in and feel like they're part of the group. They could also drink as a way to treat feelings of nervousness or anger that arise when they are in social situations.

It is also possible that people with Asperger's may become addicted to substances due to the obsessive nature of their thoughts. For example, a 2013 study suggests that autistic children would likely spend twice as much time playing video games as typical normal children.

Autism disorders seem to make people interested in always doing the same things, continuously, looking for different results each time. Just as some people might be interested in games, others may be interested in drinks and others in drugs.

THE STUDIO

A new study in Sweden suggests that autistic people who have an average or above-average IQ (I) IQ are more than twice as likely to become addicted to alcohol or other drugs as their peers. The highest risk for people who also have (ADHD) attention deficit hyperactivity disorder. This study examine the overall risk of addiction among autistic people. Is the first to examine the overall risk of addiction among autistic people. Other research is also finding unexpected common biological and psychological aspects between the two conditions.

Numerous recent studies demonstrate a kind of overlap of neural circuits and molecular signaling pathways in both (apparently distinct) disorders: autism and drug addiction.

One area involves neural circuits and neuro-modulatory systems in the striatum and basal ganglia, which play an established part in the addiction and reward.

A second area of overlap involves molecules such as Fragile Mental Retardation Protein X (FMRP) and Methyl Binder Protein 2 CpG (MECP2), which are best known for their contribution to the pathogenesis of autistic syndromes, but have recently been shown to regulate behavioral and neurobiological responses to exposure to addictive drugs. These shared pathways and molecules indicate common dimensions of behavioral dysfunction, including repeating behavioral patterns and processing aberrant rewards. Previous autism research, involving addiction, usually focused on serious conditions. Low IQs were a common thread between these topics, and addiction wasn't that relevant. This can result from the fact that people with low IQ usually have a caregiver 24 hours a day.

Autistic individuals with over 100 IQs have a better chance of taking part in addictive behaviors because they have their own distinct mind. Current studies should focus on these individuals to try to find answers.

Espen Arnevik found only 18 studies examining the overlap between autism and addiction. Each of them mainly used selected samples – such as people undergoing drug addiction treatment or those involved in the criminal justice system – rather than the general population.

Matthew Tinsley, an autistic, now 55, had always looked for alcohol and anxiety-reducing medications. Tinsley is the author of "Asperger's Syndrome and Alcohol: Drinking to Cope," one of the few books on this topic. (He has been sober since 2004.) From an early age, he took his mother's anxiety medications when he felt overwhelmed.

In college, he found that alcohol also helped facilitate socialization. "Everyone else drinks, it's socially acceptable, and if you drink, you fit because everyone is doing it," he says. "He took over." By the age of 40, Tinsley adds, he was drinking "lethal" amounts of alcohol: three liters of gin every day. This led to cirrhosis and went into rehabilitation in 2004. His diagnosis of autism in 2005 was a real relief. Once he realized there was an explanation for his sensory & social difficulties, he began to be kinder to himself and found healthier ways to deal with his anxiety.

Eric Hollander, on the other hand, deals more with behavioral addictions, such as gambling: 'I work with a lot of autistic people who have all kinds of impulsive behaviors,' says Hollander, director of the autism & obsessive compulsive spectrum programed at Albert Einstein College of Medicine in New York. "And that's one of the main goals when people come for treatment. They're either out of control in terms of Internet shopping and gaming, or they're just addicted to the Internet. "Hollander looked at the similarities between obsessive compulsive disorder, addiction, and impulsive and compulsive behaviors that occur in autistic people. He proposes that these terms, all characterized by repetitive thinking and behavior, should be grouped as "obsessive compulsive spectrum disorders" in diagnostic guidelines.

Impulsivity — acting quickly without thinking — and compulsiveness, or the inability to stop an activity once started, are both problems of self-control or "executive function." Impulsivity is strongly linked to the risk of becoming addicted; addiction is defined as compulsive drug use that persists despite the negative consequences. Autistic people show signs of both impulsivity and compulsiveness. For example, they often engage in repetitive and compulsive behaviors, dubbed "stimming" – to deal with a lack of sensory stimulation or loss thereof. In case of addiction, different types of drugs can improve or reduce the continuous feeling of anxiety and inadequacy.

10 WAYS TO BUILD INDEPENDENCE

If I had to summarize everything it takes to introduce our children to independent living, I would do so with this list. By introducing these skills in advance and building them step by step, we can help the autistic person get the tools that will allow them to be more autonomous throughout their lives.

1.Strengthen communication

If your child has difficulty with spoken language, a critical step in increasing independence is to strengthen their ability to communicate by developing skills and providing tools to help express preferences, desires, and feelings. Consider introducing alternative/augmentative communication (CAA) and visual aids. Common types of CAA include Image Exchange Communication Systems (PECS), including sign language.

2.Introduce a visual program

Using a visual program can help the transition from one activity to another with less stress. Review every element of the program with your child and then remind them to check the program before any changes. Over time, he will be able to complete this task with increasing independence, exercise decision-making and pursue activities involving it.

3.Work on self-care skills

It is essential to introduce self-care activities into your child's routine. Brushing your teeth, showering and other activities of everyday life are important life skills and introducing them as soon as possible can allow our children to master them across the board. Be sure to include these activities in your child's schedule so they get used to having them as part of their daily routine.

4.Teach your child to demand for a break

Make sure your kid has a way to request a break: add a "Pause" button on their communication device, an image in their PECS book, etc. Identify a quiet area your child can go when they feel overwhelmed. Or consider offering headphones or other tools to help regulate sensory inputs. Though this may seem simple, knowing how to ask for a break can allow your child to regain control over themselves and their environment.

5.Working on household chores

Having children who complete household chores can teach them responsibility, involve them in family routines, impart useful skills when they are older. If you consider that your child may have difficulty figuring out how to complete an entire thing, you can consider using an activity analysis. This is a method that involves dividing large tasks into smaller steps. If your child has problems at first, be sure to show the steps yourself or provide suggestions.

6.Practice skills with money

Learn how to use money is a important skill that can help your child become self-employed when walking around the neighborhood. Regardless of the skills you acquire, there are ways you can start learning the skills of money. At school, consider adding monetary skills to your child's PEI, and when you're with him in a store or supermarket, allow him to deliver the money to the checkout. Step by step, you can teach every part of this process. Your child can then start using these skills in different community settings.

7.Teaching safety skills in the neighborhood

This is a big concern for many families, especially as children become more independent. Teach road rules and other important safety indicators; familiarize yourself with public transport. Consider giving your child an identity card with their name, a brief explanation of their diagnosis, and a trusted person to contact.

8.Develop leisure skills in

Being able to devote themselves to leisure and leisure independently is something that will serve our children so much throughout their lives. Many autistic people have special interests in one or two subjects. You can help him translate these interests into age-appropriate recreational activities.

9.Teaching self-care during adolescence

This aspect is different from self-care in general. Entering adolescence and starting puberty can bring many changes for an autistic teenager, so this is an important time to introduce many specific hygiene skills. Visual aids can be really helpful in helping your child complete their personal hygiene routine every day. You could make a list of activities to help your child keep track of what to do and then hang it in the bathroom. The list could include activities such as showering, armpit washing, deodorant, tampon change, makeup, hair brushing. To stay better organized, you can put altogether a hygiene "kit" to keep everything your child needs in one place.

10.Work on professional skills

As early as about 14, our children should have some professional skills included in the EIP. Make a list of his strengths, skills and interests and use them to understand the type of professional activity that best suits him. This is a time to start planning for the future. Consider all the ways you've promoted your child's independence up to this point: communication skills, self-care, interests, activities, and goals for the future.

Chapter 16: The world of work

TEMPLE GRANDIN'S ADVICE. IDEAS FOR FINDING GOOD JOBS

Half of all good jobs are obtained through informal contacts with colleagues or friends. A person gets a great job with a major tech company because they attended a course with a professor who knew someone in the company. Another person recently got a great job in a food safety lab because his parents had met one of the managers. The lab loves its attention to detail when receiving food samples for testing. It is important to follow the exact procedures to prevent one sample from contaminating another. The secret to getting a good job when you're a little different is to avoid traditional interviews and online applications. A recent article in Kathryn Dill's Wall Street Journal indicated that automated algorithms often rule out many good applications. An autistic person needs to have the opportunity to demonstrate their skills. Some major employers are offering the opportunity for people on the spectrum to work by showing off their skills. Many enterprising parents have found a successful job for their children by asking a local company to allow them to volunteer earlier.

I learned to sell my work instead of myself, showing potential clients drawings and photos of completed projects. Creating a portfolio that showcases your work is a great way to impress potential employers. There are many job opportunities in almost every neighborhood that many parents can't see. I often ask parents, "Do you know someone who owns a business or is the manager of a store?" Sometimes they have to really think about it and then, all of a sudden, they think of someone their son or daughter might work with.

Children better start learning work skills and keep several real summer jobs before graduating from high school. The first jobs can be voluntary at the age of 11-12 in a church, community center or agricultural market. It is important for the child to learn to perform a task based on a schedule where someone outside the family is the boss.

Jobs involving many multi-tasking activities should be avoided. A crowded takeaway shop window or chaotic shop during the holiday race would be wrong choices.

A few examples of quieter working environments where autistic individuals have been successful are office supplies, auto parts shops and an ice cream parlor. For tasks to be performed in a stop sequence, the individual should receive a written checklist containing the steps. It's never too late to start working with young adults who may be addicted to video games. Video games need to be gradually replaced with something else. I know three people who have successfully replaced video games with car mechanics. Individuals learned that mechanics was more interesting than video games. Today one of the boys is repairing the trains. Transitions were made gradually and video games were slowly replaced with more hours of car work. Automotive mechanics isn't for everyone, but many of the video game fanatics are visual thinkers similar to me.

People who have my mind type are usually good at both drawing and understanding mechanical things. Some autistic people are thinkers of very good schemes in math & computer programming, while others love verbal facts. A good career choice for a verbal thinker may be specialized retail. In these jobs, the employee would be appreciated for his detailed knowledge of the products. There have been some cases of career success with car sales and corporate insurance. A large bank recently hired 2 people on the spectrum to sell specialized financial products. Social skills for specialized retail jobs can be effectively taught.

Conclusion and Bonus

And here we are, at the end of our journey.

We want to thank you for letting us into your homes, and we hope from the bottom of our hearts that this information has helped you, both informatively and practically.

We are sure that your children will be able to develop their skills thanks to the excellent work of your parents. We wish you all the best for your family.

Dear user, I would appreciate it if you would spend a minute of your time and **post a short review on AMAZON to let other users know how this experience was and what you liked most about the book.**

In addition, as of recently I decided to do a giveaway to all our readers, yes, **I want to give you a gift:** *the audiobook will be totally free for you!*

Below you will find a QR CODE that will give you direct access to this bonus (mp3 files to download directly to your device) *without having to subscribe to any mailing list or having to leave your personal data.*

We hope you enjoy it!

Also, as a publishing house, we have many more books that perhaps might be of interest to you or your loved ones in various genres (for example, cooking).

If you would like a copy, if there is a problem downloading the files, or if you simply want to share your opinion with us directly, we will be delighted to hear from you: write to author.author1001@gmail.com

A friendly greeting, we wish you the best

Made in the USA
Coppell, TX
06 June 2023